A READER'S GUIDE TO
JAPANESE
LITERATURE

J. Thomas Rimer

LIBRARY

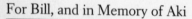

For Bill, and in Memory of Aki

In warm appreciation for their affection and encouragement

Distributed in the United States by Kodansha America, Inc., 575 Lexington Avenue, New York N.Y. 10022, and in the United Kingdom and continental Europe by Kodansha Europe Ltd., 95 Aldwych, London WC2B 4JF. Published by Kodansha International Ltd., 17-14 Otowa 1-chome, Bunkyo-ku, Tokyo 112-8652, and Kodansha America, Inc.

First edition, 1988
Second edition, 1999
99 00 01 02 10 9 8 7 6 5 4 3 2 1
ISBN 4-7700-2359-6

TABLE OF CONTENTS

After Ōe

Preface

The original edition of this guide was issued just over ten years ago, in 1988. In the intervening years, two situations have occurred which encouraged my editor, the ever-thoughtful Michael Brase of Kodansha International, to ask me if I might consider making a series of additions to the original. I therefore undertook to make these changes, and I hope that they will be useful to readers who are seeking information as to how to begin to choose from among the increasing number of translations of Japanese literature now available from all periods.

The first reason for revising the guide has to do with that proliferation of possibilities. When I began teaching Japanese literature, some thirty years ago, it was quite possible to examine and read through virtually all the works from the tradition, both classical and modern, then available in English. Now, the situation presents virtually bewildering possibilities to the general reader. I have therefore added several sections to the new edition, including "Some New Translations," which indicates the publication of new translations of additional works by authors already discussed in the body of the book. I have added as well three new sections, "Another Classical Master: Buson," "More Modern Masters," and "The Art of the Essay," all suggesting writers of great interest who were not included in the earlier guide. The section "Further Readings" has also been enlarged to contain new material of interest.

The second reason for revising the earlier edition of the guide is that, since the 1980s, Japanese literature has taken a considerable turn away from both its modern traditions and its classical heritage. Some would call these new trends "post-modern." Some applaud them, some decry them. Nevertheless, these changes have occurred, and in a new section entitled "After Ōe," I have tried to create a tentative first sketch-map of this bewildering new territory, one that includes writers of considerable potential interest to many, and in particular, I imagine, to readers younger than myself.

The only section to be dropped from the earlier edition is, interestingly enough, one I had entitled "Some Missing Books." There I gave the names of a number of writers and thinkers whose work remained unknown to readers outside Japan at that time. In the course of this decade, however, most of these representative works, miraculously enough, have now actually appeared in translation. Of the important works on my original list, only the extremely beautiful and highly influential *Shinkokinshū* (New Collection of Old and New Japanese Poetry) from the early thirteenth century still remains unavailable in a usable English translation.

Of course, my original list could now be extended, particularly in the area of modern fiction and poetry, but, as the size of that original section has now been so happily reduced, it seems best to omit it here altogether.

For those wishing to seek out more translations and biographical information on Japanese writers, I have also included a new section on "Useful Reference Books."

I have also left intact the original Preface, since it includes some general observations that are hopefully still of use.

In preparing these revisions, I would particularly like to thank Sachie Noguchi, of the East Asian Library at the University of Pittsburgh, as well as Mr. Andrew Hall, both of whom were extremely helpful in locating useful and often obscure information for me.

J. Thomas Rimer
1999

Preface to the First Edition

This book was undertaken at the suggestion of my colleague, Kodansha International's Michael Brase, who, over a cup of coffee in Tokyo two years ago, urged me to consider the fact that, in his opinion, the enthusiasms of those who translate Japanese literature into English have perhaps left the general reader a bit behind. Interest in Japan, he reminded me, rises steadily, and in the field of literature, which can provide such telling insights into the Japanese vision of themselves, their culture, and the world, more and more works of various and competing merits are now finding their way into English. Readers new to the subject and looking for individual works of Japanese literature that they may enjoy, that are representative of the Japanese tradition, and that Japanese themselves admire, have at the moment nowhere to turn for simple and practical advice on where to begin. This small book is a modest outcome of that conversation.

In planning the book, Mr. Brase and I decided to include descriptions of twenty classical works—that is, works written before the opening of Japan to the West in the latter part of the nineteenth century—and thirty modern works. Each category consists of books that are well translated and which represent, in the largest sense of the word, the Japanese tradition of excellence in literature. Based on the premise that readers should first enjoy the work of these writers directly, no studies *about* Japanese literature are discussed in detail, with the occasional exception of books that include a sufficient amount of translated material to suggest the range and accomplishments of an important author.

All, or virtually all, of these translations are in print, and most can be found in any large public library. A goodly number of them are in paperback editions. Shifts in reprinting rights may mean that some of the books listed here will later appear under the marks of differing publishers. The information as to current publishers of each of the fifty books discusses is up-to-date as of this writing, but those seeking to buy one of them at some future time may find the same translation appearing from a new publisher.

The fifty works included here range in genre from fiction to poetry, essays, and dramatic texts. In that regard, Japanese conceptions of what constitutes "literature" are very close to our own. It was possible, of course, to choose only a fraction of the books available in translation; by the same token, there are still a number of central works in both classical and modern Japanese literature, universally admired in Japan, that have not as yet found their way into English-language versions. In that sense, the art of translating from the Japanese is still a young one.

The fifty brief introductions I have written here are intentionally planned for the general reader. Specialists will doubtless have some-what different and far more nuanced responses to many of these works. Hopefully, readers who become interested in Japanese litera-ture will turn to the impressive number of sophisticated studies and commentaries on many of these works and authors, books to which my own brief set of essays owes so much. This present book is intended simply as a rough road map for the uninitiated. Some read-ers may find my enthusiasms far too inclusive ("Can he like *all* those different books so much?"), but it is not difficult to respect a series of masterpieces, which I certainly do. It will be obvious, surely, which are my personal favorites, but in all cases I have attempted to provide an angle of vision by which the reader can best approach a work which, as part of a different and developing tradition, may be diffi-cult of first access. There may also be those who feel that more con-temporary works have been unnecessarily slighted. Our goal, however, was to describe more or less the tradition. There are, to be sure, a number of novels now in translation by such gifted contemporary writers as Kita Morio, Maruya Saiichi, Yoshiyuki Junnosuke, and

Kaikō Takeshi that are of the highest quality. But to have included these writers would have meant removing an equal number of older modern masters whose works, closer to classical sources, are, I believe, in greater need of explication.

J. Thomas Rimer
1988

A Note to the Reader

For various periods of Japanese history mentioned in the text, the following general divisions (adapted from the list provided in the appendix of the standard *Modern Reader's Japanese-English Character Dictionary* by Andrew Nelson, published by the Charles E. Tuttle Co. in 1962) may prove helpful.

Yamato	300–710	
Nara	710–794	
Heian	794–1185	
Kamakura	1185–1392	
Ashikaga	1392–1568	"medieval Japan"
Momoyama	1568–1600	
Tokugawa	1600–1868	
Modern	1868–present	
Meiji	1868–1912	
Taishō	1912–1926	
Shōwa	1926–1989	
Heisei	1989–present	

Japanese personal names are given in the Japanese fashion: family name first, personal name second (thus, for example Lincoln Abraham). In addition, writers whose fame has permitted their personal or artistic name a special usage will be referred to in the customary Japanese fashion. Thus, Natsume Sōseki is usually referred to as Sōseki, while Tanizaki Jun'ichirō, equally famous and appreciated, is nevertheless referred to as Tanizaki. It might also be pointed out that those seeking to purchase copies of these or other books may need to check such sources as *Books in Print* under various possible combinations of an author's name. Even a writer as copiously translated as Natsume Sōseki, for example, has some books listed under "Natsume," some under "Sōseki," in that authoritative source.

Although each entry is meant to be self-contained, a system of cross-references has been employed to indicate relationships between authors, works of literature, and general artistic trends. Thus a reference in bold type to *Tales of Ise* or *Ueda Akinari* in the course of an essay signals the reader that there is an entire entry on that work or author. As each entry can be read independently, certain background information is occasionally repeated, so that the reader will not find it necessary to read extensively in order to glean the necessary background concerning a single book. In general, the entries themselves have been arranged in chronological order: in the classic section, according to the date the text came into existence; in the modern section (somewhat arbitrarily), according to the author's birth dates, with the exception of Futabatei Shimei, who bridges nicely the modern and classical traditions.

Some Observations on Reading
Japanese Literature

More and more readers in the West have begun to discover the very real pleasures of Japanese literature. At first encounter, the works that readers discover, particularly in the area of more modern narrative fiction, appear to meet contemporary expectations. Those readers who begin by examining the work of such often-translated modern writers as Abe Kōbō or Endō Shūsaku, for example, will find the form in which they are composed to be safely domesticated. Those who go on the explore the writings of such authors as Tanizaki Jun'ichirō, Shiga Naoya, or Kawabata Yasunari, who began their creative lives before the Pacific War, will become aware of appreciable differences—the tendency toward a certain lyricism, and a privileging of introspection—that provide a special and sophisticated means of expression authentically Japanese. Works altogether in the traditional mold (those written before the late nineteenth century, with their unusual rhetorical devices) may seem at first still more distant; yet, because of that same quality of interiority, they remain surprisingly close to our contemporary sensibilities. It is this mixture of the strange and the familiar, and in particular the tantalizing power of a half-concealed yet powerful expressiveness, that helps to give this body of literature its continuing fascination for Western readers.

Japanese literature has a long history. Like all great literary traditions, the important forms in which the Japanese have written, including fiction, drama, and poetry, remain intimately bound to the ever-shifting possibilities of the Japanese language. Written Japanese differs so much from English in terms of syntax, grammar, and rhetorical strategies that the best of translations often constitute a brilliant paraphrase. The elusiveness of these texts, and the difficulties encountered in translating them, arise to some extent from the fact that the ultimate source in the Japanese literary tradition, and so the final point of repair, is poetry.

In the Anglo-American tradition, it is customary to look to Shakespeare (with perhaps a glance over his shoulder to Chaucer) to define the fundamentals of our own literary heritage. The theater has given us as a paradigm the clash of powerful personalities and a sense of the centrality of deeds performed. Much of this concern was later transferred to narrative fiction, notably that of the nineteenth century. It is perhaps for that reason that modern Western readers, in search of the most imposing Japanese literary monument, assume as a matter of course that it must be Lady Murasaki's splendid *Tale of Genji*, written in the eleventh century. *Genji* is, without a doubt, one crucial milestone, yet the heart of the tradition goes back still further, back to poetry rather than to prose, which developed from it. Two ancient anthologies, *The Anthology of Ten Thousand Leaves* (the *Man'yōshū*) and the *Collection of Old and New Japanese Poetry* (the *Kokinshū*), first defined the hierarchy and basic nature of artistic human utterance. The primacy given there to a personal, lyrical statement set for a thousand years the aesthetic modes of response to both felt and lived experience, and provided as well the modes and parameters thought appropriate for literary expression. The tradition created and maintained by early Japanese poetry was extended into other areas, coloring in time the development of narrative prose and drama as well as that of later poetry. The introspective qualities that give *The Tale of Genji* its power could never be sustained without the poems that dot the surface of the prose text. At the core of many a great *nō* play lies a poem, doubtless familiar to the original audience, which is held in check until a climactic moment, when its recitation serves as a kind of kernel around which the rest of the play closes like a celestial onion of many layers. Even the structural logic of a modern novel by Kawabata owes as much to the elusive connections between linked *haiku* verses as it does to the necessities of a linear narrative progression.

The word "poetry," of course, is a very general one, encompassing as it does a variety of forms and rhetorical styles employed during Japan's long literary history. Certain of these details are discussed in some of the specific entries that follow, but it might be said here that the primary form that set the tradition was the *waka* (alternatively referred to as the *tanka*) form of court poetry, written in thirty-one syllables. The reasons for the dominance of this short lyrical form are many: some social, some artistic, some linguistic.

The influence of this poetry on all genres of Japanese literature has continued to manifest itself in a number of ways. One of them was, in a sense, intellectual. Early readers of Japanese literature (who were aristocrats one and all) had virtually memorized the great court anthologies of poetry and so could recognize poems, even if altered or transmuted, when they were cited in other works of art, whatever the genre. Most readers of *waka* were also composers of poetry themselves, and an intimate and working knowledge of these poems was an integral part of their social, artistic, and even religious lives. *Waka* were thus internalized, both as a literary etiquette of expressive possibilities and as a privileged means of understanding. After all, Shakespeare assumed that the better-educated segment of his audiences would understand his classical references, just as Milton freely used his elaborate knowledge of Old Testament history in *Paradise Lost*, confident that his readers were familiar with that terrain. In the same manner, later writers in the Japanese classical tradition as diverse as Zeami, the poet and playwright who perfected the medieval *nō* theater, the satirical seventeenth-century novelist Ihara Saikaku, and the great *haiku* poet Matsuo Bashō would continue to draw from this poetic river running straight down the center of the literary map, secure in the knowledge that their variations on classical themes would be appreciated.

Above and beyond the pleasures of this sort of intellectual recognition, however, there remains the importance of the basic nature of the kind of poetic expression that the *waka* makes possible. Its lyric thrust, by the very nature of the form, must be brief—moving in a spontaneous flow from the heart of the writer to the heart of the reader, where it should, if the poem is a successful one, re-create the same emotions and sympathies as in the mind and spirit of the author. Words thus become means, not ends in themselves. Japanese traditional poetry is too brief to be didactic, too intuitive to be conceptual. Other means to teach, and to preach, were available in less literary forms. One reason that traditional Japanese poetry often sounds so fresh today is due, I think, to a long championing of a natural and spontaneous expressiveness based on interior feeling. Then too, the traditional rhetorical devices of *waka*, largely unobtrusive to Western readers, do not appear to loom as large as do certain of their classical Western counterparts.

Once this pattern of a lyrical human response to the world, and most specifically to nature, had been established in poetry, classical prose writers could turn to it for literary devices with which to fashion their narrative structures. In early masterpieces, such as *Tales of Ise* and *The Tale of Genji*, sections of prose alternate with poetry like valleys that lie between high peaks and provide the traveler with sufficient time to pause and catch his or her breath before exposure to the next lofty height—a heady moment of insight, in effect, that often can only be expressed through the intensive tonality available in the poetic mode.

Many readers, when first exposed to traditional or modern Japanese fiction, are surprised to note, in comparison with Western works, a lesser emphasis on linear plot line, an apparent shying away from the sorts of powerful climaxes that, by contrast, make the great works in the Western narrative tradition seem so distinctive. Japanese literature certainly contains narrative fiction as lengthy and complex as such Western works as *Crime and Punishment, Madame Bovary,* and *Great Expectations,* but the structures and purposes of a Dickens or a Flaubert appear to be quite different from, and perhaps at odds with, equally representative Japanese works, classical and modern alike. The intent of Japanese literature is to provide the reader with a means to develop in himself or herself, through an immersion in the text, an ability to intuit the deep realities of life as perceived by the author. This kind of experience remains available for the reader even when approaching many modern novels. In *A Dark Night's Passing* by Shiga Naoya, for example, Kensaku, the protagonist, has a final mystic revelation on the top of a great mountain. His final vision has all the earmarks of a religious epiphany, and the reader, through the skill of the author, is drawn into the same process. The feelings on the part of the reader that emerge from reading such a book may be ineffable, but they can be exceedingly powerful. Thinking about those realities, or arguing about them, as opposed to feeling them, however, would require an aesthetic stance very different from that which has evolved over the centuries in Japan.

Given the long continuity of this lyric tradition, it is no wonder that, with the importation of Western literary models during the final decades of the nineteenth century and after, young Japanese writers became intoxicated by the new modalities of expression, based on Western models, that were now becoming available to them. These new possibilities constituted, in two ways, a fresh aesthetic of writing.

First, the availability, often in translation, of the example of nineteenth-century fiction, from Sir Walter Scott and Edward Bulwer-Lytton to Dickens and Tolstoy, put a stamp of approval on the kind of narrative style that permitted new subject matter: the exploration of the outer as well as the inner world of the writer. Politics, social conditions, and the clash of character could now serve as appropriate subjects for artistic treatment. New sorts of dramas, novels, and stories began to emerge in which the claims of the present could rival those of the past, and observations on contemporary society, unmediated by the set patterns of traditional literary response, took pride of place in many works of modern fiction.

A second powerful innovation, particularly visible in the art of poetry, involved the opportunity, again by appeal to European models, to create freer literary forms. The discovery by the Japanese late in the nineteenth century of, first, English and German romantic poetry, then of the French masters of symbolism, such as Verlaine, Mallarmé, Rimbaud, and most particularly Baudelaire, gave a powerful new impulse to the kind of complex imagery and ideas that had been impossible to make use of in the traditional shorter forms. Even *haiku* poets began to develop a freer alternative to that brief form, expanding its possibilities immensely.

Even so, many of these experiments were carried out in the shadow cast by the great classical precedents and the traditional insights. Many modern characters in Japanese fiction still appear to be on secular pilgrimages that, even when expressed in the ironic mode of a contemporary writer like Ōe Kenzaburō, bear more than a superficial resemblance to traditional ways of apprehending the true nature of the world and one's place in it. These old traditions, growing ultimately out of an aristocratic sensibility that can be traced back to the court of Heian Japan and before, can still serve to filter out elements not suitable to the demands of high art. The best of modern Japanese prose continues to show a sobriety and a lack of vulgarity—even as concerns the ordinary incidental vulgarity of everyday human existence—that give their stories and novels a slight, often tantalizing aura of aristocratic reserve. In the fourteenth century, Zeami, the great actor, playwright, and theoretician of the nō theater, indicated that when a character of modest background is shown on the stage, all those aspects of surface realism that detract from an understanding of the inner beauty of the character must be eliminated. Woodcutters do not scratch themselves; farmers do not spit. This appeal to a kind of grave dignity remains perhaps implicit, but certainly powerful, in much of the aesthetic of modern literature.

It may be for such reasons that there is relatively little comedy in classic Japanese literature. What there is—*kyōgen* plays that accompany the *nō*, or the social satires of a Saikaku—might best be characterized as droll, even wistful, but seldom if ever indecorous or raucous. Among all the modern novels discussed in the course of this book, none are consistently comic in tone. Such comic works abound in Japan, of course, but they are not considered by most readers there to be serious literature. Virtually none of them have been translated.

Just as modern Japanese writers have been responding to the example of Western literature, so more and more Westerners, usually through the medium of translation, are learning to expand their repertory of artistic possibilities through an appreciation of the Japanese example. No American child I know has ever been asked to write a sonnet in high school, yet virtually everyone has tried his or her hand at composing *haiku*. Since the days of Ezra Pound, poets and novelists alike have been responding to what they see as a tendency toward an elegant simplicity in the Japanese tradition. The Japanese arts are now very much a part of the contemporary international scene, and these mutual stimulations are bound to increase and expand.

The newest works of Japanese literature described in this book privilege prose over poetry, society over introspection. Yet even works created by such contemporary sensibilities as Ariyoshi Sawako, who has written on politics and pollution, or Abe Kōbō, who combines in his absurdist fables elements from such popular forms as the detective novel and science fiction, reveal the fact that the great traditions that helped shape the national sensibility continue on, even if transmuted and sometimes submerged.

The growth of population in Japan, linked with the power of mass communication and popular culture, has certainly affected the development of contemporary literature there, as in virtually every other country. The result has been to force some writers into adopting the strategy of writing difficult, avant-garde poetry or prose that can exist only for the few. In that sense, contemporary Japanese poetry has retreated from a central position to a delimited territory occupied by a new kind of aristocracy, that of the highly educated Japanese intelligentsia. Even so, the pull of poetry remains powerful among the more general population of readers. Certainly poets continue to be looked on as cultural figures of high accomplishment, almost as secular shamans. Miyazawa Kenji, for example, is widely admired and loved in Japan, yet his poetry is a good deal more difficult of access than, say, that of Robert Frost, the only poet in the United States who might be said to command anything remotely approaching general and popular reputation. Older Japanese may bewail the fact that young people are reading less and less, but corner bookstores, found in every village and town, remain full of inexpensive paperback editions of classical and early modern writers. The long tradition of Japanese literature still speaks to its youngest generation. In a sense, we who now can begin to peruse this tradition in translation are the newest set of readers. As one work of Japanese literature read and enjoyed leads us to another, and as modern works push us back to the great classic works, it would seem that, even at this point in our troubled century, we may still find ourselves capable of doing a little spiritual mountain-climbing.

TWENTY
CLASSICAL
WORKS

A Record of Ancient Matters

Kojiki

History, Myth, and Legend. Eighth Century

A Record of Ancient Matters, which is the usual translated title of the original *Kojiki*, was completed in A.D. 712 and is considered to be the first literary work in the history of Japan. To define the book in this fashion, however, is to bring false, and more modern, preconceptions to what is actually a juxtaposition of myths, history, songs, legends, genealogies, and other disparate materials from which written history, and written literature, were later made. As a glimpse into the relative beginnings of a civilization, however, *Ancient Matters* is an invaluable resource which can fascinate a modern reader with its archaic power, at once bewildering and strangely familiar.

To say that *Ancient Matters* juxtaposes diverse materials, however, is not to say that its chief compiler (indicated in the text as a court scribe, one Yasumaro) or compilers worked without guiding principles. In the first place, the work moves in loose historical progression, from the founding of the nation through the reign of the Empress Suiko (592–628), from myth to history. Within this structure, the compilers were doubtless guided by imported Chinese models of historical writing that were by then available to them at the Japanese court, possibly such famous works as the *Records of the Grand Historian* of Ssü-ma Chien (ca. 145–ca. 85 B.C.) or the *Chronicles of the Han Dynasty* compiled by Hsün Yüeh (A.D. 148–209). While there was doubtless a kind of imperial iconographical ideal of Chinese derivation which *Ancient Matters* was attempting to emulate (even if indirectly), the text itself was written in an archaic form of the Japanese language rather than in classical Chinese, which, by this time, had achieved ascendancy in Japanese court circles. In some ways, classical Chinese functioned in Japan and elsewhere as Latin did in Europe in the Middle Ages, providing a means to bring disparate cultures together as parts of a larger hegemony. The importance of this impulse by the Japanese to join a larger and more sophisticated cultural sphere can be seen in the fact that *Ancient Matters* has a virtual twin work, the *Nihongi* (sometimes called the *Nihon shoki*), which can be translated as "The Chronicles of Japan." The *Nihongi* was compiled in 720 and followed the Chinese literary and linguistic models quite closely. A comparison of the two texts, which often treat the same material, shows clearly the differences in the workings of the native and the imported modes of sensibility, a paradigm that exists in Japanese culture even today, where traditional and Western-influenced mentalities exist side by side.

The second factor that controlled the compilation of *A Record of Ancient Matters*, and perhaps to a modern reader a more subtle one, lies in the fact that the commission was an imperial one. The civil wars of 587 had given the internationalists in Japan, those wishing closer connections with China and with Buddhism, a clear hegemony over others who wished to remain apart and preferred to uphold Shintō belief. Despite its concentration on early myth, *Ancient Matters* implicitly celebrates this victory, for its texts were selected to point to the power of this hegemony. The *Kojiki*, after all, old as it is, was called *A Record of Ancient Matters* because it was intended to indicate how the legitimacy of the ruling Yamato court had come into being. Yamato legends are celebrated, while those of other competing factions are reduced, altered, or dropped altogether. The resulting document, to an objective historian, must therefore appear as an ideological one.

None of these comments, however, are meant to curb the real fascination that can be found in examining this remarkable sourcebook. Those drawn to an examination of early literary expression will find fascinating samples here in abundance, particularly in book 1, which contains mainly mythical and ancient materials. The persistent lyrical strain that looms so large in Japanese modes of expression is already visible here, even if in a rather crude form, and indeed it has become the tradition to trace the beginnings of Japanese poetry to the short verse attributed to the god Susano-o, written, according to the entry, as he built a palace at Suga, in the province of Izumo (now Shimane).

Eightfold fence of Izumo where eight clouds rise,

I make an eightfold fence to surround my wife,
That eightfold fence!   (trans. Hiroaki Sato)

Historical precedents for other genres of Japanese literature have also been sought in *A Record of Ancient Matters*. Zeami (1363–1443), the great writer of plays and theoretical works on the medieval *nō* theater, traced his art to the story of Susano-o's sister Amaterasu, the sun goddess. Angered at her brother's flagrant misbehavior, she secluded herself in a cave, thus depriving the world of light. She was tempted back outside, however, by the opportunity to see a dance, and a slightly scandalous one at that, performed by the goddess Ame no Uzume. The sun, of course, shone again. The theatrical arts, Zeami therefore insisted, could show high and felicitous purposes, sanctified alike by myth and history.

Many reading the book will be intrigued by the Orpheus-like story of the god Izanagi's descent into the world of the dead in order to seek out his lamented wife, or by the celebrated tale of two brothers. The younger brother loses the older's fishhook, and so descends to the bottom of the sea, where he encounters the palace of the god of the sea and falls in love with his daughter. *A Record of Ancient Matters* even contains a romantic hero in the figure of the legendary prince Yamato Takeru.

Book 2 moves closer to the realm of dynastic history as actual events are chronicled. From a literary point of view, this section is perhaps less vivid, containing as it does imperial genealogies, records of political turmoil, and the like. Nevertheless, there are passages here as well of effective verse, often in long and irregular forms that foreshadow the great poems in *The Anthology of Ten Thousand Leaves*. Then too, even in these historical sections, there are occasional brief sketches of the actors in these historical tableaux that bring them alive in memorable and occasionally indecorous ways. The picture of early Japan that emerges is vivid, earthy, and, in its way, charged with personality.

TRANSLATIONS
The preferred version is the Donald Philippi translation, *Kojiki*, first published

by Tokyo University Press in 1969 and now available in the United States from Columbia University Press. It is a model of its kind, written in fine style and provided with the kind of notes that serious readers and historical researchers will need. Quick comparisons with the *Nihongi*, as yet only available in the 1896 translation of W. G. Aston (presently available from Charles E. Tuttle), are made awkward, as Philippi has chosen to render the names of the many persons and places mentioned in the text using modern phonetic reconstructions of the ancient pronunciations, rather than simply using the traditional romanized spellings employed by Aston and many others since. Philippi includes these more common spellings in a glossary, however, so that the transition is easy enough to make with a little practice.

The Anthology of Ten Thousand Leaves

Man'yōshū

Poetry. Eighth Century

The *Man'yōshū*, the title of which might be translated as "The Anthology of Ten Thousand Leaves" or "An Anthology of Myriad Leaves," is the first great collection of Japanese poetry. For some Japanese readers and critics it remains the very best. Compiled sometime during the latter part of the eighth century, during the Nara period, the final version contains twenty books and something over four thousand poems, written by poets named and unnamed, and in a variety of styles. The anthology has in some ways the same canonic status in Japanese culture that the *Book of Songs* possesses for classical China. Both serve as sourcebooks for their respective cultures and provide points of repair, rightly or wrongly, for definitions of the national psyche. It should be mentioned, incidentally, that although Japan owed a great deal to Chinese literature and culture by this period, much of the poetry in *The Anthology of Ten Thousand Leaves* appears to have been written without direct reference or homage to the more sophisticated Chinese traditions. The two collections are thus quite difficult to compare.

As *Ten Thousand Leaves* represents the first extensive record of the Japanese emotional response to the world of men and nature, Japanese scholars have often turned to this collection in order to posit a comprehensive vision of early Japanese man. Some have stressed the existence of a "pure" or "sincere" quality of soul that presumably existed before the arrival of continental religion, art, and literature. These kinds of grand judgments, however, are difficult to make and sustain. The formidable linguistic challenge of translating into modern Japanese, let alone into any foreign language, texts of this kind, which are written in an archaic form of the Japanese language and filled on occasion with complex literary and rhetorical devices seldom used since, makes any level of generalization problematic. Looking over the various attempts to render the *Ten Thousand Leaves* into English suggests, rather, just how remarkable it is that we can be brought close in any way to such an archaic world. Perhaps the poems, domesticated into English, seem too close. Nevertheless, in the end it is only the greatest imaginative literature that can preserve the crucial function of thrusting us into another world. This *Ten Thousand Leaves* can do.

Readers familiar with court poetry in such anthologies as the ***Collection of Old and New Japanese Poetry***, compiled some hundred and fifty years later, will be surprised to find that, although *The Anthology of Ten Thousand Leaves* contains its share of 31-syllable *waka*, there are a variety of other poetic forms employed, notably the *chōka*, or "long poem," some of which attain considerable length. Those long poems permit a more extensive outpouring of lyric sentiment and have been particularly appreciated by modern readers, who sense in them a more natural configuration of emotional states than is possible in the *waka*, which combines brevity of form with its own complex traditions, rules, and limitations. "Long poems" were often composed as public poetry, a genre seldom used or appreciated in our century. In many of the *chōka* of this sort, there is a beauty of utterance, and an expression of poetic personality on the part of the authors, that makes them powerfully appealing.

A good portion of the best of these long poems are by Kakinomoto no Hitomaro (fl. ca. 680–700), who was active as a court poet, apparently dying before the capital was finally established at Nara in 710. His poems commemorate various activities of the imperial family and celebrate their accomplishments in obituary poems. Other are addressed more personally to his wife and family. Hitomaro's range of subject matter is great, and although he used the complex poetic devices available to him, his unique voice was not subsumed by them. By the time the *Collection of Old and New Japanese Poetry* was compiled, Hitomaro had been dubbed "the saint of poetry," and his enormous reputation has continued on down into this century. Hitomaro's poems on parting from his wife, and on her death, are among the most moving in the whole Japanese tradition.

Other famous poets of the Nara period are also included in *The Anthology of Ten Thousand Leaves*. One of them is Ōtomo no Tabito (665–731), a high government official and an excellent poet, whose works written late in life are preserved in the collection. Tabito was a supremely cultivated man for his time, and his knowledge of and sympathy for Chinese poetry permits his various verses on love, travel, old age, the pleasures of wine, and human vanity to possess a special richness. Tabito's interests and abilities were inherited by his son Ōtomo no Yakamochi (718?–85), who, like his father, brought both talent and knowledge of the Chinese tradition to his compositions. It is also believed by modern scholars that he was among those who helped compile the anthology. Yakamochi's work contains a large number of 31-syllable *waka*, and in this regard, he might be said to represent a transitional figure, whose poetic world already draws closer to the conceits of the *Collection of Old and New Japanese Poetry*.

Ten Thousand Leaves also includes works composed by far simpler people, often anonymously. Filled with fresh, sometimes homely images, many of them drawn from nature, they have an immediate appeal.

Love is a torment
Whenever we hide it.

Why not lay it bare
Like the moon that appears
From behind the mountain ledge?

(trans. Nippon Gakujutsu Shinkōkai)

The anthology also contains glimpses of poets otherwise unknown, whose work is of high beauty and suggestiveness. One of my personal favorites is the priest Manzei (fl. ca. 720), who served Ōtomo no Tabito and left behind a handful of beautiful verses.

To what shall I compare
    this life?
The way a boat
rowed out from the morning harbor
leaves no traces on the sea.

(trans. Ian Levy)

Given the inclinations of each reader, the *Ten Thousand Leaves* can be searched for linguistic, historical, anthropological, even ideological data. Unequipped with the necessarily specialized tools with which to do so, however, most English-speaking readers must fall back on their own intuitive responses, fostered in very different poetic and cultural traditions. They will be rewarded with many happy surprises.

TRANSLATIONS

Two lengthy translations are available. The earlier of them, entitled *The Manyōshū: The Nippon Gakujutsu Shinkōkai Translation of One Thousand Poems*, was first published in Japan in 1940, then reprinted by Columbia University Press in 1969. The Columbia volume contains a new and perceptive introduction by Donald Keene. The poems are chosen from the whole range of the twenty books. Ian H. Levy has begun a comprehensive translation of the entire collection. The first five books are contained in *The Ten Thousand Leaves: A Translation of Man'yōshū, Japan's Premier Anthology of Classical Poetry*, vol. 1 (Princeton University Press, 1981).

Collection of Old and New Japanese Poetry

Kokinshū

Poetry. Tenth Century

If **The Anthology of Ten Thousand Leaves** can be said to capture something of the fresh and open spirit of Japan before and during the eighth-century Nara period, then the *Collection of Old and New Japanese Poetry* (or *Kokinshū*), compiled around 920 A.D. at the request of the Emperor Daigo, can be said to set the tone, in matters literary and poetic, for the kind of court culture that would produce **The Pillow Book, The Tale of Genji,** and the court diaries. The poets of *The Anthology of Ten Thousand Leaves* used various forms of poetic expression and a wide range of subject matter; by the time of the *Collection of Old and New Japanese Poetry,* this luxuriant forest had been considerably subdued and trimmed. Most of the poets collected in *Old and New Japanese Poetry* were highly conscious of the techniques of their art and had reference to congenial models in both Chinese and earlier Japanese literary sources; in time they established the kind of poetry they wrote, the 31-syllable *waka,* as the dominant form of poetic expression. The form maintained that position until the rise of the 17-syllable *haiku* many centuries later. The *waka* ("Japanese poem"), sometimes referred to as the *tanka* ("short poem"), gained its name in contradistinction to the longer forms employed in *The Anthology of Ten Thousand Leaves,* notably the *chōka* or "long poem," of which Hitomaro's are the greatest surviving examples. At first glance, the 31-syllable *waka* seems hardly a poem at all by English-language standards since so few syllables can usually only produce a line or two of verse. The form was and is a difficult one to master. The *Collection of Old and New Japanese Poetry,* which in its twenty books sought to gather together the best of the "old" and the "new," set modes for literary allusion and became itself a sourcebook of poetical precedent that served later writers down to the present century. The development of *waka* and *haiku* alike followed a course guided by a constant dialectic interplay with this seminal collection. Twenty other official court anthologies of poetry were to follow, yet none, excepting the superb (and as yet untranslated) *Shinkokinshū* (New Collection of Old and New Japanese Poetry), assembled in the early thirteenth century, was to rival the *Collection of Old and New Japanese Poetry* in beauty or influence.

The reader coming to this collection for the first time will notice a number of unusual features seldom employed in Western poetry anthologies. Rather than grouping the poems by author, the compilers arranged them by subject matter, an artistic strategy of great import for later poetry. The first six books range over the seasons, from the beginning of spring through the depths of winter, and the pride of place given to the seasons has remained a constant in Japanese poetry. Other important categories include travel, love, congratulatory themes, and laments. Within these larger categories, some of the topics chosen were traditional and may have been assigned at various poetry-writing contests, so well described in *The Tale of Genji*, while others were composed on the basis of more personal inspiration. Within each book, the compilers arranged the poems with telling art, so that, for example, poems on melting snow are followed by those describing the songs of birds, the sprouting of grasses, then the blossoming of flowers. In one sense, each individual poem contributes to a larger artistic vision identified and shaped by the compilers. The effect for the reader is something like a journey; the traveler may stop to admire a particular scene, yet there is always a sense of forward motion. Given the brevity of the *waka* form, the method chosen by the compilers showed high artistic intuition. This model of arrangement set a pattern that was largely followed, with minor variations, in most varieties of poetic anthologies produced later.

In certain respects, the compilers of the anthology were quite articulate about their purposes and, indeed, about the larger purposes of poetry itself. Ki no Tsurayuki (ca. 872–945), a fine poet and the author of the *Tosa Diary*, composed a very influential preface, in the Japanese language (much more significant, historically, than a preface in Chinese that was also produced), in order to state a theory of poetry that set the relationship between feeling and expression for the whole court tradition. The text begins as follows:

> Japanese poetry has the human heart as seed and myriads of words as leaves. It comes into being when men use the seen and the heard to give voice to feeling aroused by the innumerable events in their lives.... It is song that moves heaven and earth without effort, stirs emotions in the invisible spirits and gods, brings harmony to the relations between men and women, and calms the hearts of fierce warriors.   (trans. Helen McCullough)

The power of song, reflecting human experience, was seen as an awesome force, one that derived from the semisacred beginnings of Japanese literature as reembodied in *A Record of Ancient Matters* and, to some extent, in *The Anthology of Ten Thousand Leaves*. Poetry was thus provided a social and spiritual function that could guide its further development. Tsurayuki and his companions saw that poetic excellence could be found in any age, and they believed that the great poets who had begun the still young Japanese tradition, notably Hitomaro, had the power to fix language in seminal images to which later poets could and should make reference; on the other hand, present and future poets must continue to examine their own authentic feelings in order to compose poetry capable of moving others. The *waka* was thus mandated to look both forwards and backwards at the same time. Poets in the long tradition that followed were required to attempt a balance between a knowledge of that tradition, allowing them to compose variants on older poems, and their own spontaneous feelings. The charge was not as simple as it seemed. At the least, poets in later generations had to know the *Collection* more or less by heart, since its poems and the philosophy of poetry it espoused quickly became pervasive.

The prestige of the anthology was such that the reputation of many poets were secured by their inclusion there. Some, in fact, have little else of their work preserved and so live in literary history because of the few samples of their poetry included. Some of the greatest of the early court poets, such as Lady Ise (fl. 900), Ono no Komachi (fl. ca. 833–57), Ariwara no Narihira (825–80), Ki no Tomonori (fl. ca. 875), and Ki no Tsurayuki himself, wrote many fine poems recorded in the *Collection*, and there are significant contributions by a number of others that reveal a widespread and exquisite sensibility in several generations of court poets.

As the *Collection* ranges over so many subjects and so many poets, it is difficult to give here any precise sense of its content, but happily it can now be read and studied in two English versions. Aside from their various merits, these two versions raise the issue of translation. All poetry is, of course, notoriously difficult to render into another language, and the *waka* presents particular problems, both because of the tremendous gap between old Japanese and modern English, and because of the brevity of the form, for which no remote analogues can be found in the history of English poetry. The strategies chosen to put these poems into English are as varied as the sensibilities of the translators who have made the attempt. Various poems have predictably attracted a number of enthusiasts, and one special pleasure available to readers is that of juxtaposing variants that suggest the beauties of a distant original. By way of example, here are four versions of a single poem, number 9 in book 1 ("Spring"), composed by Ki no Tsurayuki himself, on the subject of falling snow.

Mists rise, tree buds swell
and when the spring snow falls,
even in villages with no blossoms
blossoms come whirling down   (trans. Burton Watson)

When snow comes in spring—
fair season of layered haze
and burgeoning buds—
flowers fall in villages
where flowers have yet to bloom.   (trans. Helen McCullough)

Old and New Japanese Poetry

> when the warm mists veil
> all and buds swell   while yet the
>   spring snows drift downward
> even in the hibernal
> village   crystal blossoms fall   (trans. Rodd and Henkenius)

> With the spreading mists
> The treebuds swell in early spring
> And wet snow petals fall—
> So even my flowerless country village
> Already lies beneath its fallen flowers.   (trans. Brower and Miner)

The variations of tone and diction may seem surprising; every translator, in his or her way, has added something to the suggestively sparse original. In one sense, each of these translations can be seen as a gloss; yet, at the same time, each touches something in the depth of the original poem.

TRANSLATIONS
There are two recent and complete translations of the *Kokinshū*, one by Laurel R. Rodd and Mary C. Henkenius, *Kokinshu: A Collection of Poems Ancient and Modern* (Princeton University Press, 1984); the other by Helen Craig McCullough, *Kokin Wakashū: The First Imperial Anthology of Japanese Poetry* (Stanford University Press, 1985). Both provide considerable background on the anthology, McCullough's work extending to an entire complementary study, *Brocade by Night: "Kokin Wakashū" and the Court Style in Japanese Classical Poetry* (Stanford University Press, 1985), available as a companion volume to her authoritative translation. Hiroaki Sato and Burton Watson have translated a number of the best-known authors in the anthology in their *From the Country of Eight Islands: An Anthology of Japanese Poetry* (Columbia University Press, 1981); and the standard volume on the subject, *Japanese Court Poetry*, by Robert Brower and Earl Miner (Stanford University Press, 1961), is sprinkled with translations from the *Kokinshū*. In fact, virtually every book or anthology on traditional Japanese poetry and aesthetics contains selections from this collection, forming as it does the basis for a still-living tradition of *waka* composition that is now, remarkably enough, more than a thousand years old.

Tales of Ise

Ise monogatari

Prose and Poetry. Tenth Century

The *Tales of Ise* (*Ise monogatari*) is one of the earliest and most influential poetic works in Japanese literature. Its author or authors are unknown. Compiled sometime in the tenth century, the collection has served as a sourcebook for poetry, aesthetics, and subject matter down to the present century. Spare, almost fragmentary on first reading, *Ise* continues to fascinate and stimulate, for it provides an early glimpse of what were to become general concerns implicit in the whole Japanese view of art and the poetry of human relations.

A modern reader's first sense of surprise may be to find that the text is a mixture of genres, combining 31-syllable *waka* poetry with elegant prose sections. These prose passages usually provide a context for the lyric statements. Given the fact that the classical court *waka* form is so brief, the need for such contexts is genuine. In even earlier collections, such as **The Anthology of Ten Thousand Leaves**, for example, certain poems were assigned headnotes, a practice that was continued in such imperial poetry anthologies as the **Collection of Old and New Japanese Poetry**. In the *Tales of Ise*, their composition has become a fine art. The prose and poetry complement each other in elegant reciprocity.

The collection doubtless derives its name from a series of incidents (central to the work) which take place at Ise. It was there that the Ise Virgin, chosen from among the unmarried daughters of the high court nobility, was appointed as chief priestess to the Shintō goddess Amaterasu, worshipped at the Inner Shrine of Ise. The Virgin is visited, in this famous sequence in *Tales of Ise*, by the poet and gallant lover Ariwara no Narihira (825–80), a court official who later became the literary model for the courtly, manly lover, figuring in writings ranging from those of **Murasaki Shikibu** to **Ihara Saikaku**. The brief liaison of Narihira and the Virgin is described in a romantic fashion, pictured as halfway between dream and reality, and a similar atmosphere pervades a great portion of the other incidents as well. Although the text refers to "a man" or "a certain man," Narihira looms as the central character. Some of the poetry attributed to him in the text was written by the historical figure, some composed by others and attributed to him by the compilers.

Love, as depicted in *Tales of Ise*, often serves to draw humankind closer to an understanding of the evanescence of all earthly things. Time cannot be stopped, and worldly wisdom therefore consists of acquiescence, to the relinquishing of one's own desires. This theme will swell to a grand symphony in *The Tale of Genji*, but a similar note is struck here with brevity and poignancy.

In former times there lived a lady in East Gojō, in the Western Pavilion of the Empress Dowager's palace. Narihira visited her there, at first with no specific intentions but later in great infatuation. About the tenth day of the first month, however, she concealed herself elsewhere. Although he heard where her refuge was, it was impossible for him to go to her, and he became increasingly depressed. In the first month of the following year, when the plum blossoms were in their full glory, he went again to the Western Pavilion, remembering with longing the happenings of the previous year. He stood and looked, sat and looked, but nothing seemed the same. Bitterly weeping, he lay on the deserted bare floor until the moon sank in the sky. Recalling the happiness of the year before, he composed the poem:

> Is not that the moon?
> And is not the spring the same
> Spring of the old days?
> My body is the same body—
> Yet everything seems different. (trans. F. Vos)

Ariwara no Narihira is also shown in other contexts in the course of the collection. In one memorable scene, the courtier wades through the snow to seek out his princely patron, who has chosen to retire deep in the country as a Buddhist monk. The two meet and reminisce about the past in the fading winter light. Elsewhere, Narihira's bravery and wisdom are recounted in a number of colorful incidents.

The brevity of most sections often makes them suitable for artistic depiction. Motifs from *Tales of Ise* were used by medieval scroll painters, woodblock print artists, and many others. In the Tokugawa period, such famous artists as Ogata Kōrin (1658–1716) and others selected scenes from *Tales of Ise* to decorate such objects as screens, sliding panels, and fans. One particular favorite was the Yatsuhaṣhi or "Eight Bridges" episode, in which Ariwara no Narihira and his companions engage in a complex word game while composing alternating poems.

The structure of the *Tales of Ise*, with its alternation of prose and poetry, remained a powerful influence on later Japanese writers in virtually every genre and form. The movement of prose to poetry, narration to lyric insight, became a cornerstone of the aesthetics of the dramaturgy of the medieval *nō* theater and provided a model as well for the travel diaries of **Matsuo Bashō**. In his 1968 Nobel prize acceptance speech, **Kawabata Yasunari**, the modern novelist, mentioned the influence of *Tales of Ise* on his own work.

Elusive and slight though *Tales of Ise* may seem, and difficult as its poetry may be to translate, this evocative collection can provide even now a special fascination for readers who surrender themselves to its lyrical flow.

TRANSLATION
Helen Craig McCullough, trans. *Tales of Ise: Lyric Episodes from Tenth-Century Japan* (Stanford University Press, 1968). A beautiful and scholarly translation with full notes and references. The translation above by F. Vos is to be found in Donald Keene's *Anthology of Japanese Literature: From the Earliest Era to the Mid-Nineteenth Century* (Grove Press, 1955).

The Tale of Genji
Murasaki Shikibu

Genji monogatari

Novel. Eleventh Century

Kawabata Yasunari, in his 1968 Nobel prize acceptance speech, spoke of the influence on him, and on all of Japanese writers, past and present, of Lady Murasaki's vast and moving *Tale of Genji* (*Genji monogatari*). "*Genji* is a miracle," he said, "and it is as a miracle that the book is known abroad." Some have compared the sophistication of Lady Murasaki's insights into the court society of her period with those of Marcel Proust's on French society at the turn of the century. Both created galaxies of characters who, in their comings and goings, their moments of personal insight, and their ambiguous feelings over their own worldly commitments, are absolutely authentic and, once the frames of reference are grasped, totally recognizable by modern readers.

Given the power of the tale and its influence on such diverse traditional Japanese arts as the *nō* theater, painting, and *waka* poetry, to say nothing of the effect the text has had on such modern writers as **Tanizaki** and **Kawabata**, it is no wonder that the novel (to use our modern term, which can serve only as a rough and approximate means of identification) has spawned a whole tradition of literary criticism in Japan. Now that the book has become relatively well-known in the West as well, through translations into English, German, and French, the secondary literature in those languages is also growing apace. It is impossible to sum up all the critical points of view available; still, there is no question but that the subtle complexities of Lady Murasaki's conception certainly deserve extended commentary. The novel, however, can be fully enjoyed and savored without this body of knowledge, which may extend the significance of the text but can in no way replace it. Like all great works of literature, *The Tale of Genji* is more moving than anything that can be said about it.

If any word of caution about reading *Genji* needs to be made, it is this: be prepared to read, and enjoy, the entire text. *Genji* is full of poetic and striking incidents, all of which can be read, reread, and savored in and of themselves, but they gain their deeper significance only in terms of the larger design, which spreads across four generations. Indeed, a number of the most powerful and persuasive passages occur in the final third of the text, after the death of Genji himself. To read the first "book" alone (there are six such books in all, which together comprise a total of fifty-four chapters, some of them quite long) would be like listening to the introduction to the first movement of a Haydn symphony and then stopping before the main themes are struck. *Genji* begins lightly, when the prince is a youth. Only in the fullness of time—many, many pages later—does the handsome Genji, as do his readers alike, come to a fuller understanding of his life, centering as it does on events that lie far beyond the relatively simple beginnings chronicled in book 1.

Despite the fact that Lady Murasaki was celebrated in her time as a person of enormous accomplishment, it is astonishing to realize how little we actually know about her. Even her dates of birth and death are uncertain, although there is some indication that she may have died at thirty-seven or eight, possibly in 1014. Nor are the dates of the composition of her great work known precisely. As an attendant to the youthful Empress Akiko, Lady Murasaki had access to the highest reaches of court society, and her diary provides some revealing and evocative glimpses of her involvements with the circles in which she moved. Likewise, life in the women's quarters allowed her to know something of the emotional intrigues and aspirations of her contemporaries, and this knowledge is conveyed in her portrayal of the characters she created. In some ways, however, her life appears limited. Like other women at court, Lady Murasaki was seldom privy to the debates, assuming there were such, concerning policy and politics. To learn how the men of the court functioned, how they governed, one must turn elsewhere. *Genji* gives us rather the emotional temperature of the milieu of the times, concentrating on the ties between men and women as they span the generations.

In this regard, it can be noted that, although Prince Genji, "the Shining One," is the chief character, he often serves as a link to allow the author to create a progression of magnificently rendered women characters who pass on and off the stage. Some of these figures are romantic, like Genji's youthful love, the mysterious Yugao, some powerful and problematic, like the aristocratic Lady Rokujō. Others, like Lady Aoi, Genji's first and "official" wife, gain their full stature only in and after death. From the touching Lady of Akashi, whom Genji first meets when in exile, to the red-nosed Safflower Princess, a whole constellation of women characters appear, linked by Genji's affection and loyalty to them. Virtually all these women remain friends with the prince, even after any romantic dalliance may have ended. Some modern readers find themselves rather dismayed by Genji's attraction to so many women (what would these same readers make of the doings at the court of Louis XIV in France?). Yet actually, it is the special constancy provided by Genji's introspective sensibilities that allows for the creation of this web of complex relationships and gives a sustaining and cumulative power to the long narrative. Nowhere is this fact more evident than in Genji's long relationship with Murasaki, the real love of his life, a love that begins as a Pygmalion-like connection between tutor and girl-child, and ends, after the patient layering of so many emotional colors, only with her tragic and touching death, shortly before Genji's own demise.

It is possible to locate the design and themes of *The Tale of Genji* in the way in which the lives and assumptions of one generation go on to mark those of the next. As the narrative proceeds, Genji's son Yugiri and the son of Genji's best friend Tō no Chūjō, Kashiwagi, respond to their own situations in life by repeating (and in some degree consciously repeating) patterns of response from their fathers' generation. In this progression, the author creates her vision of the flowing nature of the human condition. Finally, with the death of Genji, himself a perfect blend of sense and sensibility and possessed of so many virile and gracious characteristics at the same time, the world of the novel truly splits apart. The last third traces the amorous careers of Niou, son of Princess Akashi, and Kaoru, who is the son of Kashiwagi. Together they might have equalled Genji; separately, they seem limited, inadequate. Niou, handsome and quick-witted, is the man of action, but his impetuousness and jealousy corrupt his attitudes and behavior alike. Kaoru shows all of Genji's exquisite sensibility and penchant for introspection, but these very virtues restrict him to a life of neurotic inaction. The tangles the two undergo with the three daughters of Prince Hachi, living in seclusion at Uji—first with Kozeri and Agemaki, then with the mysterious Ukifune—make up a highly emotional, often macabre narrative that is intensely gripping, both in the plotting of events and in its larger thematic implications. Yet Genji himself was never forced to suffer through such darkness.

The Tale of Genji represents a world in which the lives of dozens of characters are touched with that intuitive sense of the pathos of life, the supreme Heian literary value termed *mono no aware*. It was perhaps Lady Murasaki's need to express such feelings that caused the novel to be created. At one point in the narrative, Prince Genji remarks to the young Princess Tamakatsura, who loves to read the tales popular at the time, that an "author certainly does not write about specific people, recording all the actual circumstances of their lives. Rather it is a matter of his being so moved by things, both good and bad, which he has heard and seen happening to men and women that he cannot keep it all to himself but wants to commit it to writing and make it known to other people—even to those of later generations. This, I feel sure, is the origin of fiction" (trans. Ivan Morris). Most modern readers will agree that this is a tale highly worth the telling, for whatever generations there are, and for whatever that may come to be.

TRANSLATIONS
The publication of Arthur Waley's elegant translation of *The Tale of Genji*, begun in 1925 and finished in 1933, and presently available as a Modern Library Giant (Random House), provided for many years the means by which English-language readers could possess the work; and indeed, many Japanese who read English have enjoyed the Waley version, since the original text, in classical Japanese, is of fearsome difficulty for all but the specialist. (Most Japanese readers, of course, turn to versions in modern Japanese, such as the elegant "translation" by **Tanizaki Jun'ichirō**). Waley's version is slightly shorter than the original, and some of the passages he left out are of impor-

tance, particularly as they relate to certain Buddhist themes in the text. These sections became available when Edward Seidensticker published his translation (Knopf, 1976), which is absolutely complete. Seidensticker, in preparing his translation, had the benefit of the formidable scholarship that has been done in Japan on the *Genji* since Waley began his version. Nevertheless, the new version complements, rather than replaces, the earlier one. To move the Heian court society, described in such remote language, into modern times and contemporary English, powerful transpositions and transformations are required. As one critic remarked, Waley, doubtless unwittingly, selected for his new milieu an English eighteenth-century country house; Seidensticker, for his part, could not altogether escape the contemporary language of New York. The greatest pleasure, and instruction, a reader can have on the art of translation is to read the text, chapter by chapter, comparing the work of one master translator with another. Two versions thus juxtaposed help the sense of the buried original to come through. In all cases, abridgements are to be avoided.

The Ivan Morris quotation is taken from his essay "Murasaki on the Art of Fiction," in his excellent study of *Genji* entitled *The World of the Shining Prince: Court Life in Ancient Japan* (1964. Reprint. Penguin, 1979).

As I Crossed a Bridge of Dreams
Lady Sarashina

Sarashina nikki

Diary. Eleventh Century

One of the most vivid and satisfying forms of classical Japanese literature is that elusive genre referred to in this century as *nikki bungaku*, "diary literature." There has been much debate, both in Japan and elsewhere, as to what constitutes the essential nature of this group of evocative and highly personal texts. The major models for the form date to a great extent from the Heian period, and most of them were written by women. Mixing prose and poetry, fact and fiction, memory and desire, they resemble precisely no Western form, yet they are eminently approachable for modern readers, since their raison d'être is to reveal the subterranean flow of their authors' feelings. In this regard, at least, they appear virtually contemporary.

Of the many examples now available in distinguished translations, I would personally single out the *Sarashina Diary* (*Sarashina nikki*), translated by Ivan Morris with the title *As I Crossed a Bridge of Dreams*, both because of its touching, often wistful subject matter and because of the light it throws, however obliquely, on court and daily life in Heian Japan.

Curiously enough, we do not know the precise name of the author of this diary, the daughter of a court nobleman of middle rank, which seems an ironic state of affairs given the fact that we know more of certain aspects of her interior life than we do about most of our own friends whom we see every day. Lady Sarashina, as she is now usually called, spent her childhood in the country, far from Kyoto, where her father was vice-governor of Hitachi Province, northeast of present-day Tokyo. Returning to the capital when she was still virtually a girl, Lady Sarashina retained in later years a girlish shyness that marked and limited her human encounters at court and elsewhere. Such diffidence many well have lead her to an increasing interest in the contemplative life after she married and grew older.

Lady Sarashina's diary is no mere record of each passing day; rather, as Ivan Morris has noted, it serves as a means of recollecting certain patterns in her life that she felt crucial to self-understanding. In the text, she does not intellectualize these currents but, instead, juxtaposes incident with incident so that their cumulative significance is revealed. Many other events and encounters, however important they must have been in the course of her daily life, are omitted. In their place we are given the predilections, the obsessions. All that we read may not, in the ordinary sense of the word, be true. Still, there is no questioning the emotional authenticity of the text as she constructs her story, and so her life. In this sense, the diary, whatever the nature of its raw materials, can be seen as a supremely literary work.

Lady Sarashina, for one thing, is devoted to literature and, like most Heian gentlewomen, showed certain gifts as a writer of 31-syllable *waka* verse. Many of her poems, and poems written to her, dot the pages of her diary. She yearns for the high romance of the world described in *The Tale of Genji*, and she finds herself wishing again and again that she might encounter such an atmosphere of refinement, even for a single day. In one famous incident, after she has returned to the capital, her aunt manages to provide her with the loan, for the first time in her life, of a complete copy of the *Genji* (hard enough to come by, of course, as only handwritten manuscripts circulated). She immediately buried herself away for ten days, poring over the contents. Later in her life, at times of stress, her family tried to ply her with copies of other tales and stories to divert her overwrought sensibilities.

In addition to the realm of fantasy provided by literature, Lady Sarashina also had recourse to her dreams, which she often recorded in her diary, even though, as she occasionally remarks, their meaning was not always clear. Her shifting state of mind, as she moves back and forth from inner reverie to the outer demands of her life, is most effectively conveyed in such dream sequences. Reality and reverie also mix in a famous segment describing her meeting with a sensitive and thoughtful courtier who, as they discuss the beauty of the seasons, seems movingly akin to her in sensibility. After two brief encounters, however, they never meet again. And yet, Lady Sarashina's intuitive affirmation that at last she has been understood brings to her an ethereal, awed sense of imagined felicity that subtly informs other passages as well.

However striking these particular episodes of interior rumination and reflection may be, most readers will enjoy equally well Lady Sarashina's vivid accounts of trips she made with her father as a girl, as well as the pilgrimages undertaken to Buddhist temples as a married woman. Her descriptions of the lakes and forests she travels through, and of the dangers and the occasional deep pleasure she finds on these trips, make moving reading. She provides a surprisingly precise sense of place, and it does seem astounding that many of the spots described by this eleventh-century gentlewoman can still be visited by travelers and tourists today.

Self-awareness, then, is scarcely a modern literary virtue. Looking at herself, Lady Sarashina produced such a highly wrought image of her inner world that, whatever her original intentions, life was transformed into art in a way that many a novelist might well admire. Truth, real or imagined, is, in this case, more evocative than fiction.

TRANSLATION
Ivan Morris, trans. *As I Crossed a Bridge of Dreams: Recollections of a Woman in Eleventh-Century Japan.* Dial Press, 1971.

OTHER DIARIES
There are quite a number of other diaries of high literary merit that general readers may enjoy. The earliest of these, the beautiful *Tosa Diary*, was written in about 935 by Ki no Tsurayuki (ca. 872–945). Tsurayuki, a distinguished poet himself and a compiler of the *Collection of Old and New Japanese Poetry*, wrote his diary in the Japanese language. Since Japanese was favored by women—men tending to write prose in Chinese—Tsurayuki adopts the persona of a woman, and the diary, which came to serve as a model for the developing genre, mixes fact and fiction to produce a special poetic flavor. A fine translation by Earl Miner can be found in his *Japanese Poetic Diaries*, published by University of California Press in 1969. The *Kagero nikki*, translated by Edward Seidensticker under the title *The Gossamer Years: The Diary of a Noblewoman of Heian Japan*, published by Charles E. Tuttle in 1964, was composed by the sister of Lady Sarashina, and gives a remarkably frank account of the jealousy of a woman betrayed by her husband. The *Izumi Shikibu Diary: A Romance of the Heian Court*, translated by Edwin Cranston and published by Harvard University Press in 1969, is a highly charged account of an affair between the author, a famous poet, and her lover, Prince Atsumichi. Another influential diary, "The Izayoi Nikki," which served as something of a model for the kind of travel diaries written in the Tokugawa period by **Matsuo Bashō**, describes a trip made by the author, the nun Abutsu, from Kamakura to Kyoto in 1280. An English version can be found in an anthology prepared by Edwin O. Reischauer and Joseph K. Yamagiwa entitled *Translations from Early Japanese Literature* and published by Harvard University Press in 1951.

The Pillow Book
Sei Shōnagon

Makura no sōshi

Literary Jottings. Eleventh Century

Part diary, part essay, part miscellany, *The Pillow Book* of Sei Shō-nagon, written in the early eleventh century, is as difficult to characterize as its witty and perceptive author, the erstwhile rival of the author of *The Tale of Genji*, Murasaki Shikibu. Neither the life of the author nor the date of her work can be precisely ascertained, yet there is nothing whatsoever vague about her clever, clear-minded, and always eloquent account of life at the court of Heian Japan.

Because of her panache, Sei Shōnagon became the subject of a number of legends and observations, one of which was that her wit made up for her lack of beauty, another that her quick mind cut through any foolishness and pretense on the part of others. Indeed, later reputation considered her the very epitome of the cultivated, amusing, and brilliant woman who was more than a match in wit for any man. Within her Heian context, she came to resemble the kind of personality familiar in the English tradition from the comedies of a writer like William Congreve; in observing the foibles of human behavior, Sei Shōnagon's eye is as dry, and as penetrating, as that of Millamant in *The Way of the World*.

If *The Pillow Book* (*Makura no sōshi*) cannot now be classified or domesticated into a particular and comfortable literary genre, its combination of observation and reflection nevertheless served as a model, directly or indirectly, for many later works that are themselves among the greatest of the Japanese traditional classics, chief among them *Essays in Idleness* by Yoshida Kenkō. In the visual arts, Sei Shōnagon came to play a role as well. *The Pillow Book Scroll*, created in the fourteenth century, put many of Shōnagon's incidents into visual form, where they came to gain a new and expanded currency.

The reader who begins *The Pillow Book* from the first entry in Ivan

Morris's complete translation will notice what appears to be a haphazard arrangement of the various topics on which Shōnagon has chosen to comment. Memories of court ceremonies jostle with lists of things enjoyed or despised; introspective responses to the beauties of the seasons rub up against information on details of court life so accurately recorded that modern cultural historians continue to pore over them for clues on the life of the period. In that sense, indeed, *The Pillow Book* serves as a sourcebook as well as a work of what we might loosely term literature. So sure is Shōnagon's instinct, and so skillful her ability to make choices, that the smallest objective detail she records takes on an energy that can attract and hold the attention of any modern reader.

In the years after the 1890s, when *The Pillow Book* first became known to Western readers, various translators were tempted to dip into its lengthy text and pull out a few beguiling tidbits they felt might attract their readers. By 1928, Arthur Waley could remark that, in translating a quarter of the original, he had chosen virtually new material to render into English, as heretofore, "it seemed to me, the least interesting passages had been chosen." It is perhaps a sign of the growing appreciation for Japanese culture in general that the complete translation of Ivan Morris, which first appeared in 1967, has been so successful. Various passages once regarded by Western translators as repetitious, unintelligible, or dull could now be shown to hold a fascination as great as the previously translated sections. For however obscure the context, Shōnagon's commentary brings a human response at once intimate and objective. Even the structure of the book, which was found somewhat confusing to the neat ideals of the Victorian sensibility, now seems to our postmodern mentality a natural manifestation of the way our minds actually work, moving from one level to another, and from one subject to another, without apparent self-consciousness, certainly without apology.

In the end, it is the author's observant eye that, transcending time, can show us things we all can understand.

Pretty Things

The face of a child that has its teeth dug into a melon.

(trans. Arthur Waley)

Embarrassing Things

Sometimes when in the course of conversation I have expressed an opinion about someone and perhaps spoken rather severely, a small child has overheard me and repeated the whole thing to the person in question. This may get one into a terrible fix....

(trans. Arthur Waley)

Small Children and Babies

Small children and babies ought to be plump. So ought provincial governors and others who have gone ahead in the world; for, if they are lean and desiccated, one suspects them of being ill-tempered.

(trans. Ivan Morris)

Squalid Things

The back of a piece of embroidery.

The inside of a cat's ear.

A swarm of mice, who still have no fur, when they come wriggling out of their nest.

The seams of a fur robe that has not yet been lined.

Darkness in a place that does not give the impression of being very clean.

(trans. Ivan Morris)

Some commentators have suggested that one reason for the freshness of Shōnagon's observations lies in the fact that she did not intend them to be read by others. Her account of how the manuscript was discovered might well have fitted under her rubric of "unpleasant things."

When the Middle Captain of the Left Guards Division was still Governor of Ise, he visited me one day at my home. There was a straw mat at the edge of the veranda, and I pulled it out for him.

This notebook of mine happened to be lying on the mat, but I did not notice it in time. I snatched at the book and made a desperate effort tò get it back; but the Captain instantly took it off with him and did not return it until much later. I suppose it was from this time that my book began to be passed about at Court.

(trans. Ivan Morris)

There are, of course, occasional passages that, since Shōnagon names names, might well have brought annoyance, yet surely her contemporaries must have been as surprised and beguiled as we to watch her sensibilities play over the objects and events that made up the fabric of their lives, providing them, had they only guessed it, with the only immortality they would know.

TRANSLATIONS
The abridgement prepared by Arthur Waley, entitled *The Pillow-Book of Sei Shōnagon*, was first published by George Allen & Unwin in 1928 and has continued to be made available in a variety of imprints. Waley's own witty commentary is delightful, and his informal account of the author's actual life and times can serve as a genial introduction to the full Ivan Morris translation of the same English title, first published by Columbia University Press in 1967 and presently available as a Penguin paperback. Waley is not replaced by Morris; read in tandem, they produce a higher ratio of delight than either can give alone.

Tales of Times Now Past

Konjaku monogatari
Popular Tales. Twelfth Century

Many of the great monuments of early classical Japanese literature belong, not surprisingly, to the category of what in modern terminology might be defined as products of high culture, written by aristocrats or other relatively erudite and well-educated people for a fairly small coterie of readers. *Tales of Times Now Past (Konjaku monogatari)*, however, although edited by a person or persons of culture, provides the best glimpse we can probably obtain of the popular traditions of medieval Japan. Replacing the introspective milieu of the Heian courtier is another view of a universe populated with a highly varied cast of characters, from ancient Chinese sages to Japanese woodcutters. Magic and sorcery take a central role, and the elevated emotions of the nobility, as pictured in works like *The Tale of Genji* or *The Tale of the Heike*, although sometimes in evidence, are now broadened to encompass a wide variety of human responses to the comedy, and the occasional tragedy, of life. There are noble characters in this collection of tales, but there are jealous ones, lecherous ones, and dangerous ones as well.

Tales of Times Now Past is perhaps the best known of quite a number of collections of legends and other popular tales assembled during the medieval period. Arguably it has remained the most influential. Although evidently little known when the manuscript was first compiled, the collection came to serve as an important sourcebook during succeeding eras. A number of well-known stories eventually found their way into other works of literature, particularly in dramatic form, where they were reworked as the basis for *nō*, *kabuki*, and *bunraku* plays. In the modern period, Japanese artists and intellectuals, attempting to better understand the feelings and attitudes of these remote generations, have read over these stories with a renewed interest; some, like **Akutagawa Ryūnosuke**, created famous modern versions, notably "Rashōmon" (Rashō Gate), which have become modern classics themselves.

The author or compiler of this enormous collection has not been positively identified, but the stories were evidently assembled early in the twelfth century. The original manuscript was to contain thirty-one "books" or chapters, arranged systematically by topic. The first five contained stories of Buddhism in India, the next five tales of China with an emphasis on Buddhist narratives. Books 11 to 20 ranged over a variety of tales on Buddhism in Japan, while the final books brought together secular tales of various kinds. Some sections, however, were evidently left unfinished, so the original design as we have it is not complete.

Given the fact that *Tales of Times Now Past* was assembled in the twelfth century, when popular forms of Buddhism were spreading throughout the country and into all levels of society, it is not surprising that so many of the stories deal, at least formally, with religious subjects, and indeed a certain number of them seem to be included for their didactic messages. Yet the effect on the modern reader is far more varied, and far richer, than the model of a pious fable might suggest. The tales seem to have been chosen basically because they are good stories, full of human interest, and their plots, sometimes simple, sometimes extremely complex, usually contain many of the typically vigorous elements that make up any exciting popular narrative. It is true, certainly, that the tales describing India and China are somewhat more formal in manner than those concerning Japan, since many appear intended to suggest solemn moments in high antiquity. Yet even in these cases, the satiric eye of the storyteller can locate pompousness and fraud as soon as it appears.

In one important sense, a collection such as this serves as a telling corrective to more refined works of philosophy or literature. These tales indicate artlessly the limits of what ordinary people understood of the high religious traditions. There are few references to abstruse doctrines or transcendental considerations. Priests and laity alike are judged by how they act. The Buddha is wise and the Chinese ancient sages clever because of what they accomplish, not merely because of what they may propound, or what they might symbolize by their presence. And although there are a good deal of magical and supernatural goings-on recorded in many of these stories, a recognizable humanity pervades. Even in the midst of a Chinese Buddhist hell, a kind thought for a living relative can do wonders.

No complete translation of this voluminous collection exists, or is likely to. The standard manuscript contains some 1,200 tales. Marian Ury in her translation has selected only 62 of the total. Nevertheless, she has chosen wisely in providing representative stories from all sections of the original, so that the compiler's intended plan, with its progression from India to China and then to Japan, and from religious to secular considerations, remains clear. In addition, as the translator explains in her lucid and useful introduction, her choices were made to appeal to "all those who, like myself, are fond of stories and are interested in how they are told." Her principle is certainly effectively applied, for virtually every one of these pithy accounts sets an atmosphere and makes its point with economy and often with considerable wit. Annotations are kept to a minimum, just enough to provide the reader with the proper bearings, and although the oral "storytelling" aspects of the Japanese text (repeated phrases, stock epithets, etc.) have been somewhat reduced in translation, the English versions represent an accurate rendering of the often spare originals.

Those readers who take an interest in European, African, or other Asian folk stories and legends will of course be able to draw suggestive comparisons with much that is recorded here, but such comparative interests are by no means necessary in order to fully enjoy the kind of world that is presented in this collection. The vigor and piquancy of medieval Japan are so suggestively described that most of these stories can bring that distant world much closer to us than might be imagined possible; and on the whole, the journey is a highly entertaining one.

TRANSLATION
Marian Ury, trans. *Tales of Times Now Past: Sixty-two Stories from a Medieval Japanese Collection.* University of California Press, 1979.

OTHER COLLECTIONS
Two other book-length translations of medieval story collections are available. One, *Collection of Tales from Uji*, translated by D. E. Mills and published by Cambridge University Press in 1970, is highly annotated and aimed at the scholarly reader. Royall Tyler's delightful *Japanese Tales* (Pantheon Books, 1987) takes another approach, retelling a number of stories in a fresh and contemporary idiom, including some important stories taken from *Tales of Times Now Past.* In addition, there are two more specialized collections of Buddhist tales available in English, *Miraculous Tales from the Japanese Buddhist Tradition: The Nihon Ryōiki of the Monk Kyōkai*, translated by Kyoko Nakamura (Harvard University Press, 1973), and *Sand and Pebbles* of Mujū Ichien, translated by Robert Morrell (State University of New York Press, 1985).

The Poetry of Saigyō (1118–90)

The Buddhist monk Saigyō lived in a turbulent period. He began his life as a courtier but turned to the religious life in his early twenties. The rest of his days were spent in a variety of hermitages and in traveling as a mendicant monk to both the eastern and northern regions of Japan. One of the most renowned poets of his day, Saigyō left a splendid legacy of *waka* verse and quickly came to serve as a spiritual role model for many who followed him in the Way, notably the *haiku* poet **Matsuo Bashō**. For many, Saigyō is the greatest of all traditional poets, combining compassion, enormous literary skill, and spiritual profundity.

By abandoning the confinements of court life, Saigyō was able to turn to composing poems that touch on his own most personal experiences, thus broadening by his example the range of possibilities within the *waka* tradition. Saigyō was in close touch with all the greatest poets of his time, most of whom were attached to court or Buddhist ecclesiastical circles, and thus a certain percentage of his poems do deal with the sorts of assigned topics typical of his period. Even in such a milieu, however, Saigyō often found fresh and attractive approaches to such traditional themes as the seasons, love, travel, and other set themes. His meditative verse in particular achieves a rare individuality and depth.

Given the brevity of the *waka*'s 31-syllable form, Saigyō sought to perfect a system of extended metaphor that gave his images of nature a powerful symbolic resonance. The moon, already an accepted image for Buddhist enlightenment, served the poet on a number of occasions as a means to suggest the possibility of transcendence.

So taken with
The faultless face and radiance
Of an alluring moon,

My mind goes farther ... farther ...
To reach remote regions of the sky.   (trans. William LaFleur)

The seasons, redolent of the natural cycle of growth and decay, provided Saigyō with a means to illustrate man's eventual need, as Buddhists believe, to abandon his craving to possess a world which, however solid it may seem, is destined to change and elude his grasp.

Gazing at them,
these blossoms have grown
so much a part of me,
to part with them when they fall
seems bitter indeed!   (trans. Burton Watson)

Saigyō's nuanced use of such images becomes all the more remarkable when a large selection of his verse is read, so that the poet's subtle shifts in tonality and meaning within the strictures of the *waka* form can be strikingly revealed.

A powerful and attractive personality stands behind Saigyō's poetry, most clearly sensed in the many verses that deal with his spiritual quest. In particular, he embodies in his poetry the human longing for companionship and the ordinary human responses of human life that stand in contrast to the lonely rigors and austerities of the Buddhist Way.

Even a person free of passion
would understand this sadness:
autumn evening
in a marsh where snipes fly up.   (trans. Burton Watson)

In later Japanese literature, Saigyō's persona became as important as his poetry. He became the subject of poems by other *waka* poets, an important character in a number of *nō* plays, even a kind of iconographical image to be drawn and painted by artists. This man, so intensely human, both approachable and austere, both in and out of the world, continued to serve as a durable role model in Japanese culture, a symbol of a human being, all too human, who struggled toward and surely obtained enlightenment. Bashō wrote of him and created *haiku* variations on his poems in *The Narrow Road to the Deep North* and elsewhere. Saigyō can still remain a potent force in modern works, such as the astonishing 1955 short story by **Ariyoshi Sawako,** "The Village of Eguchi."

Ultimately, it is perhaps that sense of life as a pilgrimage which gives Saigyō's poetry such resonance within Japanese culture, and indeed it is on this theme that he has written his most remarkable poetry. The best of these poems exist outside of time. The reader who finds himself or herself sharing Saigyō's premises will be drawn close to him and, through him, to the experience itself.

> Passage into dark
> Mountains over which the moon
> Presides so brilliantly ...
> Not seeing it, I'd have missed
> This passage into my own past.   (trans. William LaFleur)

TRANSLATIONS

Despite the centrality of Saigyō in the Japanese tradition, no adequate complete translation of his poetry has yet been attempted. Saigyō's own collection of his *waka* contains some 1,500-odd poems. William LaFleur's collection *Mirror for the Moon* (New Directions, 1978) provides translations for over 170 poems, and Burton Watson has rendered 64 into English in the anthology *From the Country of Eight Islands: An Anthology of Japanese Poetry,* edited in collaboration with Hiroaki Sato (Columbia University Press, 1981). Translations by other hands can be found in virtually every collection or anthology of traditional Japanese verse. A translation of the Ariyoshi Sawako story mentioned above, incidentally, can be found in the *Japan Quarterly,* vol. 18, no. 4.

An Account of My Hut
Kamo no Chōmei
Hōjōki

Literary Jottings. 1212

Kamo no Chōmei (1153–1216) lived through tumultuous times, and his poetic diary, the 1212 *Account of My Hut (Hōjōki)*, which chronicles his retreat from society, remains the classic expression of the psychology of a Buddhist recluse in traditional Japanese culture. It represents an ironic, occasionally wistful statement of a man who has abandoned society for the consolations of meditation and art. Along with **Saigyō**, the archetypal wandering poet-priest, Chōmei helped set down the traditions of the roving artist who retired from the world in order to transcend the ordinary vicissitudes of life. Chōmei helped provide the model for the conduct and aspirations of such great figures in the Japanese literary tradition as **Yoshida Kenkō**, **Matsuo Bashō**, and **Ryōkan**. His poetry is less revered than that of the later Tokugawa masters, but *An Account of My Hut* is one of the most admired and studied of all classical literary texts. Its complex and sometimes winsome atmosphere can fortunately be conveyed in English as well.

Chōmei was brought up in the capital city of Kyoto, the son of a prominent Shintō priest, who died when the writer was a young man. Chōmei showed an early vocation for writing verse and eventually found himself involved in the poetry circles that had formed around the Emperor Go-Toba. Go-Toba held the throne from 1183 to 1198, when he retired and continued to exercise power from behind the scenes. As a youngster, Go-Toba had suffered through the dislocations of the 1185 civil wars between the feuding Taira and Minamoto clans, chronicled in *The Tale of the Heike*, and Chōmei lived through that difficult period as well. Perhaps those events colored Chōmei's outlook on life, or perhaps his basic temperament, reinforced by the Buddhist doctrines he came to study, led him to seek a life apart. In any case, Chōmei took Buddhist vows and retired from his active life at court. After a period of traveling about, he built a hermitage overlooking the beautiful Uji river, south of the capital, a locale already famous because of its importance in the later chapters of *The Tale of Genji*. There Chōmei continued to write poetry, commentaries on poetry, and, most importantly, *An Account of My Hut*.

The theme of evanescence runs through all of the *Account*, and this atmosphere is nowhere more beautifully captured than in the opening passages of the work.

> The flow of the river is ceaseless and its water is never the same. The bubbles that float in the pools, now vanishing, now forming, are not of long duration....
>
> ... The dew may fall and the flower remain—remain, only to be withered by the morning sun. The flower may fade before the dew evaporates, but though it does not evaporate, it waits not the evening. (trans. Donald Keene)

Chōmei's *Account* uses this theme and expands it through a series of metaphors and comparisons. One of them involves the pride of men and the houses they build, structures that vanish through neglect, fire, or political imperatives, such as the brief shift of the capital in 1177. Famine and earthquake alike can kill and destroy men and their pretensions. Chōmei describes events of this kind that he has witnessed, and his vignettes of human suffering are extraordinarily vivid. Although often understated, the scenes he pictures linger long in the reader's mind.

Chōmei goes on to describe the changes he came to observe in his own attitudes toward the world. He chooses to do so in terms of living quarters. He began, Chōmei recounts, in an elegant house during his childhood days, then moved to smaller and smaller quarters, until at last he came to construct his legendary square hut, "fashioned for the last leaves of my years," which represented a space only "a bare ten foot square and less than seven feet high." Chōmei describes his elegant living arrangements within this tiny space and indicates how he spends his time playing music, reciting the Buddhist sutras, and walking through the mountains and fields, often in search of some spot made famous in the history of poetry. Chōmei thus becomes the kind of "temporary man" that the realities of his life have convinced him to become. "The hermit crab chooses to live in little shells because it well knows the size of its body. Knowing myself and the world, I have no ambitions and do not mix in the world. I seek only tranquillity; I rejoice in the absence of grief" (trans. Donald Keene).

Buddhism teaches withdrawal from desire as a means to transcend the pain of present life. Chōmei attempts the process, yet is shrewd enough to know that each choice brings with it its own dangers. Is it not perhaps a sin, he wonders ruefully, to love his little hut so much?

At once elegant, powerful, and ironic, *An Account of My Hut* leads the reader back through the text itself to the personality of its author, a man who possesses within himself the capacity for ennui, wisdom, despair, and wonder. In this regard, Chōmei and his responses to the world seem not remote at all.

TRANSLATION
Donald Keene's translation of *An Account of My Hut* can be found in his *Anthology of Japanese Literature: From the Earliest Era to the Mid-Nineteenth Century* (Grove Press, 1955).

Essays in Idleness
Yoshida Kenkō

Tsurezuregusa

Literary Jottings. Fourteenth Century

The revelation of personality in literature is often said to have begun in the West with the essays of Montaigne in the sixteenth century. In the Japanese tradition, there are two antecedents of high charm and great stylistic merit, *The Pillow Book* of Sei Shōnagon (ca. 1000) and the remarkable collection of essays, observations, and aphorisms of the courtier-monk Yoshida Kenkō (1283–1350), whose comments and reflections have delighted and instructed readers down to the present day.

Kenkō came to mix with the highest artistic and political circles and so was able to observe the accomplishments of the court culture of his time. He was born into a family of Shintō priests, and his poetic skills gave him access to the emperor's court in Kyoto, although he took Buddhist orders in 1321, after the death of his patron, the Emperor Go-Uda. Living in seclusion outside the capital, Kenkō traveled to a variety of places, including Kamakura, the seat of shogunal power. Widely read in the Chinese and Japanese classics, he shows himself in *Essays in Idleness* to be a man of letters who loved learning and yet wore his scholarship lightly. He returned to Kyoto toward the end of his life, and it is thought that the 243 sections that make up this collection were composed largely during those last years. There are a variety of theories as to how the various fragments were put in order, but none can be definitely proven. Since its discovery, however (the oldest manuscript is dated 1431), *Essays in Idleness* has been studied, quoted, even parodied. Kenkō's superb style and quick, cultivated mind allowed him to create the finest—and still the most enjoyable—work of its kind in classical Japanese literature.

The various entries in the collection are highly irregular in length. Some are only a sentence or two, others several pages. The fact that they flow together so naturally from subject to subject, moving smoothly from introspection to observation and back again, make the text quite accessible to a modern reader. Familiar as we are with the conventions of stream-of-consciousness fiction, we can read Kenkō as almost a contemporary figure, witnesses to the movements of his mind, the shifting course of his thoughts. This is the starting point that allows familiarity, yet the real fascination of the book resides in its ability to lead us into an understanding, and a sympathy, for ideas and attitudes quite removed from those of contemporary life, either in Japan or in the West.

Many of Kenkō's attitudes spring from his study of Buddhist texts, coupled with his observations on the political vicissitudes of his day. As an outside observer living in partial retirement, Kenkō saw the grasping for power around him as a sign that all the rewards of life in this world represent an illusion that must be overcome. Nothing, he felt, can be firmly grasped or held forever. The natural cycle of rise and fall, birth and decay, must rule the actions of all men. These ideas, so fundamental to writers and thinkers in medieval Japan, are expressed in other great works of the period, notably in Kamo no Chōmei's *An Account of My Hut* and *The Tale of the Heike*, where the political and religious implications of such a world view are stressed. Kenkō moves these concepts of the cyclical nature of life into the realm of aesthetics. Many of his observations on the nature of the beautiful have become the classic explications in the Japanese tradition. Profound beauty, Kenkō stresses, can truly exist only when a sense of time is present in the mind of the beholder. If everything were to continue on for eternity, nothing would truly catch our human fancy. Transiency makes a flower beautiful because we know the petals must fall. So, by extension, a flower in the bud or a tree with the leaves falling in late autumn are more beautiful than they might be in the fullness of their seasons, since, for the sensitive observer, they show by their very nature the image of the evanescent, always subject to change. Much of subsequent Japanese art is indebted to the power of Kenkō's insight and example.

Kenkō was an astute observer of the social order as well, and few escaped his penetrating wit. A man of good will himself, he disliked pretense and vulgarity in any form. Priests, courtiers, warriors, country bumpkins, all became the object of his observations, and he was never reticent to use ridicule. Kenkō saw his period as one of decline, and in holding up the standards of the past, he found many in the present wanting in discretion, thoughtfulness, and human wisdom. Kenkō never seems malicious, but he can often be sharp, and very funny.

The fact that Kenkō wrote of the particulars of his society means that a modern reader will, of course, need a great many details explained. In this regard, the translation of *Essays in Idleness* most generally available, that of Donald Keene, is exemplary in every way. His version provides both a sense of the charm of the original and the scholarly and historical apparatus needed to make the point of each section clear.

In that respect, the arrangement of the printed text is particularly felicitous, since notes follow each individual section.

"The pleasantest of all diversions is to sit alone under the lamp, a
book spread out before you, and to make friends with people of a distant past you have never known," writes Kenkō in Keene's translation.
He was thinking of the poets of China, but many generations of readers
have developed a similar affection for Kenkō's essays, and for him.

TRANSLATION
Donald Keene, trans. *Essays in Idleness: The Tsurezuregusa of Kenkō*. Columbia
University Press, 1967.

The Tale of the Heike

Heike monogatari

War Chronicle. Fourteenth Century

"The bell of the Jetavana temple tolls in every man's heart to warn him
that all is vanity and evanescence" (trans. Kitagawa and Tsuchida). So
begins this great and complex tale of the 1185 civil wars waged between
two great clans, a conflict that altered the whole course of Japanese
history and culture. In one way, the long narrative of these battles and
their dour consequences can be seen as a dramatic manifestation of the
idea expressed in that one sentence: man's seeking for fame, security,
and happiness in this world is, by the very nature of the human condition, doomed from the start.

The Tale of the Heike exists both inside and outside history. In one
sense, the book is a chronicle of the tumultuous years leading up to the
struggles in which even the emperor must die, and climaxing in the battle of Dannoura, in which the power of the Heike perished forever.
There were many groups vying for power at the time, chief among
them two great clans, the Taira (also referred to as the Heike, another
pronunciation for the written characters "Taira family") and the
Minamoto (also sometimes called Genji, an alternative reading for the

words "Minamoto clan"). The Taira had long served the emperor, and in the generation of Kiyomori, the arch-villain of the piece, they are determined to rise above their station and supplant even the most noble and ancient clan, the Fujiwara, who had always been closest to the imperial family. Kiyomori's arrogance and pride arouse the ire of many and cause a series of plots against his family. Eventually the Minamoto rise up to suppress the Taira and, in doing so, bring new values to the circles of power in medieval Japan. The Minamoto were not cultivated aristocrats familiar with the court, the kind of elegant, understanding men described in *The Tale of Genji*, but men of military might, sure of will and hungry for power. Although there are many among them who show true nobility, much of *The Tale of the Heike* is elegiac and expresses a yearning for the beauty of a peaceful court culture that could no longer continue. Ruth Benedict, in her famous book *The Chrysanthemum and the Sword*, posited a basic dichotomy in the Japanese character, dividing various attributes into the aesthetic and the militant. In literary terms, *The Tale of the Heike* is the sword, *The Tale of Genji* the chrysanthemum, that sensitive and resplendent culture so deeply mourned in the medieval classic.

For a modern reader, *The Tale of the Heike* may most seem to resemble some sort of historical novel, but it was not composed to be read in that fashion. Virtually every character in the story is based on historical accounts. No major events have been created. Certainly, early audiences believed it to be a truthful account. For them, in addition, the *Heike* was a moral injunction, an account of how men at all times may go astray through the sin of pride. In that sense, the book is a moral document that transcends history. The text does not always preach, but the weight of its Buddhist insights is powerful indeed. Thus a foreign reader who absorbs the text with some literary sympathy can gain invaluable access to the unarticulated assumptions about the human predicament that have governed Japanese thinking since the medieval period and, in some areas, still prevail today.

The *Heike*, however, is certainly not a work of sustained introspection. The military battles described there are of the most swashbuckling sort, and a host of vivid characters crowd its pages. The dashing hero Minamoto Yoshitsune, the evil Kiyomori, the exiled monk Shunkan, the enlightened warrior Kumagai, Goshirakawa, the cloistered emperor who attempts to control the whole progress of the war behind the scenes, and a dozen or so others are so vividly re-created and presented that they came to serve as models for characters in countless *nō* dramas, *kabuki* and *bunraku* plays, and a number of modern works as well, including powerful dramas by **Kinoshita Junji** and others. These vivid historical figures likewise appeared in scroll paintings and other works in the visual arts. The *Heike* has always been, and is likely to remain, a potent work of popular art that inspires high art.

Given the development of the text as it has come down to us, this popularity is not so surprising. The authors are unknown, and what we have now is a text taken down in 1371, in the version presented by a famous chanter of the period. The story exists in many variants, and while early versions may have been based, according to recent research, on a relatively short account of the wars (thus the historical veracity), the various episodes were embroidered by chanters, who took the tale all over Japan, reciting it with a musical accompaniment to audiences that were doubtless largely illiterate. In that sense, the *Heike* is a sort of folk epic; yet, unlike Homer's *Iliad*, it began as a sophisticated written account to which oral elements were added. The *Heike* in that regard may well be unique among classic works in world literature, combining as it does courtly and popular ideals in close and untroubled juxtaposition.

The *Heike* contains, of course, a good deal of cultural baggage that English-language readers must acquire. There are two translations available. The newer of the two, by Hiroshi Kitagawa and Bruce Tsuchida, is complete and contains an excellent introduction and copious notes that help the uninitiated through the undergrowth of political and religious terminology that can invariably confuse. A certain number of readers maintain an attachment for an earlier translation by A. L. Sadler, first published in 1928. Sadler's work is heavily abridged, as he selected what he took to be the major scenes and attempted, often with considerable success, to match the tonality of the magnificent language of the original with a slightly archaic English that suggests on occasion the King James Bible. Sadler strove to convey the moral tone that pervades the Japanese text, and his Western linguistic analogues sometimes strike the proper weight more than those of Kitagawa and Tsuchida, whose language is relatively simple. There is a peculiar pleasure, in fact, to be gained by reading both translations side by side.

Modern scholarly and popular interest in *The Tale of the Heike* has produced a number of retellings of the original, and one of them, *The Heike Story*, by the popular novelist Yoshikawa Eiji (1892–1962), has been partially translated into English. The version available concentrates on earlier portions of the story. Yoshikawa brings psychological considerations to the fore, and the more archaic elements in the *Heike* tend to recede, especially those dealing with religion. The narrative, in this version, is surely tighter and closer to the modern mentality, yet invariably the awesomeness, the striking foreignness of the historical and literary conceptions (even to a modern Japanese reader) are diminished. The loss is significant. *The Heike Story* has excitements that repay a reading, and some of the moral vigor of the original shines through, but at best it provides an adjunct to its powerful parent.

TRANSLATIONS

Bruce Tsuchida and Hiroshi Kitagawa, trans. *The Tale of the Heike.* Tokyo University Press, 1977. Distributed in the United States by Columbia University Press.

A. L. Sadler, trans. *The Ten Foot Square Hut and Tales of Heike.* 1928. Reprint. Charles E. Tuttle, 1971.

Yoshikawa Eiji. *The Heike Story.* Trans. Fuki W. Uramatsu. Charles E. Tuttle, 1956.

As this book goes to print, Helen Craig McCullough has produced a new translation (*The Tale of the Heike*, Stanford University Press, 1988), which will undoubtedly prove an invaluable means of coming to grips with this great epic.

Nō Theater
Fourteenth and Fifteenth Centuries

The *nō*, which began in medieval times, constitutes what in this century has often been termed total theater: chant, mime, music (instrumental, vocal, and choral), dance, masks, and poetic texts forming an entire aesthetic environment. The aim of these highly coordinated dramas is not to re-create any reflection of realism, in our modern sense of the word, but rather to suggest a kind of ethereal and profound beauty, one that lurks beneath the surface of things, unamenable to direct expression. This beauty, referred to as *yūgen* in Japanese, represents the highest reach of dramatic and poetic art as practiced in this period.

A variety of writers and poets have composed texts for the *nō* theater, which reached perhaps its most innovative peak with the work of Kan'ami (1333–84) and his son Zeami (1363–1443). The continuing popularity of the *nō* required the composition of plays down to the latter half of the nineteenth century, when, as Western influences became increasingly pervasive, it became a basically classical theater with few new additions to a now historic repertory.

In the context of this integrated dramatic form, the play texts themselves constitute only one element of the whole. In a sense, they are closer in function to, say, an opera libretto than to any playscript in the modern, Western sense. In spite of the spare nature of many of their texts, the best of the *nō* plays are dramatic masterpieces of the highest rank. When *nō* texts became known in the West early in this century, such important figures as Yeats, Ezra Pound, Bertolt Brecht, the French poet Paul Claudel, and the British composer Benjamin Britten took an intense interest in the form and attempted to compose *nō* dramas in terms of their own personal vision of a total theater.

As in opera, the musical forms employed in the *nō* dictate to a certain extent the form that the play text takes. In that regard, the structures of *nō* plays are generally similar. Prose and poetry alternate, and a gradual quickening of tempo as the play proceeds prepares the audience for the climax. Plots are often drawn from classical tales, such as *The Tale of Genji* or *The Tale of the Heike*, so that the audience's interest is far less focused on what may happen as on why it happened, a dramatic strategy that helps direct the movement of the play toward the interior world of the characters represented, objectified in the poetic lines that they speak.

The events of the plays usually follow a set course. The drama begins with the entrance of a Buddhist pilgrim or other similar person, who comes upon some relic or memento of a famous person, often long dead. Showing a sympathy for that person, the pilgrim asks questions of the main character, who enters at this point in the play. As the questioning proceeds, the main character, who at first appears to be an ordinary person, may reveal himself or herself (although, in fact, all parts are played by male actors) as the ghost of the person for whom the pilgrim has shown sympathy. As the play moves toward its climax, the chief character, in a sequence of powerful poetic intensity, often relives the emotions—rage, love, shame, regret, terror, sorrow, chagrin—that still bind him or her to this earth. Then, the character will vanish as the pilgrim prays for the soul of the spirit manifested to him. The main action of the play, therefore, is a reenactment of memory. There is no confrontation between the main character and the pilgrim; indeed, they work in tandem to increase the power of the emotional moment that represents the dramatic core of the play.

Within this general structure, however, the individual texts are remarkably varied in structure, poetic power, dramatic urgency, and tonality. Subjects range from gods and warriors to women, madmen, even supernatural creatures. Many of the finest classic plays were written or revised by Zeami, who in the centuries after his death took on legendary status. A vast number of texts were at one point ascribed to him. Modern research would indicate, however, that the number should be narrowed to no more than sixty-odd pieces. Among them, there are English translations of a number of the best, including *Lady Aoi* (trans. Arthur Waley), based on the famous scene of exorcism in *The Tale of Genji*; *Atsumori* (trans. Arthur Waley), adapted from a moving incident in *The Tale of the Heike*; and *Izutsu*, another adaption, this time from *Tales of Ise* (trans. in volume 2 of the NGS series). Zeami's father, Kan'ami, is perhaps best known for his masterpiece *Matsukaze*, which was possibly revised by Zeami and is arguably the most exquisite play in the whole repertory (to be found in the Keene volume).

Of the 250-odd plays that constitute the standard repertory, perhaps 80 now exist in some form in English translation. There are many masterpieces yet to be made available, but those we do have provide eloquent testimony to the poetic power of this ancient theatrical form.

It should be mentioned that the *kyōgen* comic plays, usually interspersed with the *nō* in a full day's traditional program, are quite delightful in their own right, even when read on the page. The comedy of *kyōgen* relies on stock situations familiar the world over—the foolish master tricked by his wily servants, the country bumpkin seeing through the city slicker, or the philandering husband caught by his clever wife. The aim of these little comedies is to delight rather than to elevate, but they strike a remarkably refined tonality, never ugly, always pleasing in their good spirits.

TRANSLATIONS

The two best collections of *nō* plays for the general reader are *Twenty Plays of the Nō Theatre*, edited by Donald Keene (Columbia University Press, 1970) and Arthur Waley's *Nō Plays of Japan* (Grove Press, 1957). Those interested in seeking out additional translations will find the three-volume set *Japanese Noh Drama* published in Japan from 1956 to 1960 by the Nippon Gakujutsu Shinkōkai to be of high value, but they can be hard to locate.

The most satisfactory volume of *kyōgen* translations remains the prewar collection prepared by Shio Sakanishi, *Japanese Folk Plays: The Ink-Smeared Lady and Other Kyogen*, first published in 1938 and presently available as a reprint from Charles E. Tuttle.

Five Women Who Loved Love
Ihara Saikaku
Kōshoku gonin onna

Stories. 1686

For those who find much of Japanese literature perhaps too introspective, with a tendency to the elegiac, the ribald and worldly-wise tales of Ihara Saikaku (1642–93) will prove a refreshing antidote to virtually all the high-minded pieties. Modern critics often refer to the many prose works of Saikaku as "novels," but in fact he fits neatly into no Western canon. Reading him, even in translation, can move the spirit of the reader in a quicker and more paradoxical manner than most narrative fiction can be expected to match. Saikaku's ironic touch is lightning-fast, stemming as it does from poetic sources.

Part of the reason for the success of this witty style, of course, can only be explained by the author's peculiar genius, but his early career as a humorous writer of verse provided important training. Saikaku was roughly a contemporary of the great *haiku* poet **Matsuo Bashō**. Both lived during the long Tokugawa reign of peace, when the growth of cities and towns allowed the first real flowering of the merchant class, which, both as patron and as subject matter, began to play a significant cultural role. Writers and poets who several generations before would have found patrons among the aristocracy and the warrior class were now writing and publishing (thanks to the spread of literacy and printing alike) in what looks remarkably like a prototype for the modern mass market. Saikaku was, in this sense, a commercial writer. He responded to his public and earned his living from his readers.

Just as did Bashō, Saikaku began his literary career composing what is now termed comic *haiku* poetry, but was actually referred to at the time as *haikai*, comic linked verse. One way in which this form was practiced during this period involved linking various short verses together for comic effect. In 1677, Saikaku began a series of literary marathons in which, rather than composing links with his colleagues, he composed all the poems himself. In 1684 Saikaku set the all-time record: 23,500 links at one sitting. All this bravura and extemporaneous poetizing showed off his remarkable wit and verve. And as a public performance, it was an immensely profitable one.

Two years before, Saikaku had turned to the writing of prose. His first tale, *The Man Who Loved Love*, a work that served in part as a satire on *The Tale of Genji*, was such an immense success that Saikaku began to concentrate more and more on works of a similar sort, sometimes illustrating them himself. During the remainder of his career, Saikaku's subject matter ranged widely. He composed stories dealing with merchants, samurai, and personages from the provinces. All show his wit and, along with it, his compassion.

A good deal of Saikaku has been translated, but nothing, to my mind, provides a more genial introduction to his many collections of stories than his 1686 *Five Women Who Loved Love* (*Kōshoku gonin onna*), a collection of stories showing five variants on the eternal theme of the passions that can flare up to consume men and women. The various heroes and heroines who grace its pages show a commodious range of responses to the absurd situations into which their author puts them, and in true *haikai* style, Saikaku whisks the reader from scene to scene, incident to incident, in an exhilarating, even breathtaking manner. Each story is less narrative than a series of brilliant related vignettes. Each moves so quickly that they must be experienced; it would take longer to describe them.

Among the five cautionary tales, each reader will have his or her own favorite, but I must confess that my own is the third story, "What the Seasons Brought the Almanac Maker." If this one has a moral, it must be something to the effect that, if you lose yourself in passion and forget the outside world, you will only bring grief on yourself. This hoary chestnut, however, seems not the point but rather the pretext for a remarkable concoction of wry adventures. A certain almanac maker decides to take a wife; he marries the beautiful Osan, and all goes well for the new couple until, during his absence, she falls head over heels in love with Moemon, the young man who has been brought in to look after the husband's business affairs. They eventually run away and pretend to commit suicide together, so as to throw their pursuers off the track. After suffering various misadventures and indignities, they are tracked down because of the chattering of a peddler and brought to trial. The fact that their final execution may strike the reader as ironic rather than sad suggests something of the effectiveness of Saikaku's witty and ironic style.

Some of Saikaku's effects in stories such as these are created by the use of surprise, some by comic juxtaposition. In both respects, like many great humorists, Saikaku creates a sense of emotional distance in order to allow sufficient space for the comic impact. In one of the opening passages in the story, for example, a group of young men are lounging about on the street, watching the women who go by. Voting for their various candidates for the most elegant beauty, they, and so the reader, find themselves at first quite excited by one of the ladies passing by.

> Her sash was of folded taffeta bearing a tile design. Around her head she had draped a veil like that worn by courtladies; she wore stockings of pale silk and sandals with triple-braided straps. She walked noiselessly and gracefully, moving her hips with a natural rhythm. "What a prize for some lucky fellow!" a young buck exclaimed. But these words were hardly uttered when the lady, speaking to an attendant, opened her mouth and disclosed that one of her lower teeth was missing, to the complete disillusionment of her admirers.

Reality never matches desire. In this surprise juxtaposition, Saikaku strikes a comic note that continues to resound throughout the tale.

In modern times, Saikaku has often been termed a realist, and it is certainly true that his stories deal, albeit in a highly self-conscious way, with the foibles of those ordinary people he saw living around him. To the reading public of his day, the fragrant, poignant court society pictured in *The Tale of Genji* doubtless seemed as removed and romantic as it does to us today. In that sense, Saikaku might, minimally, be called a realist in that he chose to write about contemporary life. Nevertheless, in terms of his literary art, it seems to me a mistake to read into his work much of any larger or deliberate social criticism, as some modern critics in Japan have attempted to do. Saikaku set out to amuse, and his brilliant techniques linking realistic detail to fantastic event, his ability to puncture cliché, and, perhaps most important of all, his acute powers of observation provide a firm basis for his humor. In Saikaku's case, distance lends not enchantment but clarity of vision. No writer in Japanese literature possesses quite his eye for significant, one might almost say poetic, detail. Certainly, no one uses it so surely.

TRANSLATION
Ihara Saikaku. *Five Women Who Loved Love*. Trans. Wm. Theodore de Bary. Charles E. Tuttle, 1955.

OTHER WORKS BY IHARA SAIKAKU
The best one-volume collection that allows a sampling of various works by Saikaku is the Ivan Morris anthology *The Life of an Amorous Woman and Other Writings*, published by New Directions in 1963, which includes most of that remarkably funny work as well as selections from several other Saikaku works. Among other translations well worth reading are the Ben Befu translation of *Worldly Mental Calculations* (University of California Press, 1976), G. W. Sargeant's masterful rendering of *The Japanese Family Storehouse or the Millionaire's Gospel Modernized* (Cambridge University Press, 1959), and the Caryl Ann Callahan version of *Tales of Samurai Honor*, published by *Monumenta Nipponica* as a monograph in 1981.

The Narrow Road to the Deep North
Matsuo Bashō

Oku no hosomichi

Poetic Travel Diary. 1702

Matsuo Bashō (1644–94) is the one name from classical Japanese literature that is familiar throughout the world. Hiroaki Sato has in fact gathered together "a hundred frogs," a vast group of translations of

Bashō's celebrated *haiku*, an indication of the attention that has been paid to this poet since he was first discovered by Western writers in the late nineteenth century.

> The ancient pond
> A frog leaps in
> The sound of water   (trans. Donald Keene)

Bashō is revered in Japan as a saint of poetry, yet the 17-syllable *haiku* he perfected had its basis in the kind of earthy charm and humor that would seem to make sainthood a bit unlikely. In transmuting the *haiku* into a means capable of expressing elevated sentiments, Bashō brought elements from the older courtly poetic tradition, long crystallized into the 31-syllable *waka* and its fixed sentiments and vocabulary, down to earth again. Bashō once said something to the effect that the world of *waka* is represented by willow trees, the world of *haiku* by mud snails. Certainly the wry and human touch he brought to his consummate art makes his poetry ever fresh and approachable.

This charm, however, may well serve to disguise for the casual reader the fact that Bashō was a profoundly serious artist, whose work can be read and pondered for spiritual depths, however pleasant it may be to splash around in his shallows. Nowhere can these qualities be better seen than in his long poetic diary *The Narrow Road to the Deep North* (*Oku no hosomichi*), first published in 1702, eight years after his death. It is the longest and, in received opinion, the greatest of his travel accounts, although several of the others, in particular *The Records of a Weather-exposed Skeleton* and *The Records of a Travel-worn Satchel*, contain passages in prose and poetry of the highest accomplishment. Bashō wrote the diary as a literary re-creation of an actual journey he made to the then remote reaches of northern Japan, a trip begun in 1689 and lasting for over two years. In this diary, which he kept reworking and revising until his death, he mixed fact, fiction, poetry, and prose to create the record of a journey that moves both geographically and spiritually, one strand mixing with the other on virtually every page. Read and reread with care, *The Narrow Road to the Deep North* can reveal more qualities still basic to Japanese cultural attitudes than perhaps any other work in the whole canon of classical literature. For once, the highest of reputations is truly deserved.

By the same token, *The Narrow Road to the Deep North* is not a religious work. Composed in a secular age, it remains, for all its incipient religious overtones, firmly in the world of literature. This diary annexes much of the great literary tradition that had gone before it, and in the power of its accomplishment it suggests other works that will follow its example. As with other great works of highly wrought prose and poetry, the text is virtually untranslatable in the most literal sense. An elegant paraphrase seems the only possibility.

A work as rich as *The Narrow Road to the Deep North* can be "read" in countless ways. Here, I would like to make only a few brief suggestions that may help the reader understand something of its larger purposes. One such issue involves Bashō's solution to a problem that he, like so many others composing in the *waka* and *haiku* tradition, had to face: that of finding a method to set off reverberation of meaning in a poetic form so short that it might pass as a simple declarative sentence in English translation. In the court-poetry tradition, headnotes were often supplied to individual *waka*, thus providing a setting and perhaps suitable historical or emotional context in which the poem might be better understood. Bashō expands and develops this kind of contextual material into a highly evocative form of narrative that serves to personalize the context in terms of the poet's own intimate thoughts and feelings. By leading the reader through the movement of the poet's own responses to the world he experiences, Bashō prepares the way for the poem, so that the emotional weight of a brief *haiku* can be felt with full impact. Indeed, Bashō's prose often approaches the controlled language of poetry, so that reading *The Narrow Road to the Deep North* is like moving in and out of some magnetic force field: the pull may be strong or weak, but the poetic "tension" is always there.

Bashō's juxtapositions, moving from prose to poetry, then back to prose again, often follow an evolving pattern, proceeding from highly selected details of his actual travel to some historical explanation of the spot he visits, next to the examination of any prior literary response, and finally to his own felt moment of truth. In some places too often celebrated in history and poetry, Bashō cannot produce any poetic response at all, as at the famous islands of Matsushima, near Sendai. At others, such as Ichinoseki, Bashō's musings on the horrors of civil war—sharpened by recollections of his much beloved Tu Fu (712–70), the great poet of T'ang-dynasty China who suffered through such battles—produce at the end of this sequence a *haiku* on the futility of war that, experienced in the larger context of the preceding passages, becomes supremely moving.

Allied to these formal considerations is Bashō's ability to serve as a kind of artistic seesaw. His works, particularly *The Narrow Road to the Deep North*, because of the artistic attitudes and assumptions it embodies, can provide modern readers with a travel account, and so a guidebook, with which to enter the world of classical Japanese culture. Bashō says at the outset of his journey that he wishes to visit the north country in order to "seek out what those before him sought," and so in his travels he cites the work of his spiritual mentors in previous generations, Saigyō in particular. Bashō wishes to see for himself the sights that moved and excited other poets centuries before. In that sense, Bashō is a pilgrim. And although he insists that his is a trip made for poetry, not for religious understanding, his preference for Saigyō, a Buddhist of high moral and poetic ideals, suggests that Bashō too is seeking enlightenment, at least on his own terms, by developing his powers of intuition and artistic insight. There is a justly famous portrait of Bashō painted by the great artist and *haiku* poet Yosa Buson (1716–83), in which the master appears garbed as a traveling mendicant priest. Bashō himself might have rejected such a role, such an image, yet he filled it. In our time too, when artistic insight is often privileged, Bashō's path through introspection to enlightenment is one that we certainly respect. His humor and wit also help make the shift of consciousness from ordinary daily perceptions to privileged insight, from prose to poetry, all the more convincing.

TRANSLATIONS
There are all manner of translations of this highly complex and elusive text. On

one hand, Donald Keene's translation of lengthy excerpts from the diary, included in his *Anthology of Japanese Literature: From the Earliest Era to the Mid-Nineteenth Century* (Grove Press, 1955), strikes a fine balance between scholarly understanding and literary skill. Sid Corman's version, done in collaboration with Kamaike Susumu and entitled *Back Road to Far Towns: Bashō's Oku-no-Hosomichi* (Grossman, 1968), sends Bashō through the land of Jack Kerouac to produce a highly contemporary "journey" which, although it contains striking successes in terms of modern poetic language, may represent too much of a paraphrase, too vast a transition for many. For the general reader who wants to examine the text complete, there are two fine translations, that of Earl Miner, in his *Japanese Poetic Diaries* (University of California Press, 1969), and the version of Nobuyuki Yuasa, whose *Narrow Road to the Deep North and Other Travel Sketches* (Penguin Books, 1966) also contains reproductions of delightful illustrations by Buson, including the portrait mentioned above, in addition to translations of the other travel sketches. The charming collection of the Bashō frog translations, mentioned above, can be found in Hiroaki Sato's *One Hundred Frogs: From Renga to Haiku to English*, published by Weatherhill in 1983.

The Love Suicide at Amijima
Chikamatsu Monzaemon

Shinjū ten no amijima

Puppet Play. 1721

Chikamatsu Monzaemon (1653–1724), one of the earliest of the Tokugawa dramatists, was arguably the greatest, and his legacy still forms the backbone of the *bunraku* and *kabuki* repertory. Of all the plays he wrote, *The Love Suicide at Amijima* (*Shinjū ten no amijima*) is certainly, at least to the modern taste, his masterpiece. It has been translated twice and forms the basis for a celebrated 1969 film of Shinoda Masahiro entitled *Double Suicide*, which has been shown widely abroad.

Those able to attend theater performances in Japan often assume that Chikamatsu wrote for the *kabuki* theater, since many of his plays can most often be seen, sometimes highly adapted, in that form. Yet in fact, during most of Chikamatsu's career, the art of *kabuki* acting was in its infancy. Virtually all of Chikamatsu's best plays were written for the puppet theater, then termed *jōruri* and now most often referred to as *bunraku*. In the aesthetics of *bunraku*, the puppets were employed as a means to illustrate visually the story told by the master chanter, whose performance was intended to dominate the entire conception. In that regard, reading a Chikamatsu play translated into modern English gives a somewhat false impression of its effect in the theater, since the translation perforce assigns the names of the characters to their speeches, which appear to be punctuated by occasional comments from the narrator. In actual performance, however, the chanter plays all roles, rendering all voices, giving all the lines, from the cries of howling babies to angry crowds. His single voice is accompanied by the dramatic sound of the samisen, a small guitar-like instrument that can provide strong rhythmic and dramatic pacing. A functioning Chikamatsu text, therefore, more resembles the libretto for a musical performance such as an opera than it does a modern, Western dramatic text.

In terms of psychology and philosophical content, however, Chikamatsu's plays are surprisingly modern, particularly his so-called *sewamono* or "domestic dramas," which have retained their popularity through the centuries. In his day, Chikamatsu was especially appreciated for his rather swashbuckling historical dramas, such as *The Battles of Coxinga* (*Kokusen'ya kassen*), usually based on Chinese or Japanese historical sources, but as tastes changed later in the Tokugawa period and thereafter, these failed to hold the stage, much as in the case of, say, the historical dramas of Voltaire and Dryden, highly popular in the Europe of their day.

From our contemporary point of view, one remarkable thing about a drama like *The Love Suicide at Amijima* is that its protagonist, the paper merchant Kamiya Jihei, is an ordinary man, with all his warts and weaknesses showing. At the time of the play's composition in 1721, there had been few if any attempts on the Western stage to suggest the possibility of tragic elements in the stories of ordinary men, as opposed to those concerning kings and princes; indeed, one may have to come down to Ibsen, or even Arthur Miller, to find this consistency of focus on the emotional potential for real tragedy in ordinary, recognizable lives.

In any event, a play like *The Love Suicide at Amijima* is not really a realistic drama in any twentieth-century sense. The use of the puppets themselves, with their fixed expressions, provides a measure of aesthetic distance. The audience knows from the beginning who is the hero, who the villain. True enough, many of Chikamatsu's plays, *Amijima* among them, represent dramatizations of actual events of recent occurrence. Rival dramatists often vied to present their theatrical versions of an actual scandal, murder, or suicide as quickly as possible. Rather than moving his play along by such devices as suspense, however, as a modern dramatist might do, Chikamatsu concentrated rather on trying to find a means to portray *how* certain events, happenings already known to the audience, had come to pass. In the case of *Amijima*, Chikamatsu, by then in his late sixties and the grand old man of the theater, managed to interview those on the periphery of the tragedy before immortalizing his hapless lovers on the stage.

The outlines of the plot of *Amijima* can be quickly told. Jihei has fallen in love with Koharu, a nineteen-year-old courtesan, abandoning for her sake his wife and children. Trapped in a complex set of tensions between duty and passion, all persuasively laid out during the course of the first two acts of the play, Koharu and Jihei, "caught," as Koharu says, "by obligations from which I could not withdraw," decide to commit suicide together. They do themselves in, at the conclusion of the third and final act, at Amijima, an island in the bay of Osaka. The earlier sections of the play are lively and occasionally rather racy in their bantering scenes, juxtaposed with stretches of intense dialogue. In the long last scene of the play, however, Chikamatsu, showing himself master of a different sort of language altogether, allows his play to reach a level of real tragic grandeur. The two lovers have now come to realize that, within the limitations of their lives as defined for them by the rigid strictures of their own society, in which a Neo-Confucian sense of obligation played such an important part, they can find no possibility of happiness together on earth. Only in death might they escape society and find each other out of time. The language of this last scene, appropriately, becomes highly poetic and heavily Buddhist, with an emphasis on the transitory nature of life on this earth. The lovers hope as they die to be reborn together, perhaps to live as husband and wife "in every world to come until the end of time."

Chikamatsu's special skills as a dramatist make the characters and their extreme situation both credible and sympathetic. There are many realistic, often comic, touches early on in the drama, and the shift to the different atmosphere required by the final scene is achieved with consummate skill. It might be noted that, through the use of a narrator, Chikamatsu has found within his own dramatic tradition a solution to the problem that has bedeviled so many modern dramatists, that of showing the greatness and complexity of the emotions of ordinary men and women who, by virtue of their station in life, cannot speak with great eloquence in the context of a realistic dramaturgy. Chikamatsu's skillful blending of dialogue and narration provides a satisfying means to give that larger view.

In a famous interview, Chikamatsu remarked that the art of the puppet theater lies in "the thin margin between reality and unreality." With unerring skill, Chikamatsu followed this principle through success after success. However complex the cultural baggage of Tokugawa language, behavior, and history may be, the emotional dilemmas of the characters in a play like *Amijima* emerge with striking clarity. They can, through the persuasiveness of Chikamatsu's powerful sympathies, still elicit deep-felt responses from contemporary audiences and readers alike. Indeed, it is just this play of Chikamatsu's that so moves the twentieth-century protagonist in Tanizaki's *Some Prefer Nettles*. Chikamatsu's specifics may seem distant, even alien, to this generation in both Japan and elsewhere, but once the spectator is caught up in the world his characters inhabit, their milieu takes on an immediacy that can be keenly felt even today.

TRANSLATIONS
A scholarly translation of *The Love Suicide at Amijima: A Study of a Japanese Domestic Tragedy by Chikamatsu Monzaemon* by Donald Shively, with full notes and background information, was published by Harvard University Press

in 1953. In 1961, Donald Keene published his persuasive translation of the play as one of eleven he rendered into English in his *Major Plays of Chikamatsu*, published by Columbia University Press. Four of these translations, including *Amijima*, are contained in a paperback volume, *Four Major Plays of Chikamatsu*, published by Columbia University Press in 1961.

The Treasury of Loyal Retainers
Takeda, Miyoshi, and Namiki

Chūshingura

Kabuki Play. 1748

The stuff from which legends are made, this 1748 play, written by Takeda Izumo, Miyoshi Shōraku, and Namiki Senryū, remains the most popular traditional drama in Japan. First conceived for the puppet theater, then the greatest vehicle for serious dramatists, the play was soon adapted for *kabuki*. In this century, *The Treasury of Loyal Retainers (Chūshingura)* has provided the basis for countless modern theatrical, film, and television adaptations. A complex story encompassing eleven acts in the original, the drama involves so many aspects of plot and social significance that it has virtually created its own complete and self-sustaining world. Later playwrights often put that world to their own uses, using minor figures in the original to form a link to whole sets of newly created characters and situations which came to exist, as it were, in the shade of their vast dramatic parent tree.

The Treasury of Loyal Retainers is based on, and energized by, a series of tumultuous events that took place in 1701. In that year, Asano Naganori, the daimyo of the fief of Akō, not far from the present-day city of Okayama, was invited to officiate at a high ceremony. The inexperienced young lord received the necessary instructions in etiquette from the shogun's official Kira Kōzukenosuke, but failed to provide the customary bribe. Kira then so goaded Asano that he slashed out at the older man with his sword, committing the gravest offense possible in the eyes of the shogunate. As a result, Asano was ordered to commit suicide and his lands were confiscated. After Asano's death, forty-seven of his trusted retainers, now masterless samurai (*rōnin*), made the decision to avenge what they considered to be the unwarranted demand for the death of their master. Concealing their true motives, the band pretended to disperse. They finally brought their plottings to a culmination in February of 1703, when they broke into Kira's heavily guarded mansion and killed him. Public sentiment was largely on their side, but their actions were an affront to shogunal power. After considerable delay, the *rōnin* were sentenced to death but given the privilege, usually reserved for high-ranking officials and samurai, of committing ritual suicide rather than facing execution.

This incident of the forty-seven *rōnin*, which appeared to threaten the whole complex balance of power engineered by the Tokugawa regime, made the men into national heroes. Within a few months after their deaths, a play on the subject of their vendetta was staged. It was quickly closed down by the government censors. Three years later, in 1706, **Chikamatsu Monzaemon** added material concerning the *rōnin* to a play he had already composed. The earlier drama had been set in the fourteenth century, and he relocated the incident of the forty-seven *rōnin* in that earlier period in order to avoid any contemporary references that might attract censorship. Later plays, of which there were many, continued to set the scene in the earlier time. Dramatists continued as well to use the fictitious names assigned to the main characters by Chikamatsu. Thus the 1748 play as performed today has a partial pedigree through these earlier versions.

In contrast to the brevity of Chikamatsu's play, *The Treasury of Loyal Retainers* of 1748 grew extremely complex, with the addition of a whole tangle of plots and subplots. Intricate as this later version became, however, the climax, as in the original version, was represented by the attack on the mansion of Moronao (the name given to the historical Kira).

The theme of the *Treasury* is loyalty, both to master and, by extension, to abstract principle. Each important character in the play is presented with a test in order to see whether he or she is worthy of carrying out the often painful duties that loyalty demands. In the course of those eleven acts, the tests presented are varied and ingenious. Some, but not all of them, are based on historical fact. Complicated as the various events may seem when the play is read for the first time, they unravel themselves with superb logic on the stage, since the spectator then has the necessary time to grasp the increasingly complex relationships as the drama slowly unfolds. Full performances, in fact, last at least eight hours.

As the play was originally written for *bunraku* puppets, the various characters, as Donald Keene points out in the introduction to his translation, are fixed in their general demeanor by the kind of puppet head employed. The drama therefore cannot gain its effectiveness through psychological introspection, since the audience knows at once who is hero, who is villain. Rather, the play moves by employing swift, vivid, and heroic gestures. The characters are not intended to be realistic in any modern sense. The web of events in which many of them find themselves caught may often seem exaggerated. Still, those tests are there, like the barriers in John Bunyan's *Pilgrim's Progress*, to test the mettle of the heroes as they proceed toward their goal. Chief among them is the leader of the *rōnin*, Yuranosuke, who inspires his colleagues to great deeds and undergoes a number of excruciating tests himself, including the famous scene in the Gion teahouse where, in order to throw his enemy Moronao's enemies off the scent, he must appear to insult his dead master. The role of Yuranosuke is one of the greatest in the entire repertory of the traditional Japanese theater.

The Treasury of Loyal Retainers is not *King Lear*. It is not a highly introspective or philosophical study but a brilliantly conceived popular drama. Not only is the play gripping in its own right; its evocation of the samurai mentality throws long shadows in Japanese society even today. It is no wonder that the play, whether staged for actors or puppets, still holds the boards decade after decade. *The Treasury of Loyal Retainers* is one of the keys that can elucidate, with dignity and sympathy, many assumptions still alive in the behavior and culture of contemporary Japan.

TRANSLATION
Donald Keene, trans. *Chūshingura: The Treasury of Loyal Retainers, a Puppet Play*. Columbia University Press, 1971.

⚜ Tales of Moonlight and Rain
Ueda Akinari

Ugetsu monogatari

Stories. 1776

Ueda Akinari (1734–1809) is in many ways the most fascinating Japanese author of his century. The kind of eerie atmosphere that he was able to create in his ghostly stories has become well-known in the West through Mizoguchi Kenji's 1953 film *Ugetsu*, an evocative adaption of elements in Akinari's best-known work, *Tales of Moonlight and Rain (Ugetsu monogatari)*. Akinari is a master storyteller who can, through the art of suggestion, fashion tales that blend macabre elements reminiscent of Edgar Allan Poe, with powerful insights from the religious to the erotic that give a genuine profundity to his stories.

An adopted child, Akinari was never able to ascertain the identity of his real parents. He was often sickly and suffered from a severe case of smallpox, which marked his personality as well as his body. As a young man he wrote a number of light satirical pieces. In his middle years, he took up the study of medicine and became a respected practicing physician. At the same time he had an interest in the movement then current among the intellectuals of the day that involved a rigorous philological study of the Japanese classics. Akinari produced important commentaries on several of the works discussed in this volume, among them the *Collection of Old and New Japanese Poetry*, *The Anthology of Ten Thousand Leaves*, and *Tales of Ise*.

Tales of Moonlight and Rain, published in 1776, reveals Akinari's skills as a scholar and philologist, but those talents are well submerged in his telling of these romantic and often chilling stories. Akinari wrote in his preface that great literature has the ability to cause "a deep note to echo in the reader's sensibility wherewith one can find mirrored realities of a thousand years ago." He was speaking of Lady Murasaki and *The Tale of Genji*, but his words describe equally well the purposes of his own work.

Akinari's tales range over a wide variety of periods and subject matter. The first of them, "White Peak," consists of a first-person narrative that concerns the political upheavals of the twelfth century, as relayed by the ghost of a deceased emperor to the wandering poet-priest Saigyō. The tale is constructed somewhat in the narrative style of a medieval nō play. "Chrysanthemum Tryst" is an elegant re-creation, with significant variations, of a Chinese Ming-dynasty tale of a young man whose best friend joins him after death. "The House Amidst the Thickets," which provides much of the material for the Mizoguchi film, chronicles the adventures of a husband home from the wars who eventually discovers that his wife has become a ghost. "Bird of Paradise," which takes place on Mt. Kōya, the famed Buddhist temple complex south of the ancient capital of Nara, provides another mixture of ghosts and politics. This particular story so inspired the American writer Lafcadio Hearn, resident in Japan at the end of the nineteenth century, that he composed his own version using some of Akinari's themes. "The Cauldron of Kibitsu" is an erotic tale of jealousy and magic, based on older Japanese sources, while the mysterious fish swimming through the pages of "The Carp That Came to My Dream" originally appeared in an older Chinese tale. "The Lust of the White Serpent," another tale of sorcery and eroticism, has roots in both Chinese and Japanese classical texts. The final two stories deal with particularly unusual material. "The Blue Hood" recounts the startling results of a Zen priest's homosexual attachment to a young companion, while "Wealth and Poverty," the last story in the collection, provides an ironic debate on the role of money in society.

All these stories have complex roots, and their original readers (along with scholars ever since) were fascinated to observe just how Akinari reworked, and made his own, these often famous precedents, many of which, incidentally, are available in English translation. Modern readers, be they Japanese or foreign, no longer carry that kind of cultural baggage. Such knowledge is helpful in judging the exact nature of Akinari's special genius, and it is of the highest interest to observe Akinari's dialogue with his own sources across cultures and centuries. However, general readers can proceed directly to the tales themselves. They will not be disappointed.

TRANSLATION
Ueda Akinari. *Ugetsu Monogatari: Tales of Moonlight and Rain.* Trans. Leon Zolbrod. University of British Columbia Press, 1974.

OTHER WORKS BY UEDA AKINARI
Another collection of Akinari's stories, *Tales of Spring Rain (Harusame monogatari)*, in a translation by Barry Jackman, was published in 1975 by University of Tokyo Press and is available in the United States through Columbia University Press. Compiled and written toward the end of Akinari's life, these stories show the depth of his scholarly researches, but an enjoyment of them demands a greater knowledge of traditional culture. While revealing the author's sensibilities, they are on the whole of less immediate appeal than those in *Tales of Moonlight and Rain.*

The Poetry of Ryōkan (1758–1831)

Ryōkan, a Zen Buddhist priest, calligrapher, and writer of meditative verse, has long been a cultural hero to many in Japan. During his lifetime, he joined, in his own way, that long line of poet-recluses stretching from **Saigyō** and **Kamo no Chōmei** to **Bashō**. Ryōkan, like them, attempted to find a means to withdraw from society in order to transcend it. Like the *haiku* poet **Issa**, on the other hand, he sought out the spiritual dimensions of his existence at least in part through his contact with ordinary and simple country people. In this regard, both poets differed from some of their more austere predecessors, who often had ties with the court nobility. Both, perhaps for that reason, wrote poetry that is at once approachable and profound.

Ryōkan was born in the northwestern province of Echigo (now Niigata), in the area writers such as **Kawabata Yasunari** sometimes referred to as the "snow country." There the weather is severe, and the winters long and cold. Interestingly enough, Issa was also brought up in a rather similar spot. So many legends have sprung up concerning Ryōkan's life that disentangling fact from fiction has become a complex affair. Suffice to say that Ryōkan, for reasons that remain not altogether clear, decided to enter the priesthood at seventeen. His father, the headman of his village and something of a *haiku* poet in his own right, apparently committed suicide some twenty years later, and this event may have confirmed Ryōkan in his vocation as a wandering mendicant priest.

After many years of travel, Ryōkan eventually settled down in his native province, in a small hut on the slopes of Mt. Kugami, near the coastline that faces the sea of Japan some twenty miles south of the present-day city of Niigata. There he remained for the remainder of his life.

Despite his present high reputation as a poet and calligrapher, Ryōkan presumably never thought of himself as an artist in the usual sense of the word. His poetry represented rather a record of his search for enlightenment. He seems to have traded poems with his brother and with friends in the region who loved literature, notably the Buddhist nun Teishin, with whom he carried on an extensive exchange. Ryōkan's poetry was collected by others.

Reading Ryōkan's record of his days can be, even through the medium of translation, a moving and often exhilarating encounter. His walks through the forests he knew so well, his sessions of meditation, the games he played with the local children, all remain fresh and authentically moving experiences. Many readers have been particularly attracted to Ryōkan's introspective poems, in which he confesses the difficulties, and the loneliness he felt, in the solitary task of enlightenment he had set for himself.

A modern reader can enter Ryōkan's world with relative ease, but a careful perusal of his poetry will show that the monk was a profound student of ancient literature, both Chinese and Japanese. Like Ueda Akinari and other writers and intellectuals of his period, Ryōkan developed an ardent and sustained interest in *The Anthology of Ten Thousand Leaves*, and there are many traces of that enthusiasm in his poetry. He also studied with great care the *Collection of Old and New Japanese Poetry* and other classical Japanese poetry anthologies. Most important of all was the poetry of Han-shan (Cold Mountain), the name given to the famous Chinese Ch'an (or Zen) Buddhist recluse of the T'ang dynasty (618–907), whose self-reflective religious poetry has continued to play a role in China and Japan since it first became known. Many of Ryōkan's poems represent attempts to grasp the ineffable through the use of certain literary metaphors and other techniques employed by Han-shan. By reusing the images of his awesome predecessor, Ryōkan doubtless hoped to draw closer to him and to the truth that Han-shan sought. Read together, Han-shan and Ryōkan disclose certain striking similarities, suggesting that they gave themselves to similar processes of mental and physical training in order to achieve enlightenment.

Ryōkan chose to compose his poetry in many forms. In Japanese he wrote both 31-syllable *waka* and 17-syllable *haiku*. Many of his longer poems were composed in classical Chinese. Chinese poetry written by Japanese had a long and illustrious history, stretching back to the Heian period and before. Such a tradition might roughly be compared to the composition of Latin prose and poetry by medieval monks and scholars in a variety of European environments. During Ryōkan's time, educated people could read such verse with relative ease. It has only been in this century, as training in reading classical Chinese was displaced by the study of European languages, that the Chinese verse of such poets as Ryōkan has become very difficult for contemporary Japanese readers, who are often forced to read a paraphrase in modern Japanese, just as, say, readers of the Latin poetry of John Milton must seek English translations.

Whatever the linguistic difficulties of the originals, however, Ryōkan's poetry, either in the original or in translation, is always engagingly personal, never remote.

> One narrow path surrounded by a dense forest;
> On all sides, mountains lie in darkness.
> The autumn leaves have already fallen.
> No rain, but still the rocks are dark with moss.
> Returning to my hermitage along a way known to few,
> Carrying a basket of fresh mushrooms
> And a jar of pure water from the temple well.
>
> (trans. John Stevens)

Brief as it is, a poem such as this places the reader and the poet in a close and vivid proximity.

Many readers find a special pleasure in Ryōkan's poetry written in the classical Japanese forms, in which he often combines the simplest of images to suggest the personality of the poet as he proceeds on his quest.

> In my begging bowl
> violets and dandelions
> jumbled together—
> I offer them to the
> Buddhas of the Three Worlds   (trans. Burton Watson)

Whatever the form employed, Ryōkan's divine simplicity and gentle austerity strike a note that, in the midst of contemporary self-consciously affluent cultures on both sides of the Pacific, can serve as a corrective to our contemporary values. So Ryōkan is read in Japan, and so, an increasing readership in English would seem to agree, can he be elsewhere.

TRANSLATIONS

Readers of Ryōkan are fortunate in that three studies and anthologies have appeared, each contributing to an understanding of the poet from slightly different perspectives.

John Stevens, trans. *One Robe, One Bowl: The Zen Poems of Ryōkan*. John Weatherhill, 1977.

Burton Watson, trans. *Ryōkan: Zen Monk-Poet of Japan*. Columbia University Press, 1977,

Nobuyuki Yuasa, trans. *The Zen Poems of Ryōkan*. Princeton University Press, 1981.

Those wishing to read the Han-shan poems will find a persuasive collection of translations by Burton Watson in *Cold Mountain: 100 Poems by the T'ang Poet Han-shan* (Columbia University Press, 1970).

The Year of My Life
Kobayashi Issa

Ora ga haru

Poetic Autobiography. 1819

Three *haiku* poets are generally regarded as the greatest traditional masters of the form. The work of these three, taken together, can suggest the depth, richness, and diversity of Tokugawa culture; no one of them can illustrate it fully. **Matsuo Bashō** (1644–94) brings a certain austerity from his Buddhist heritage to his vision of the world. Yosa Buson (1716–83) displays in his poetry the richness and elegance of high cultural and artistic traditions, revealing the metaphorical power of the Chinese-inspired literati ideal on the Tokugawa artistic mentality. Kobayashi Issa (1763–1827) came from a poor mountain village, and his poems show a compassion, a humanity, and a kind of surface simplicity that have given him a reputation as the poet of the common man. Yet Issa is no less elevated in his thoughts and responses than his two illustrious predecessors, and his flashes of insight into the meaning of his homely surroundings, as revealed in his *haiku*, come as close to larger truth as any poetry of the period.

Classical Works

All three poets traveled extensively. Bashō's **Narrow Road to the Deep North** is the best-known of the Tokugawa *haiku* travel journeys, but Issa's *The Year of My Life (Ora ga haru)*, which records certain of the poet's thoughts and movements in the year 1819, possibly inspired by the example of Bashō's travel diaries, is wrought with equal care. It blends fact and fiction, memory and direct experience, into a touching account of the poet's responses to life, ranging from his delight in the seasons to his stunned sadness at the death of a dear child.

If at this time in his life Issa traveled less than Bashō, it was doubtless because he had a family, and then too, because he was finally able to settle down and live in his father's house, where he had so long rightfully belonged. Issa's father, a farmer, became a widower when Issa was two; when he remarried, the boy found himself shunted aside by his foster mother. Sent as an apprentice to Edo when a teenage boy, Issa continued to live an extremely difficult life, traveling and working at odd jobs, all the while slowly learning to perfect his craft. His poetry began to attract attention when he was in his thirties, yet he was still forced to travel and work hard until his fiftieth year, when his stepmother finally relented and allowed him to inherit the property that his father had long wanted him to have. Issa returned to his village and married. *The Year of My Life* was written during this relatively calm and happy period in Issa's life. In his full maturity, Issa seemed to have reached a plateau of calm. More difficulties were to follow later, however, including the death of his wife and his other children, and the destruction of his property by fire. At the time of the composition of *The Year of My Life*, however, the poet had obtained at last a certain sense of calm and tranquillity.

It is difficult to characterize this poetic diary, an evocative mixture of prose and poetry divided into twenty-one chapters. Each incident has its own flavor, its own nuances. The incidents recorded often seem outwardly plain and simple, perhaps too slim even for the comment they receive, yet the ease and charm with which they are related often serves to mask a powerful metaphysical thrust in which a simple incident, like a rock thrown into a pond, can produce infinite ripples.

In chapter 8, for example, Issa records the struggle of a chestnut tree to remain alive. Each spring the tiny tree sends forth a few green shoots. Each winter the weight of snow breaks off the trunk at its roots.

Seven years have passed in this way—seven cycles of frost and stars. But this poor tree has neither the strength to put forth fruits and flowers, nor the good fortune quite to die. Existence is a continuous struggle to remain simply one foot high.

Issa sees himself to be like the tree, and so describes himself. The tone is laconic, the beauty obvious.

The climax of *The Year of My Life* is surely the section concerning the death of his beloved daughter, related in chapter 14. The poems there, and their surrounding text, are too long to be cited here, but those passages, culminating in Issa's famous poem on the difficulties that humanity finds in accepting the reality of evanescence, rank with the most beautiful in traditional Japanese literature.

Along with such longer, sustained sections, there are short vignettes that reveal charming incidents and insights. Issa's images are often unusual, combining as they do his sense of the now highly developed *haiku* tradition and his own idiosyncratic powers of observation.

Standing close together,
Stags are licking
The first frost and ice
Off one another's coats.

A small patch
Of green rice
Is all the ornament
My house affords.

Earthbound, emotionally responsive to everything he sensed around him, unafraid even of vulgarity, Issa may well be, as some critics would have it, the ultimate democrat in the history of *haiku* poetry. Whatever the source of his appeal, however, Issa's observations make him altogether approachable.

> Beneath the bright
> Cherry blossoms
> None are indeed
> Utter strangers.

TRANSLATION
Kobayashi Issa. *The Year of My Life: A Translation of Issa's Ora ga Haru.* Trans. Nobuyuki Yuasa. Rev. ed. University of California Press, 1973.

Mr. Yuasa is well-known for his translations of Bashō, and his efforts with this particularly elusive text, from which all the quotations above are taken, are largely successful. Some of Issa's *haiku* disclose their oblique meanings only with difficulty even in the original, and in their transposition into English, occasionally meaning and sense become flattened. Nevertheless, this small book provides a fine introduction to the poet. Another small collection of translations of poems by Issa, *The Autumn Wind: A Selection of the Poems of Issa* by Lewis Mackenzie (Kodansha International, 1984), was first published in England in 1957 by the firm of John Murray. The selection gives a broad sampling of Issa's work, rendered into English with gusto and style.

THIRTY
MODERN
WORKS

Drifting Clouds
Futabatei Shimei

Ukigumo

Novel. 1887–88

In the 1850s, writers of prose in Japan were still using the kinds of classical diction and modes of thought familiar from the works described in the first part of this book. By the 1890s, however, novels of considerable interest were being composed in a modern, European mode. Such a transformation seems extraordinary, regardless of the quality of the works created. This revolution was possible largely because of the example set by the writer Futabatei Shimei (1864–1909), and in particular because of the power and skill of his remarkable novel *Drifting Clouds* (*Ukigumo*), published in two sections in 1887 and 1888. The novel is a remarkable product indeed for a man in his early twenties, whatever his background.

Futabatei (to use the pen name taken by Hasegawa Tatsunosuke) developed his vocation as a novelist through a number of seemingly arbitrary yet crucial encounters with other extremely gifted men. In the beginning, Futabatei hoped to enter the Army Officer's School, but failed the examinations because of poor eyesight. He then decided to attempt a diplomat's career and entered the Foreign Language School in Tokyo, where, contemplating what he thought to be the coming strategic needs of Japan, he began the study of Russian. There he fell under the sway of a remarkable teacher, Nicholas Gray. Gray was a Russian-born, naturalized American citizen who passed on to his students not only a love of the language but of Russian literature as well. Gray read aloud in the evenings, thrilling the young Japanese in his charge with the flow and the inflections of the great nineteenth-century novels he so much admired. From this experience, Futabatei came to realize that, in the creation of a narrative sensitive to the psychological aspects of its characters, a close tie was needed between the spoken and written languages. At that time, no such connection existed between written and spoken Japanese. Futabatei was confirmed in this insight when he met the young critic Tsubouchi Shōyō (1859–1935), who was equally interested in the problems of creating a contemporary written language responsive to the changes that were coming so rapidly to their Westernizing society. Shōyō's main enthusiasm was for Shakespeare, and he would later go on to translate the whole corpus of the plays into Japanese. He much admired Russian nineteenth-century literature as well. Shōyō and Futabatei engaged in intense discussions on these topics, and Shōyō also served as a friendly commentator and critic of Futabatei's efforts to write his own fiction, providing useful suggestions as to both structure and language.

Futabatei particularly admired Turgenev. While he was writing *Drifting Clouds*, he translated at the same time portions of *Sportsman's Sketches*, developing for the two projects a new colloquial language based on aural values. Readers were happily astounded by both. Turgenev's example certainly helped Futabatei to understand how to shape his own narrative, and the young Japanese writer acknowledged at every point his debt to the Russian master, as did so many other writers around the world, Henry James among them. Nevertheless, *Drifting Clouds* is an entirely independent work.

The greatest break with Japanese tradition that Futabatei achieved was his giving priority to the development of character over plot. The novels of Takizawa Bakin (1767–1848), for example, popular a few generations earlier, were historical romances crammed with characters, plots, and counterplots. Brilliant in their way, they were ill-suited to the portrayal of details of character development or modulations of feeling. There was literally no room for such concerns in the thick tangle of incident so popular with nineteenth-century Japanese readers. In *Drifting Clouds*, on the other hand, Futabatei cut his cast of characters down to four: Bunzō, a young man out of work, Osama, his landlady, Osei, her daughter, with whom Bunzō falls in love, and Noboru, a young man on the rise in the world who also vies for Osei's hand in marriage. Much of the action of the novel is interior, as characters reflect on their own motives and speculate on those of the others with whom they come in contact.

The novel is rich in psychology and devastating in its criticism of a Japanese society grown materialistic and self-seeking. Bunzō represents the thoughtful outsider, the one who stands aside, watching and sometimes worrying over the foibles of his contemporaries. Noboru (whose very name suggests the meaning "to climb up"), on the other hand, has sold himself to the system without even acknowledging the fact, fawning over his superiors like an enthusiastic lapdog. Osei, and her mother, must choose between these two models of behavior.

Futabatei shows compassion for his characters, yet he does not hesitate to reveal their comic sides. Osei is prey to every Western fad, Bunzō is often childishly weak-tempered, and Noboru preposterous in his desire to please. The book is filled with amusing glimpses of such foibles, and yet each of these young people remain fresh and authentic. The creation of such a work at this moment in Japanese literary history must be judged as at least a minor miracle, and its success provided an encouraging model to the brilliant generation of writers that were to follow.

The composition of the book was by no means simple. Futabatei worked on the last part of the novel for several years, but the final published version nonetheless breaks off before Osei can make any decision as to which young man she will choose. The author left behind various notes as to how he wished the novel to end, some of them contradictory, and there has been a good deal of scholarly ink spilled over what his best intentions might have been. In many ways, however, this open-ended conclusion is altogether appropriate for the kind of psychological truth that Futabatei wished to convey. Life rarely comes in neat packages, and *Drifting Clouds* joins the ranks of other great and perhaps unfinished works of Japanese fiction, notably *The Tale of Genji*, that attest to the openness of life and the art that attempts to capture it.

TRANSLATION
The complete text of the novel is contained in Marleigh G. Ryan, *Japan's First Modern Novel: Ukigumo of Futabatei Shimei* (1967. Reprint. Greenwood Press, 1983).

OTHER WORKS BY FUTABATEI SHIMEI

Two of the author's later novels, *An Adopted Husband* (1919. Reprint. Green-wood Press, 1969) and *Mediocrity* (Hokuseido, 1927) were translated into English several decades ago. The latter is out of print but well worth seeking out. Less remarkable than *Drifting Clouds* perhaps, they nevertheless contain absorbing characters created by a master novelist.

Wild Geese
Mori Ōgai

Gan

Novel. 1911–13

Mori Ōgai (1862–1922) is along with **Natsume Sōseki** one of the giants of Japanese literature in the Meiji period (1868–1912). If his work seems more difficult of access to English-language readers than Sōseki's, it is doubtless because the traditions on which Ōgai drew, and his own en-thusiasms, involved conceptions of literature at some remove from our own Anglo-American assumptions. Sōseki loved *haiku* and studied in England, where he absorbed the Victorian traditions of fiction. Ōgai had a particular interest in the older forms of history writing in Japan, which in turn often hark back to erudite Chinese models. Ōgai studied medicine in Germany, where he acquired a passion for European literature that allowed him to bring into a newly developing Japanese literary tradition the possibility of creating texts filled with philo-sophical resonance, based in particular on his admiration for the work of Goethe and the German romantics. Readers in the United States and England are familiar with those traditions, but less comfortable, as certain elements important to them seem to lie outside the frame-work of the purely "literary" as understood in London or New York. For many readers, Ōgai may thus seem overly abstract, perhaps too austere. Nevertheless, in his own restless literary experiments, ranging from his translations of romantic German poetry and Ibsen's dramas to the composition of his own poetry, dramas, fiction, and historical tales, Ōgai represents one pole in the Japanese literary world, and his success as a writer and a thinker have long given him the status of a cultural hero.

It is difficult to single out any particular work of Ōgai's that can demonstrate the way in which he combines his sense of historical milieu with his own interior response to what he witnessed or imagined. Ōgai, even in the midst of a frantically busy career as a writer and government bureaucrat (he eventually became Surgeon General of the Japanese Army), characterized himself as a "bystander," one who observed life, emotional or political, as history in the making. Many of his works are short, and at least one of the most striking remains unfinished. Perhaps the work that best sums up his profound understanding of the complex relationship he felt to exist between self and society is his 1910 novel *Seinen* (Youth), which chronicles the life of a young intellectual in Tokyo, but this cornerstone of Ōgai's oeuvre remains as yet untranslated. *Shibue Chūsai*, Ōgai's historical re-creation of the mentality of the late Tokugawa period, is, on the other hand, because of the formidable amount of historical detail provided, doubtless untranslatable.

Wild Geese (Gan), written in 1911–13, remains a favorite among Japanese readers and was the subject of a famous Toyoda film of 1953, abroad usually called *The Mistress*. Part of the appeal of this work may lie in the fact that, for its original Japanese readers at least, the novel represented a historical account in which Ōgai attempted to re-create the life of Tokyo some thirty or more years before in order to portray the beginning of a modern mentality in his character. This particular dimension of the novel's success is invariably blunted for a modern reader, for whom 1913 may seem as remote as 1881. Nevertheless, the strongly conceived characters are touching and their actions convincing.

"This is an old-fashioned story," Ōgai begins, and then proceeds to set up a set of links by which the reader moves from the world of the narrator to that of a fellow student named Okada, then in turn to the life of a young woman whom Okada has seen but never spoken to. The changing mentality of this young woman, Otama, comes to provide the focus of the story.

As in the traditional *kabuki* melodramas, Otama has been married off to a certain Suezō, an unpleasant moneylender, in order to aid the foundering family fortunes. However, Ōgai uses this "old-fashioned" plot line as a framework in which to display a modern understanding of the heroine's psychological plight. After forcing herself to become the wife of the moneylender, Otama comes to the realization that she has in fact made a conscious choice. In turn, this newfound ability to reflect on her own conduct brings about an incipient sense of independence and freedom, just the opposite of what a reader might have expected in a truly "traditional" narrative.

Otama's quickening sense of self allows her, in time, to act independently as well. She yearns to escape the overwhelming sense of loneliness that her new self-understanding has brought in its wake. Okada, the student, often passes her house on his walks through the city, and eventually they speak to each other. Their nascent relationship, however, tantalizing as it seems, never finds consummation. Okada (like Ōgai) leaves Tokyo to pursue his studies in Germany, and Otama waits, in the full pain of her self-awareness, for an opening into life that her society cannot provide her.

Although the story has literary precedents, Ōgai reverses them. He does not show the traditional happy ending implicit in the cultural myth of the handsome student who rescues the girl he loves, choosing rather to point out the inevitable pain felt by those who manage to develop a sense of interiority in a still traditional society. Ōgai felt such pressures in his own life, and he bore them stoically and without regret. In this regard, *Wild Geese* can serve as a useful introduction to the author's larger concerns with the often tragically conflicting demands of self and society. Ōgai's favorite quotation from Goethe, perhaps his favorite European author, reads as follows: "How may one come to know oneself? Never by contemplation, but only by action. Seek to do your duty, and you will know how it is with you. And what is your duty? The demands of the day." Ōgai attempted to live out these words, and he knew to the fullest the difficulties and ambiguities involved in coming to grips with the implications of Goethe's observation.

TRANSLATION
Mori Ōgai. *Wild Geese*. Trans. Kingo Ochiai and Sanford Goldstein. Charles E. Tuttle, 1959.

OTHER WORKS BY MORI ŌGAI
A number of Ōgai's important works have been made available in English, some of them in specialized journals such as *Monumenta Nipponica*. Closest to *Wild Geese* in theme is *Vita Sexualis*, written in 1909 and available in translation by Kazuji Ninomiya and Sanford Goldstein (Charles E. Tuttle, 1972). In this work, Ōgai creates an ironic account of the sexual awakening of his protagonist. David Dilworth and the present writer edited and translated two volumes of Ōgai's late historical fiction, *The Incident at Sakai and Other Stories* and *Saiki Kōi and Other Stories*, both published by the University of Hawaii Press in 1977. Ōgai's reputation in Japan, more often than not, rests on these historical accounts (at once accurate and highly imaginative) of the lives and moral dilemmas lived through by a variety of characters, ranging from Chinese monks to Tokugawa samurai. Special mention should be made of Edwin McClellan's moving *Woman in the Crested Kimono* (Yale University Press, 1985), in which the author sets out to re-create, rather than translate, the remarkable account provided by Ōgai of late Tokugawa life contained in his remarkable *Shibue Chūsai* of 1916, mentioned above.

The Poetry of Masaoka Shiki (1867–1902)

There is perhaps no figure more able to symbolically represent the excitement, and the pain, of the rapidly evolving Meiji period (1868–1912) than the poet Masaoka Shiki. In a remarkable burst of intellectual energy, Shiki recast the traditional 31-syllable *waka* (or *tanka*) and the 17-syllable *haiku* so that they might gain renewed currency in a new literary atmosphere already heavily influenced by Western models. Once this was accomplished, the poet fell ill and died a slow and painful death from complications brought on by tuberculosis. These final days were also transformed into poetry, demonstrating Shiki's ability to create great art from health and illness alike.

Educated like all his contemporaries in the Chinese and Japanese classics, Shiki began his artistic training under one set of literary assumptions; then, as he became exposed to Western works of art and literature, he set about applying newer and broader perspectives to the art of writing. And yet Shiki was not a scholar of literature; in fact, he was apparently an indifferent student. But his powerful ability to juxtapose and synthesize allowed him to evaluate the traditions of Japanese poetry, particularly with regard to the *haiku*, and to create in his own work a new set of possibilities for a form which—after the work of the three great Tokugawa *haiku* masters, **Matsuo Bashō**, Yosa Buson, and **Kobayashi Issa**—had reverted to a kind of parlor game of matching syllables. Shiki read voraciously the work of these and other masters. In his critical writing, he restored Buson to a position of prominence in the eyes of his contemporaries and provided a critical framework for the appreciation of Bashō's writings that has been adopted by modern Japanese readers ever since. Reading Shiki's remarks on his illustrious predecessors has a very different effect from the kind of remarks, however stimulating, generally made by scholarly writers and commentators. In Shiki's case, one poet is writing about another. The sense of discovery is palpable. It is for such reasons, perhaps, that Shiki's essays were, and still are, widely read. Then too, his editorial talents allowed him to serve as a writer and editor for several magazines concerned with art and poetry.

One aspect of Shiki's art that drew on his education in traditional Japanese attitudes concerned his profound and continuing interest in the synthesis of the visual and literary arts that was typical of the Tokugawa literati mentality, as evidenced in the work of an artist like Buson, who painted as well as composed poetry. Buson, like Bashō and many other poets of the period, drew their ideals from their image of the Chinese gentleman, by definition gifted in poetry, calligraphy, and painting, seen as sister arts. Shiki admired such a synthetic vision. Yet he had been affected as well by the penetration into Japan of the ideals and practices of Western-style sketching and oil painting. His friendship with the gifted young Western-style artist Nakamura Fusetsu (1866–1943), before the painter left for Paris to study in 1901, led Shiki to a new sense of the visual possibilities of art and of the relation that might be established between that art and a new kind of *haiku*. Both could represent a fresh way of seeing. The collaboration between the two, begun with so much intensity, might well have continued after Nakamura returned to Japan in 1905, but by then Shiki was already dead.

In the course of his intellectual exchanges with Nakamura, Shiki became convinced of the need for *haiku* to make manifest what he called a "sketch from life." Poetry must be grounded, he felt sure, in the realities of the thing observed. Shiki began therefore to include images altogether new to the form, based on his own fresh powers of observation.

> spring rain:
> browsing under an umbrella
> at the picture-book store   (trans. Janine Beichman)

> From the trellis
> sponge gourds dangle down, each one
> where it pleases.   (trans. Makoto Ueda)

This ability to observe closely and exactly took a new and powerful inward turn when Shiki's final illness began, following his service as a war correspondent in 1895, during the Sino-Japanese War. Eventually bedridden and in exhausting pain, Shiki turned his eyes, literally and spiritually, on what he saw around him. All his ambition and energy were now forced to reduce themselves to what he could make of his room, his bed, and his own exhaustion. Finally, unable to move, only his eyes could search out new sensation.

again and again
I ask how high
the snow is

(trans. Janine Beichman)

Shiki's last works bear witness to the various moods that overtook him as he slipped toward death. He combined prose and poetry and placed his own sketches with his writing, thereby creating a modern form of poetic diary that, while it owed something to the precedent of Bashō, possessed a striking modernity in both psychological intimacy and subject matter. Shiki had made the old forms usable in the twentieth century, but at the greatest possible cost to himself. Shiki's friend **Natsume Sōseki**, in his 1913 novel *The Wayfarer*, has his protagonist lament that "from walking to rickshaws, from rickshaws to horse-drawn cabs, from cabs to trains, trains to automobiles, automobiles to airships, airships to airplanes—when will we ever be allowed to stop and rest? Where will it finally take us?" Shiki, more than a decade before, had felt the same restlessness, and his very intensity of belief in the ideals of poetry may have helped exhaust him. As we trace this trajectory through Shiki's work, the Meiji period, with all of its cultural strivings, comes vibrantly alive. So, too, does the reality of a human being contemplating his own annihilation. In this regard, Shiki's art is timeless.

TRANSLATIONS

Strictly speaking, there is as yet no volume entirely made up of translations by Shiki. The excellent biography of the poet by Janine Beichman, *Masaoka Shiki* (1982. Reprint. Kodansha International, 1986), however, contains copious translations of his poetry and prose and so can be well recommended on several counts. In addition, her bibliography makes reference to other translations of Shiki scattered in various anthologies and collections. The quotation from Makoto Ueda in the text above is taken from *Modern Japanese Haiku: An Anthology* (University of Toronto Press, 1976).

Kokoro
Natsume Sōseki

Kokoro

Novel. 1914

No modern novelist is more revered in modern Japan than Natsume Sōseki (1867–1916), and of his dozen or more novels, most of which have achieved classic status among readers there, none has been given greater respect than *Kokoro*, written in 1914. The culmination of Sōseki's attempt to plumb the depths of the loneliness of modern man, the book has a directness that remains extraordinarily moving, despite the fact that Sōseki's theme of psychic separation has since become something of a commonplace in world literature.

The title of the novel is difficult to render into English. Edwin McClellan, whose elegant translation provides a privileged means to approach the original, was doubtless wise to leave the word in Japanese. The dictionary definitions of *kokoro* range from "heart" or "mind" to "soul," "spirit," and "intention." All of these apply to the subject of the book, which examines motivations that in time reveal the core of the personality of the protagonist, an intellectual who lives in retirement. It is his state of mind, and his story, that Sōseki wishes to delineate. Although some of the specifics of the story, set in 1912 at the end of the modernizing Meiji period, are important to the development of the plot, the protagonist represents for Sōseki a modern everyman who, looking into his own soul, finds only loneliness and solitude; his sole comfort remains his clarity of vision concerning himself.

Sōseki has chosen not to name his characters, thus providing something of an archetypal quality to them and their situations. The novel is divided into three sections, all presented in the first person. The first two sections are narrated by a young student who, at the beginning of the novel, meets an older man. The two strike up a friendship. The student calls the older man *sensei*, a term of respect that means "teacher" or, more accurately, something like the French word *maître*. The Sensei, in the long third section of the book, tells in a letter of his own moral decline and fall. Here too, the names of the other important characters are presented in as abstract a fashion as possible. The Sensei's close friend is simply known as K, and the girl with whom both fall in love is called Ojō-san, which is not a name but a form of address that might be rendered as Young Lady. All the characters in the book thus rise above the specificity of their names and personal situations.

Sōseki's ingenious structure for the novel mirrors beautifully the themes he wished to explicate. The narrative is planned in such a way that the reader begins to uncover the deepening layers of truth about the Sensei in just the same way as does the student, whose voyage of self-discovery, as well as his increasing understanding of his mentor's state of mind, brings him closer and closer to the frightening moral truth. The student first sees the Sensei talking with a foreigner; he seems conversant with the world of learning and culture. As the student gets to know the Sensei and his wife better, however, he comes to realize that at the heart of this urbane and often compassionate man, there lies something cold and broken. The Sensei in turn tries to warn the warmhearted, ardent young man that life in its fullness will show other, darker sides. The youth, however, has stirred the deadened sense of humanity within the Sensei, and the final letter from him to the student calls forth a true confession. That long letter is, in effect, an extended suicide note.

The Sensei's own journey to self-awareness, which he wishes to chronicle as an admonition to his young friend, gains depth and poignancy as the Sensei's moral concerns are placed against the larger ones of his changing society, in which egotism has begun to replace the commonality of older social structures, a process that the author saw as inevitable. The Sensei commits suicide in 1912, not long after the ritual death by suicide of General Nogi Maresuke (1849–1912), the famous general of the Russo-Japanese War. Nogi himself had followed in death, in the old samurai fashion, his leader the Emperor Meiji. As the Sensei points out, Nogi's suicide represents the last of the old values; his own situation is rather that of a man caught between two worlds posing separate and often conflicting values.

Kokoro

In such bald summary, *Kokoro* may sound relentless and unrelievedly grim, but in the reading, the book is compelling in its evocation of the moral complexities of human relations, where much remains unarticulated, even between friends. The silences in the novel become as pregnant with meaning as the conversations. In this respect, Sōseki, who studied for a time in England and wrote on, and admired, such English writers as Meredith and Swift, pays homage to the reticences of his own classical literary tradition. In that regard, *Kokoro* indeed serves as a bridge into the heart of things, relative both to the specifics of Japanese culture and to the human condition in general. Those who read it will be unlikely to forget the Sensei, for the mirror Sōseki holds up can shine into any heart, whatever his or her cultural background. *Kokoro* has had a long life, both in the original and in translation, and it will surely, and deservedly, continue to do so.

TRANSLATION
Natsume Sōseki. *Kokoro*. Trans. Edwin McClellan. Regnery/Gateway, 1957.

OTHER WORKS BY NATSUME SŌSEKI
Sōseki has been well translated, and most of his important works have now appeared in English. Beginning with his early, humorous novels such as *I Am a Cat* (Putnam, 1982) and *Botchan* (Kodansha International, 1972), both delightful satires on the foibles of society in Sōseki's day, later poetic works such as the poignant and evocative *Three Cornered World* (Putnam, 1982) and the final, darker works leading up to *Kokoro* are now available. Among these, those of special interest are *Sanshiro* (Putnam, 1982), an often humorous chronicle of a young man from the country up to study in Tokyo, *Mon* (Putnam, 1982), the story of a man who searches for, and fails to find, a meaning for his life in traditional Japanese religion, *And Then* (Putnam, 1982), an account of a man who attempts to break out of his own egotism through love, and *The Wayfarer* (Wayne State University Press, 1967), which examines loneliness from varying social and family angles. Several other works of high merit are also available, among them *Grass by the Wayside* (University of Chicago Press, 1969), an autobiographical novel touching on the difficulties of Sōseki's marriage, and *Light and Darkness* (Putnam, 1982), his longest, most ambitious and unfinished last work, in which the author sought to find a way to transcend the inevitable prison he felt that the modern ego had and must become.

Encounter with a Skull
The Five-Storied Pagoda
The Bearded Samurai
Kōda Rohan

Tai dokuro, Gojū-no-tō, Higeotoko

Novellas. 1890, 1891–92, 1896

Kōda Rohan (1867–1947) lived a long life. A boy when the Meiji period and its Westernizing influences began, he published his first work in 1889 and continued his literary and scholarly endeavors until the 1940s. Rohan became a famous writer as a young man; then, as Japanese literature moved closer to the influences of European models, his work seemed to take on a strongly classical tinge. Indeed, his erudite language, as many Japanese commentators have pointed out, has made him more and more difficult to read for younger generations. With his interest in classical Chinese and Japanese literature, Rohan brought many of the literary ideals of the Tokugawa period (1600–1868), exemplified in the learned and fanciful writings of authors like Takizawa Bakin and **Ueda Akinari**, into the twentieth century. However, a friend of **Mori Ōgai**, who shared many of the same intellectual and literary interests, Rohan also looks forward to the austere historical narratives of **Inoue Yasushi**. In that regard, Rohan's work provides a crucial link in the ongoing classic strain still important in modern Japanese letters.

Rohan's significance, however, is by no means contingent upon such links. He was regarded as a major writer throughout his long career, and now that a sampling of his work is at last available in English translation, his skill as a storyteller is apparent. If the style of these tales seems, at first reading, somewhat controlled and remote, a careful perusal shows a penetrating command of psychology, a superb sense of timing, and a moving and romantic vision of the role of art in life.

The three long stories now available in English (perhaps better termed novellas) were all written during the earliest phase of Rohan's long career and thus cannot suggest the whole range of his developing concerns. What they do reveal, however, is the enormous skill of a young man, still in his twenties, already able to blend a highly romantic imagination with a formidable knowledge of Chinese and Japanese literary and historical precedents. Written in 1890, when the author was only twenty-three, "Encounter with a Skull" attains a level of sophistication quite comparable to that of Ueda Akinari in his masterpiece *Tales of Moonlight and Rain*. Akinari's ghost stories come to mind because some of the same elements are involved. Rohan's protagonist, a young man who unwittingly stumbles on a mysterious woman living in a forest, shares the same general model as Akinari's young scholar in "The Lust of the White Serpent," who also finds himself face to face with a beautiful, mysterious woman who lives in a remote spot. Beyond that point, however, the stories move differently. Rohan begins with his narrator firmly in the present. He has been recuperating from an illness "in April, 1890," near the famous lake Chūzenji at Nikko, north of Tokyo. Wishing to take an unfamiliar path out of the mountains, the young man hires a guide, who leads him partway through the snowy pass, then points him in the right direction and leaves him to his own devices. As he wanders through a mysterious forest, he comes upon a beautiful young woman, who offers him food and lodging for the night. There is a masterly contrast between their charming banter and the young man's rising conviction that he is in the presence of a magical, perhaps demonic figure. As the night goes on, the woman recounts her own highly romantic story, then allows the young man to leave as the sun is about to rise. In his purity and innocence he has escaped, but from what he only learns after he returns to civilization.

"Encounter with a Skull" contains many Buddhist elements, and such themes are even more apparent in "The Five-Storied Pagoda," first serialized in 1891 and 1892 and now surely his most famous work. With the story set in the Tokugawa period, a consciously old-fashioned language is employed by the author, evident even in translation, which gives the reader a sense of looking at a frieze (or a woodblock print, if you prefer), wherein a legend has been captured in both its mundane and fabulous aspects, worked into a conscious artistic whole. The story concerns the rivalry between two men for a contract to build a pagoda at a great Edo Buddhist temple presided over by the saintly abbot Rōen. Genta, a superb craftsman and astute businessman, assumes the contact will be his; the simple carpenter Jūbei, whom many regard as a fool, stakes his life on the fact that he will be able to surpass himself and build a perfect structure. The story masterfully contrasts the mentalities of these three men. Rohan achieves the climax of his romantic and ethical tale with perhaps the fiercest storm in all Japanese literature—certainly, at least, the most colorfully described. The conclusion is startling yet inevitable.

"The Bearded Samurai," composed in 1896, discloses another aspect of Rohan's intellectual prowess. The tale concerns a series of complex events in Japanese history that occurred in the decades preceding the unification of the country in 1600 by Tokugawa Ieyasu. At this juncture, the three great generals Oda Nobunaga, Toyotomi Hideyoshi, and Tokugawa Ieyasu are all grappling for supreme power, and each of the smaller clans perforce must attempt to follow one or the other of this trio of titans. The casual reader may find the swirl of events Rohan describes somewhat difficult to follow at first, but eventually, in the maze of moral undercutting that takes place, a seemingly minor character, a certain bearded samurai, takes the center of the stage. This samurai, in his retelling of an incident important to his own path of moral awakening, provides a powerful statement on the horrors of war. Rohan uses both historical and literary sources for his account, drawing in particular on the incident of the death of the boy-warrior Atsumori, a central incident from the medieval *Tale of the Heike*. The effect of the story is rather like reading the best of the Mori Ōgai historical narratives or watching a late Kurosawa samurai epic. Indeed, the 1980 Kurosawa film *Kagemusha* involves some of the same historical characters that function in Rohan's narrative. Rohan, like Ōgai and Kurosawa, seeks to define the real moral issues faced by his characters. All the historical complexities help provide nuance and color to the central moral confrontations. Once the reader has learned to follow the details of the narrative, "The Bearded Samurai" seems, in the end, a tale told with remarkable economy.

These three long stories only begin to suggest the richness of Rohan's best work. Hopefully, these successful English versions may spur on other translations of writings by this poet-scholar whose moral sense is matched so beautifully by his aesthetic intuitions.

TRANSLATION
Kōda Rohan. *Pagoda, Skull, and Samurai: Three Stories by Rohan Kōda*. Trans. Chieko Irie Mulhern. Charles E. Tuttle, 1985.

Comparing Heights
Higuchi Ichiyō

Takekurabe

Story. 1895–96

Modern Japanese literature can boast a dozen or more women novelists of the highest accomplishment. There are impressive precedents for this flowering of talent, beginning in the Heian period with Murasaki Shikibu, author of *The Tale of Genji*. In the medieval and Tokugawa periods, however, few women achieved prominence in the arts, possibly because the requisite educational opportunities were generally denied them. Higuchi Ichiyō (1872–96), whose work bridges the end of the traditional Japanese literary tradition and the beginnings of the modern era, heralds the return of women to the profession of writing. She was one of the first to overcome the restrictions of her milieu and find for her prodigious talents an artistic outlet. But Ichiyō is no mere transitional figure. She is one of the most accomplished writers of the modern period.

Reading Ichiyō's work in the original gives a considerably different impression than doing so in translation. The themes she often chooses, the lives of those who inhabit the world of the pleasure quarters, can be found as subject matter as far back as **Saikaku**; others, like **Nagai Kafū**, were to carry forward these themes well into our century. In English, the freshness of Ichiyō's psychological treatment of her characters seems paramount. Her style in the original Japanese, however, growing out of the comic tradition of Saikaku and his followers, is somehow redolent of classical texts, despite its fresh content. For Japanese readers, this odd, sometimes startling combination of new wine in old bottles brings a very particular pleasure. Stripped of this classical language, Ichiyō in English shows off her path-breaking concerns in the clearest fashion.

Having shown precocious talent, Ichiyō died at the age of twenty-four. Given the astonishing quality of her best writing, and the skill with which she assimilated new literary ideas, her early death was an enormous loss. The difficult circumstances of her life, however, made this perhaps inevitable. As a child, when both her parents were still alive, she showed a great interest in literature and even tried her hand at writing poetry in the classical forms. With the death of her father, however, she was forced to make an exhausting effort to support herself. In 1893, she attempted independence by opening a small confectionery shop near the Yoshiwara pleasure quarters, which failed. But this experience provided her with the opportunity of knowing something of the lives of those who inhabited the Yoshiwara, and their postures and attitudes formed the basis for much of her writing. The delightful comic stock characters that people the world of a Saikaku novel now take on the nuances of flesh and blood, as though cartoons had been transmuted into deftly realistic pen-and-ink sketches.

Strictly speaking, Ichiyō was less a novelist in the accepted sense of the word than a writer of short stories and novellas. Some of her accounts are only a few pages long, and some, like the 1895–96 *Comparing Heights* (*Takekurabe*), approach the complexity of a novel. Thanks to the excellent recent volume of translations by Robert Danly, much of Ichiyō's best work can now be savored in English. I must confess a particular fascination for the 1895 story "Troubled Waters" (*Nigorie*), in which the author has taken the kind of love-suicide story familiar (perhaps too familiar) since the era of the domestic dramas of **Chika-matsu**, then infused it with a sense of psychological reality that allows the reader to enter into the mental states of her troubled characters.

While all her works hold a similar fascination, few readers would dispute the supremacy of "Comparing Heights."

The central image of the story can be traced back to *The Well Curb* (*Izutsu*), a famous *nō* play by Zeami, which in turn draws on an incident in *Tales of Ise*. In these original sources, the two main characters, reminiscing on their childhood and how they grew to be adults, recall how they had compared heights by making marks on the side of a well. The *nō* play is deliberately nostalgic in tone, and that same shadow of incipient sadness casts itself over Ichiyō's modern story. The memorable characters she has created are still children, yet they are poised on the edge of adulthood, when they will perforce lose their spontaneity and their lives take their preordained courses. Eventually, all of their friends—the lovely Midori, Nobu the Buddhist priest-to-be, Chōkichi and his "back street gang"—all will disappear into the busy life of the quarter to work out the rest of their unremarkable destinies. In the moments touched upon in the story, however, Ichiyō's creations have just arrived at the instant of adolescent self-awareness. As they look around at one another, the quick flow of their shifting perceptions of themselves and of each other are caught up in a series of incidents that, like photographs taken with some mysterious psychic camera, reveal a glimpse of certain truths that they themselves had not previously perceived.

Comparing Heights is a group portrait. The youngsters remain in the foreground, but all kinds of people who inhabit the quarter are sketched in the background with quick strokes of significant detail. No one who reads the story will easily forget, for example, Nobuyuki's priest father, who makes an honest woman of his touching common-law wife. Yet it is in the fluctuating moods of Ichiyō's heroine, Midori, that the author best captures the atmosphere she wishes to convey. The moment when Midori attempts to help Nobuyuki with the broken thong on his sandal, only to find herself held in check by feelings she had never before experienced during her "tomboy" childhood, is one of the most moving evocations of adolescence in the literature of any country. Here, and elsewhere in her work, Ichiyō approaches genius.

Edward Seidensticker's elegant translation of *Comparing Heights*, which he calls *Growing Up*, is contained in Donald Keene's anthology *Modern Japanese Literature: From 1868 to Present Day* (Grove Press, 1956). Robert Danly's *In the Shade of Spring Leaves: The Life and Writings of Higuchi Ichiyō, a Woman of Letters in Meiji Japan* (Yale University Press, 1983) provides his version of the story, which he calls *Child's Play*, plus evocative English renderings of eight other shorter works and a fine biography of the author.

Before the Dawn
Shimazaki Tōson

Yoakemae

Novel. 1929-35

Despite a formidable reputation as a fine poet and premier novelist of Meiji and Taishō Japan, Shimazaki Tōson (1872-1943) has remained, for the English-reading public, something of a buried giant. His novels are lengthy and complex, and so have long daunted the enthusiasms of potential translators. With the triumphant appearance in 1987 of a fine English version of his most significant and longest work of fiction, *Before the Dawn* (*Yoakemae*), however, Tōson's compelling vision of the Westernization of his country is finally available to readers outside Japan. Tōson's long novel took him many years to write. The first segments appeared in 1929; the remainder required another six years to complete. Tōson was already a famous novelist when he undertook this enormous effort, and its publication was to cap his career.

Tōson was the son of an important village official on the old Kiso road, an important mountain artery in Tokugawa times that connected remote areas to the major road networks near what is now the modern city of Nagoya. Tōson was eventually able to use his family history as background for his novel, but before that his career was to take many twists and turns. His formative years were spent in Tokyo, where he came in touch with Western literature and thought, most importantly through his contact with the writer and philosopher Kitamura Tōkoku

(1868–94), a Byronic figure who inspired an idealistic generation of disciples before creating consternation and shock for friends and readers alike by his suicide. Tōson, upset and disillusioned, left Tokyo and became a teacher in the northern city of Sendai. There, in a calmer atmosphere, he began to experiment with new forms of poetry, writing the first really successful attempts at long verse in the modern manner, poems that would quickly come to have a profound effect on the development of the new poetry in Japan. Tōson's concerns, however, soon shifted to prose. First he created a series of fresh sketches describing local life in the north, and then, in 1906, an epoch-making novel, *The Broken Commandment* (*Hakai*), in which his sense of the tensions in contemporary Japanese society were encapsulated in his account of a teacher and a young man of the *eta* or outcast class, who faced bravely the hypocrisy of the world around him. Tōson's next novels, such as *Haru* (Spring; as yet untranslated) and *The Family* (*Ie*), began to draw more specifically on his personal experiences. In 1913 Tōson went to France, and after his return to Japan during World War I, he published one of his most striking works, *Shinsei* (New Life; as yet untranslated), an account of his own spiritual rebirth in a European setting.

Tōson was a lively correspondent while in Paris, writing with insight and vigor of the artistic and intellectual brilliance of the "capital of light." At the same time, however, his inevitable and growing sense of isolation and loneliness in an alien culture led him, as his diaries and other writings indicate, to reflect both on his own personal past and on the recent past of his country, which had changed so remarkably since the coming of the Europeans and Americans in the 1850s. Undoubtedly it was this extended trip outside his own cultural milieu that forced Tōson to contemplate the composition of a narrative describing the significance, on both a human and a national scale, of Japan's recent history. Once home, he began to undertake considerable research in order to reconstruct the kind of life his father had led, an existence that by the 1920s seemed almost impossibly remote. In a sense, Tōson was trying to catch a last glimpse of the past before it slipped away forever, just as **Mori Ōgai** had attempted to do in his monumental historical account of the Edo physician Shibue Chūsai.

In *Before the Dawn*, Tōson combined his ability to express larger social concerns, as he had done in *The Broken Commandment*, with his technique of delineating the personal, interior life of the characters, a skill he was to perfect in the novels written afterward. Tōson chose for his main focus a re-creation of his father, Hanzō, who had witnessed and been sorely afflicted by the vast changes that had come to Japan. Moving relentlessly back and forth from Hanzō's small world to the whole shifting society, Tōson juxtaposes individual and national responses to the coming of the West so that one level illustrates and explicates the other. Hanzō's sympathies for the common man and his distaste for the old feudal system make him an advocate of what he perceives to be changes for the better, yet he is eventually betrayed by the new order. Hanzō's own idealistic beliefs and convictions seem of little use to a society bent on material gain, as if to prove the doctrine of the survival of the fittest. Living in a remote area as he does, Hanzō must learn of various historic events through secondhand accounts, and this structure permits Tōson to write at length about the larger issues with which the country was grappling during that period. Some of these accounts, like the lengthy soliloquies in French classical drama, occasionally seem to suggest that the real excitement is happening offstage, but the composite picture these incidents provide remains nonetheless compelling.

Caught up in these changes—the fall of the old system of government, the outbreak of local rebellions, and the advent of a new bureaucracy aimed at creating for Japan a parity with the West and its perceived values—Hanzō can scarcely understand his own reactions and certainly not the responses of many who surround him, particularly the men who possess the "new mentality" of burgeoning Tokyo. The doggedly idealistic Hanzō, faced with so many difficulties, becomes prey to melancholia. He begins to drink to excess and slowly moves from the status of eccentric to that of madman. Back in his native village, he is finally locked in a woodshed, like some wounded King Lear, where he dies shortly afterward. The year is 1886.

For all the cumulative power of Tōson's account of Hanzō's life, the book has other focuses as well. In particular, some of the set pieces, such as those describing certain battles at the end of the Tokugawa shogunate, provide a wealth of specific detail that recall the kind of loving and painstaking research that Tolstoy put into the composition of the historical frescoes in *War and Peace*. Then too, Tōson's ability to portray the clash of ideas and ideologies in terms of human response allows even an unprepared reader to grasp the differences between Buddhism, Confucianism, and Tokugawa "native studies," at least in terms of their human dimensions.

Perhaps only a novel written with this much care, and this much passion, can make the realities of this crucial period so alive, and so compelling, for Western readers. Indeed, many Japanese have formed their own sense of the implications of the coming of the West to their country through their perusal of this dark and thoughtful narrative. Tōson's greatest qualities as a writer, his simplicity and sobriety, are well employed in the service of this final homage to his family and their generation. Long, sprawling, occasionally unfocused, *Before the Dawn* is as real as life itself. The hours spent reading it will provide a sense of a time, and a complex opportunity, still seen as central to contemporary readers in Japan. And the story is one in which we, as Westerners, are intimately involved as well.

TRANSLATION
Shimazaki Tōson. *Before the Dawn*. Trans. William E. Naff. University of Hawaii Press, 1987.

OTHER WORKS BY SHIMAZAKI TŌSON
Two earlier novels have been translated into English, both published by the University of Tokyo Press and available in the United States from Columbia University Press. *The Broken Commandment*, translated by Kenneth Strong, appeared in 1974. *The Family*, translated by Cecilia Segawa Seigle, was published in 1976. Most of Tōson's major works, with elegantly rendered translations of significant passages, are well described in Edwin McClellan's *Two Japanese Novelists: Sōseki and Tōson* (University of Chicago Press, 1969), which also presents an overview of the work of **Natsume Sōseki**.

A Certain Woman
Arishima Takeo

Aru onna

Novel. 1919

Within the range of modern Japanese literature, there are many skillful and evocative portraits of women. Some of these characters accept their fate, some fight against it. But nowhere is there a character as powerful, or at such odds with herself, as Yōko in Arishima's famous novel *A Certain Woman (Aru onna)*. Yōko springs to life on the opening page, and the reader, mesmerized, can only abandon her on the threshold of death in the final paragraphs. Her very intensity makes her the exception that reveals the level of discretion and decorum customarily brought to the portrayal of the battle of the sexes in much of Japanese literature, classical and modern alike. **Saikaku, Nagai Kafū,** and the others who deal with the sensual aspects of human relationships tend to suggest the erotic through indirection. Arishima, in a tremendous feat of the creative imagination, has moved himself inside the skin of his central character. Some critics have suggested that, just as Flaubert could say, "Madame Bovary, c'est moi," Arishima could have made a similar claim for Yōko. She may well be the most powerful, the most disturbing woman in modern Japanese fiction.

Arishima's innate creative energies are responsible for Yōko's being, but his imagination was surely spurred on by many of his own life experiences. Born in 1878 to a wealthy family with considerable land holdings in Hokkaido, Arishima came early under the influence of Protestant Christianity, then a strong attraction within intellectual circles in Japan. A trip to study in America, however, brought him a sense of disillusionment with what he perceived to be the narrow thinking of the Christian community. In the end, his voyage out of Japan put him in touch with Western literary accomplishment, exposing him to works and writers that were to remain influential in the development of his own art—Ibsen, Tolstoy, and Walt Whitman. Back in Japan in 1907, having abandoned his religion, Arishima replaced it with a career devoted to writing and teaching, working with other like-minded intellectuals to introduce into Japan the kind excitement he found in Western high culture.

A Certain Woman, published in its final version in 1919, has remained the most widely read of his many works, and the novel is surely the strongest and most probing of all his literary creations. Arishima modeled his heroine on the actions of a real woman, the wife of a noted novelist known to him personally. Arishima's lightly fictionalized account of her actions on a trip to America served as the basis for an earlier version of the novel published in 1911–13. The latter half of the finished book, however, appears to have come entirely from his imagination. Like Flaubert, Arishima apparently created a character only to watch her take on a life of her own. All the details added to give a sense of reality to the story came from the writer's lived experience: thus the disdain for straight-laced and hypocritical Christians, and the conviction that Japanese women remained trapped and imprisoned because of their inferior social status. Yet *A Certain Woman* plunges still deeper, into the core of human personality. In that sense the novel deals boldly with the grip that the erotic impulse can have, at least implicitly, on every human being. Arishima's daring exploration of this impulse gives the book its ultimate force.

Yōko, the protagonist, is glamorous, forceful, beautiful. Married to a promising journalist, then divorced, she is soon pressured into a proper marriage with Kimura, an earnest young Christian businessman living in America. Reluctantly she agrees to the union, then undertakes the long voyage to Seattle by sea. By the time she has arrived there, however, she has begun an affair with Kuraji, a handsome purser on the ship. Her body has awakened for the first time to its full erotic potential, and, completely caught up in the relationship, she feigns illness, remains on board, and returns to Japan with Kuraji. The variations on the fever chart of their emotions are described by Arishima with the skill of a D. H. Lawrence.

After the couple returns to Japan, they continue to live apart from society as the scandal of their relationship spreads. The latter part of the novel traces Yōko's downward spiral. Kuraji, fired from his job, is trapped into taking up illegal pursuits and eventually forced to disappear. Yōko's behavior becomes more and more erratic: she is cruel to her declining circle of friends, haughty and difficult with her lovely younger sisters, and eventually mentally ill herself.

Arishima's skill ultimately lies, it seems to me, in his ability to present his material without moralizing about it. A variety of characters in the course of the story pronounce judgement on Yōko; yet, seen from the vantage point of her own emotional intensity, their remarks never cut to the heart of the matter. It is not surprising, perhaps, that those who preach the loudest, the Christian believers, are sketched in the most disdainful way by the author. Some readers have understood Yōko as a woman suppressed by society, but the text seems to suggest something else as well, the author's vision of a woman caught in the full grip of an elemental force so powerful that, once it is unleashed in her, neither she herself nor the society in which she lives can contain it. She can only destroy herself.

Despite this remarkably modern theme, Yōko in her final degradation comes less to resemble Ibsen's Hedda Gabler than some of the wicked and erotic heroines of the nineteenth-century *kabuki* plays written by Tsuruya Namboku or Kawatake Mokuami, women who will undertake any evil action in order to insure their continuing hold over their paramours. Back in Japan, Yōko decides to continue to accept money from her unsuspecting fiancé, Kimura, who remains in America. She manages to convince Kuraji, who to this point has behaved honorably, to agree to her swindling the young man. The scene strikes a powerful, melodramatic note that recalls the vampire murderesses so famous in the theater of the preceding decades. In *A Certain Woman*, Arishima has created a gorgeous sort of infernal machine; once Yōko is wound up, she can follow only one destructive path, straight to the end.

By the time the novel was finished and published, Arishima had become deeply discouraged by the selfishness he found in society. Unable to find a means to deal with that despair in artistic terms, he himself was to flounder spiritually: in 1923, he and his mistress committed suicide. That act has been seen as bringing a symbolic end to the idealism prevalent in the intellectual and artistic circles that Arishima had long stood for. *A Certain Woman*, however, suggests that the author may have located a new country of darkness, one that put him at painful odds with some of his previous convictions. Such is the tension that propels this remarkable novel.

TRANSLATION

Arishima Takeo. *A Certain Woman*. Trans. Kenneth Strong. Tokyo University Press, 1978. Available in the United States from Columbia University Press.

A Strange Tale from East of the River
Nagai Kafū

Bokutō kidan

Novella. 1936

Nagai Kafū (1879–1959) stands, like **Mori Ōgai** and **Natsume Sōseki**, as one of the early giants of modern Japanese literature. Although he lived a good deal longer and saw a great deal more of an evolving Japanese society, Kafū resembles the two others in that he was instrumental in bringing to Japanese prose and poetry the example of European literature. Sōseki's study of British fiction helped shape his own goals as a novelist, while Ōgai provided his readers with important models from German romantic and modern fiction and poetry. It was Kafū, however, who, through his love of French literature and culture, brought the work of Verlaine, Baudelaire, Zola, and Maupassant to Japanese intellectual and artistic circles. As a translator, an essayist, and a novelist in his own right, Kafū combined his intuitive sympathy for French life with his own respect for traditional Japanese literature to create a succession of works filled with a sinuous self-awareness and a sensual egotism that perhaps makes him at once the most decadent and the most elegant of all modern Japanese authors. Kafū's work is not to every taste, but for those who allow themselves to enter into the special world to which he bears witness, his works explore a range of human experience and sensation that any reader can recognize as lying, even if dormant, within himself. I use the word "himself" because, for many women, Kafū seems slightly distasteful; for them, he remains a man's author. Kafū describes women with an extraordinary degree of nuanced observation, yet many of his female characters are forced to remain to some extent as playthings, willing or unwilling, of the narcissistic men who hold them in thrall.

Kafū has been fortunate in attracting the formidable skills of Edward Seidensticker as a translator, whose rendering of Kafū's novella *A Strange Tale from East of the River* (*Bokutō kidan*) captures to a remarkable degree the effectiveness of the original. In this story, most of Kafū's major concerns are touched on in a particularly evocative way. Written in 1936, the novella was at first a serialization, to be published in book form in 1937. The narrative, written in the first person, has a plot, but only a slight one. The focus is rather on the changing moods of an aging author, himself in the process of writing a novel, who begins a brief affair with a prostitute who lives "east of the river," in one of the poor sections of Tokyo that lie beyond Asakusa. The narrator first wanders about in that depressed area, seeking a proper setting for his new work. Caught in a sudden rainstorm, he offers his umbrella to a woman in kimono, who takes him to her home and out of the storm. They strike up a friendship, and he soon begins borrowing elements from their developing relationship for use in his writing. The story, and the story-within-a-story, thus reflect back on each other like confronting images in subtly shifting mirrors.

And yet, however skillful the techniques employed, the real power of the story lies in Kafū's ability to conjure up the hot summer and the nostalgic yet strangely powerful glamor of the poorer districts that the protagonist continues to visit. Kafū's narrator, like the author himself, disdains the superficial modernity of Tokyo and constantly seeks out traces of an older, more authentic culture. Often these searches take him to the most neglected parts of the city. "Better," the narrator states, "to seek happiness in finding the remains of a beautifully woven pattern among castaway rags than in finding spatters and stains on a wall proclaimed immaculate." The real story, then, is about the decaying city within the city of Tokyo.

In novellas such as *A Strange Tale from East of the River*, Kafū set out to create a world known to few of his readers, since most of them had surely never ventured into such obscure parts of the capital. For that reason perhaps, Kafū's descriptions of the buildings, the heat, the clothing, even the mosquitoes, is wrought in such persuasive detail that the reader is drawn, fascinated, into the setting.

Despite the presumed decadence of the subject matter, the narrator, again mirroring the author, remains something of a moralist as he protests the hypocrisy of the new city and what he takes to be its sham middle-class morality. Indeed, Kafū never hesitated to speak his mind, either through his characters or in his essays. His independence of mind never faltered. In the period just after the war, Kafū was revered as a writer who never became in any fashion a proponent of the overly patriotic values that swept the country during the 1930s. His wartime diaries reveal the observations of a powerful personality who maintained a clear head and the necessary distance from everything around him.

Elegant, erotic, aristocratic, Kafū's writing has a special and complex flavor. Although he cannot suit every taste, many regard him as a chronicler of the very highest quality, one who has captured certain elements that belong to a true Japan rarely visible in the "official" versions so often served up for Western consumption. Winsome, antisocial, yet capable of great enthusiasm, Kafū remains a unique and personal voice.

TRANSLATION

A Strange Tale from East of the River is contained in Edward Seidensticker's *Kafū the Scribbler: The Life and Writings of Nagai Kafū, 1879–1959* (Stanford University Press, 1965). Other shorter works, notably his highly regarded "River Sumida," plus sections of longer novels, are included, along with biographical and critical material. The book is one of the very best available in the whole field of modern Japanese literature.

The Poetry of Santōka (1882–1940)

The reader who believes that art transcends its own times will surely take solace and inspiration from the work of Taneda Santōka (1882–1940), a remarkable Zen priest and poet of our century who produced poetry as personal and profound as that of his illustrious predecessor and spiritual mentor, **Ryōkan** (1758–1831). Like Ryōkan's poetry, Santōka's work can best be understood as a record of his quest for spiritual enlightenment, the kind of voyage that can be undertaken in any era. Readers in our increasingly secular age may first be drawn to Santōka out of a sense of nostalgia, but in reading his poetry they will immediately come face to face with a strong will and the personality of a man who, whatever his personal weaknesses, appears quite unafraid to live on the very edge of society, far from its received values and expectations. Santōka explores, or re-explores, realms that are commonly believed no longer to exist.

Santōka (a pen name the translator John Stevens has rendered "Burning Mountain Peak") began his life as an ordinary young man with some interest in literature. His father was a local politician who owned a certain amount of property. Santōka began writing *haiku* in college, where he also slipped into a pattern of heavy drinking. Married, then separated, he drifted from job to job until, after what may have been a suicide attempt, he was sent to convalesce in a Zen temple. This proved the turning point in his spiritual life, and in 1925 he was officially ordained as a Zen priest. Santōka went here and there begging for his sustenance, short trips turning into longer pilgrimages. Sinking into drunkenness again, he was rescued by friends, who found him a small cottage to use as a hermitage. This served as a base for his walking trips, which took him through many parts of Japan, begging, writing, drifting. Some of these trips were undertaken in order to seek out certain traditional sites holy to Buddhists in Japan, some without apparent destination. A number of his poems were published during his lifetime, and indeed he achieved a degree of fame. But worldly attention was apparently of little interest. He once told a newspaper reporter, "I'm one of society's warts."

Santōka's free-style *haiku* poetry, like his life, appears stripped to the essentials.

> No path but this one—
> I walk alone.   (trans. John Stevens)

> Walking into the wind,
> heaping abuse upon myself.   (trans. James Abrams)

Walking, walking, he traveled on. Like his great poet predecessors, stretching back through **Bashō** to **Saigyō** and beyond, Santōka perceived that movement, in and of itself, provided a sense of elevated awareness that might in turn lead to some higher level of understanding.

> Stretching out my feet;
> Some daylight still remains.   (trans. John Stevens)

> A steady autumn drizzle,
> one road, straight ahead.   (trans. James Abrams)

Laconic, deceptively simple, these brief vignettes allow the reader to penetrate special instants in the poet's journey, creating an empathy of strong feeling between poet and reader.

For all the timelessness of this spiritual landscape, Santōka is quite able to record our own century when he feels the need.

> At the tobacco shop
> no cigarettes,
> a cold rain falls.   (trans. James Abrams)

The deep, cool moon
Appears between the buildings.   (trans. John Stevens)

The moon, traditionally a Buddhist symbol for enlightenment, remains; only the milieu has changed.

Haiku being as difficult as they are to render into English, it sometimes helps to contrast translations of the same poem in order to uncover layers of implicit meaning. Here, for example, is a famous poem in which, by extension, walking may serve as a symbol for the difficult, unending search for self-understanding.

Going deeper,
And still deeper—
The green mountains.   (trans. John Stevens)

I push my way through,
push my way through,
green mountains   (trans. James Abrams)

There are few answers in Santōka's poetry, only signs of his continuing search. Success, failure, and frustration are courageously recorded.

Thinking of nothing,
I walk among
A forest of withered trees.   (trans. John Stevens)

Difficult as Santōka's life and art may be to describe, the reader who examines these *haiku* with care and sympathy can experience something of them both. The poems are so close to the heart of the man that one seems a reflection of the other. The reader's interest can begin with either.

There are two collections of translations presently available, both quoted from above. Those by John Stevens are gathered together in his book *Mountain Tasting: Zen Haiku* (John Weatherhill, 1980). The second group can be found in a long and useful essay on the poet by James Abrams, entitled "Hail in the Begging Bowl: The Odyssey and Poetry of Santōka," published in the autumn 1977 issue of the scholarly journal of the Japanese humanities *Monumenta Nipponica*. It is well worth seeking out.

The Poetry of Takamura Kōtarō (1883–1956)

Takamura Kōtarō was one of the seminal artistic figures in modern Japan, making considerable contributions as critic, poet, and sculptor. In all three fields, his creative activity was an inspiration to the work of others. Kōtarō's poetry, in particular, is a telling record of his trajectory through the complex changes that Japan underwent during his lifetime, serving for many readers as a sometimes exultant, sometimes painful commentary on his age.

The son of a woodcarver well-known for his Buddhist images, Kōtarō first assumed he would continue in his father's profession and so entered the Tokyo School of Fine Arts in 1897 to study sculpture. Founded a decade before, the school provided excellent academic instruction for painting and sculpture in both traditional and Western modes. For many Japanese of the period, the first encounter with Western art (itself in a period of great flowering) was to be an extremely powerful one, helping them to create a fresh vision of the way in which art might affect society. For Kōtarō, his contact through photographs with the sculpture of Rodin proved decisive. He decided that he must find a way to study abroad, at the time an expensive and culturally daunting task. He went first to New York, then eventually to his cherished destination, Paris, in 1908, where he managed to find the funds necessary to sustain himself for almost a year. His moving encounters with that city are described in his poetry, as is his later sense of disillusionment on returning to Japan, where, he felt, cultural life remained in a perilous state of transition.

Kōtarō now became a spokesman for the kind of artistic commitment he had witnessed in the activities of the Post-Impressionist artists in Paris. His essays on the creative role of the artist, notably his famous "Green Sun" manifesto of 1910, had a profound effect on his generation. Art, Kōtarō insisted, must spring from the authentic interior vision of the one who creates it; artistic success does not consist of mere technique but rather derives from the manifestation of an inner truth grasped intuitively by the artist.

All through this tumultuous period in his life, Kōtarō had been writing poetry. At first he composed *haiku*, the 17-syllable poems still highly popular in the generations after such poets as **Bashō** and **Kobayashi Issa**. Then he experimented with new-style *waka*, a freer version of the classic 31-syllable poetic form, to which poets at the turn of the century now turned for self-expression. Kōtarō's trip to Europe, however, introduced him to the work of such great Western poets as Rimbaud and Baudelaire, and within a few years of his return from France he was writing his best work in long poems composed in the vernacular. The beauty of this poetry helped bring about a linguistic revolution.

Kōtarō married in 1914. His wife, Chieko, was a highly educated painter and an activist for women's rights. Each understood and supported the efforts of the other, and their union seemed a perfect one. In 1931, however, Chieko became depressed, then mentally ill, and her steady decline continued until her death in 1938. Kōtarō's poems dealing with his concern for his wife—in health, sickness, and then in death—are among the most admired poetic sequences in all modern Japanese literature.

By the beginning of World War II, when Kōtarō was in his late fifties and doubtless suffering from mental fatigue due to the death of his wife, he had turned to writing verse of a nationalistic sort. By the end of the war he had retired to live alone in the country, not to return to Tokyo until 1952, when he accepted a commission for a final work of sculpture at the age of sixty-nine. In 1956, succumbing to the same disease that had struck down the mentally ailing Chieko twenty years before, he died of tuberculosis.

All of these events, and Kōtarō's responses to them, are recorded in his poetry.

A number of individual poems by Kōtarō have attracted translators over the years, but it was not until the publication of Hiroaki Sato's book-length selection from the poet's work that the full range of his lyric vision became known outside of Japan. Sato's choice from the corpus of poems is varied and judicious. The poems written on Kōtarō's European experiences—in particular his encounter with the cathedral of Notre Dame in Paris—show the enthusiasm the poet felt as his artistic horizons opened out ("I became an artist in Paris," he wrote), and those describing his work as a sculptor are surprisingly successful. Sato has included some of the late postwar poems as well, in which the artist looks back on his past, especially on his foolishness during the war years. By the end of that period he could write, in sadness, "... serene, with nothing left / I enjoy fully the beauty of the desolate."

The centerpiece of the book, however, as well as of the poet's own work, are the Chieko poems. Sato has included twenty-six of them, and they touch on all aspects of the couple's relationship. The poems describing her madness are the most moving of all. In some, the poet learns to witness new truths through her increasingly childlike vision. In others, he can only trail behind her without understanding. "Chieko sees what one cannot see / hears what one cannot hear." The poems on her death, notably "Lemon Elegy," are intensely moving, particularly in the contrasts between objects and feelings.

Kōtarō's closeness to his dead wife continued on. It is fitting indeed

that one of the last poems included in the book, "Report (to Chieko),"
is a brief and touching account of the changes for the better that Japan
had undergone since the war. Kōtarō wanted her, in spirit, to know
about them.

TRANSLATIONS

Sato, Hiroaki. *Chieko and Other Poems of Takamura Kōtarō*. University Press of
Hawaii, 1980.

Takamura Kōtarō. *Chieko's Sky*. Trans. Soichi Furuta. Kodansha International,
1978. Furuta includes a slightly different selection of the Chieko poems and
provides a translation as well of a prose essay by Kōtarō concerning his wife.
The book is beautifully illustrated with photographs of paper cutouts made by
Chieko herself.

A Dark Night's Passing
Shiga Naoya

An'ya kōro

Novel. 1921–37

Throughout his long life and after, Shiga Naoya (1883–1971) has remained for his countrymen one of the most revered of all modern
Japanese writers. His enthusiasms mirrored certain important intellectual currents of his time, and his virtual silence after completion of the
novel *A Dark Night's Passing* seems, in retrospect, the inevitable outcome of the spiritual quest he thought to chronicle in that ambitious
and eloquent work.

Like many intellectuals and artists of his generation, Shiga was deeply impressed by his early contact with Christianity, notably through his
meeting the renowned writer and thinker Uchimura Kanzō (1861–
1930), whose powerful essays on the Christian life had an enormous
influence. Filled with enthusiasm for new means of self-expression,
Shiga joined forces with **Arishima Takeo** and others to found a new
magazine of art and literature, *Shirakaba* (White Birch), which, dur-

ing its thirteen years of life, introduced the best of modern Japanese and European fiction, poetry, critical writing, and art (in reproduction) to the Japanese public. During this time Shiga was to develop his own skills in composing short stories as well as other works that might best be described as semi-autobiographical essays. Many of these works are extremely accomplished and can rank with the best of their kind in modern Japanese literature. Fortunately, a number of these short pieces are now available in excellent translations.

By 1923 Shiga had published most of his long novel A *Dark Night's Passing*, but the final chapters were to take him well over a decade to complete. As the novel is to some extent autobiographical, it may be that Shiga had to live out, in his fashion, just the kind of spiritual adventure that his novel sought to relate. Basically, his story traces the ascent of a modern man—egocentric, willful, full of self-doubts—a man who eventually frees himself of uncertainty, nihilism, and despair to move to a state of spiritual understanding and, with it, a rare exhilaration. At all stages of this account, Shiga's sense of the journey is compelling.

The novel opens with a brief reminiscence of an unhappy childhood related by the protagonist, Tokitō Kensaku. The account centers on events that took place when Kensaku's cold and unyielding father, following the death of the boy's mother, hands him over to be raised by his grandfather. The grandfather, in a further complexity, maintains an ambiguous relationship with a young woman named Oei, who we later learn is indeed his mistress. It is such a past, here briefly glimpsed, that sets in motion the forces that are to shape Kensaku throughout his youthful and middle years.

After the death of his grandfather, Kensaku lives with Oei, with whom he develops a complex emotional relationship. In a constant state of unease because of the treatment he continues to receive from his relatives, Kensaku leaves Tokyo for Onomichi, a beautiful town on the hills rising above the Inland Sea. There he experiences his first powerful contact with the beauty of nature. Still in an emotional turmoil, however, Kensaku returns to Tokyo, thinking to marry Oei. There he learns that he is the son not of the man he always thought his father, but of his grandfather, who had seduced his mother when his father was traveling. Completely crushed, Kensaku seeks consolation in writing.

Kensaku's restlessness begins to dissipate as his contacts with Zen Buddhism and the classical literature of the Orient increase. Eventually he moves to Kyoto and marries. A sense of harmony begins to enter his life. While on a trip, however, his wife is seduced by his best friend, placing Kensaku in the same position that his father had been in a generation before. This device of repetition is as effective here as a similar technique employed in *The Tale of Genji,* where first Genji, then his son, experience the same patterns of attraction to women. Kensaku comes to realize that his pervading sense of spiritual malaise has come about through his own egotism. He realizes that he must transcend this "I," the sense of self that gives him such pain. Toward the end of the novel, Kensaku decides to make a pilgrimage to Mt. Daisen, a magnificent cluster of peaks near the Japan Sea in Tottori Prefecture. Historically, the spot has long served as a pilgrimage center for Buddhists. These final sections of the novel represent those relatively few pages that took Shiga so long to write. In them, he achieves the amazing literary feat, in prose, of creating a genuine poetic and mystical experience.

In the moments described there, Kensaku comes to terms with nature (one is tempted to write Nature) as well as with his own human nature. "He could feel his mind and his own body both gradually merging into this great nature that surrounded him.... To be gently drawn into it, and there to be restored, was a pleasure beyond the power of words to describe." In the intensity of his experience, Kensaku collapses. When his wife arrives at the mountain temple where he is resting, she discovers him to be grievously ill, yet strangely tranquil. She now finds herself as close to him as he has become to nature. Both characters are mute. Shiga, having gone as far as the limits of what he felt words might express, surely felt that he had reason to cease writing.

It is not surprising that this deeply serious and often enthralling book has retained its power to move Japanese readers, for it touches on some of the grand themes that belong to the finest Japanese traditional literature, those predilections that privilege the power of intuition and a search for transcendence. Those convictions, so important for writers ranging from **Saigyō** to **Bashō**, live on in *A Dark Night's Passing*, recreated in authentic twentieth-century terms.

TRANSLATION

Shiga Naoya. *A Dark Night's Passing*. Trans. Edwin McClellan. Kodansha International, 1976. One of the truly great translations of modern Japanese literature and fully worthy of the novel.

OTHER WORKS BY SHIGA NAOYA

There are a number of Shiga's shorter works available in translation. Two collections call for special mention. William F. Sibley's *The Shiga Hero* (University of Chicago Press, 1979) includes evocative translations of ten stories. Lane Dunlop's fine collection of Shiga's work, *The Paper Door* (North Point Press, 1986), contains seventeen.

The Poetry of Ishikawa Takuboku (1886–1912)

Ishikawa Takuboku may be credited, along with **Masaoka Shiki** (1867–1902), with having brought the venerable 31-syllable *tanka* (or *waka*) into the realm of modern poetic possibility. Takuboku was only a teenager when Shiki died, and the younger writer was likewise to have a short life and a painful death. If the two are to be compared, Shiki's work maintains a balance between traditional images of nature and the poet's personality; next to Takuboku's obsessive interiority, it appears merely transitional. Whereas Shiki projected the anguish of his final illness onto the increasingly small number of experiences available to him from the confinement of his hospital bed—snow outside the window, a few falling petals—Takuboku plunges directly inside himself, attempting to express what he senses to be the disintegration of his own mind.

> How sad to have a mind
> Without desire to recover from disease—
> O the *why* of this mind!   (trans. Shinoda and Goldstein)

Even in Takuboku's *tanka* written in other, happier periods, the personality of the poet often occupies the center of the poem with an intensity that seems new to the form.

> Urged on by something nameless,
> I pick up the pen—
> O this morning with fresh flowers in a vase!
>   (trans. Shinoda and Goldstein)

Poetry, Takuboku insisted, could only be at its most genuine a truthful record of the poet's inner life. At one point he wrote, "Poetry must not be what is usually called poetry. It must be an exact report, an honest diary, of the changes in a man's emotional life. Accordingly, it must be fragmentary; it must not have organization." In creating works according to this aesthetic, Takuboku succeeded brilliantly. Paradoxically, describing the specifics of his mental and emotional life, he achieved a remarkable universality. In his best poetry, the reader peers through the prism of Takuboku's specific situation to catch a glimpse of all humanity beyond. There is virtually always a shock of recognition.

Takuboku's life, despite its earlier enthusiasms, was grimmer than many. Born in a poor section of northern Japan, he was precocious and found himself a published poet at sixteen. He traveled to Tokyo and came to know a number of leading writers, including the highly gifted feminist poet Yosano Akiko and her husband, Yosano Tekkan. Takuboku was unable to make a living, however, and he returned home to find work in various cities in Hokkaido, first as a teacher, then as a newspaper editor. In 1908, aching to return to Tokyo, Takuboku left his family behind and came to work as a proofreader for the *Asahi Newspapers*. He began to publish his own poems, but, as his so-called *rōmaji* diary clearly shows, he led a frantic and marginal existence, both economically and spiritually. By 1911 he found himself in the hospital. A year later he was dead of tuberculosis at twenty-six. His posthumously published *tanka* collection, *Sad Toys* (*Kanashiki gangu*), made him famous.

The very first poem in Takuboku's 1910 collection, *A Handful of Sand* (*Ichiaku no suna*), provides an image of the poet strikingly different from any that precede it. **Matsuo Bashō**, whose work provided the model for so many modern *tanka* and *haiku* poets, allowed his personality to emerge by indirection; his juxtaposition of ponds, willows, crows, and dozens of other familiar images permitted the reader to grasp something of the nature of the artist by the way in which he put those images together. Now, the poet becomes the poem.

> on a white strip of sand
> on a tiny island
> in the eastern sea
> drowned in tears
> I play with a crab   (trans. Carl Sesar)

The nervous pace of modern urban life, which was to give **Natsume Sōseki** so much grief, was altogether familiar to Takuboku.

> just felt like
> a train ride—
> when I got off
> there was
> no place to go   (trans. Carl Sesar)

And always, that inescapable self was there too.

came to
a mirror shop
what a jolt—
I could've been
some bum walking by   (trans. Carl Sesar)

The title for Takuboku's posthumous collection, *Sad Toys*, was a
phrase taken by his editors from an essay he had written on the art of
the *tanka*, in which, among other things, he attempted to explain to
himself the fact that he needed to write poetry. "Though I try to justify
myself," he confessed, "I cannot help but admit I have become a victim
of the present family, class, and capitalist systems and the system of
trading in knowledge. From the clock I turned my gaze to a doll thrown
down like a corpse on the *tatami* mats. Tanka are my sad toys." The
reference to "capitalist systems" may appear to strike a peculiar note,
but the term indicates a side of Takuboku's poetic efforts which,
although extremely important in the development of modern Japanese literature, has so far received little attention from his translators. Takuboku was profoundly disturbed, as were many contemporary
writers and intellectuals, by the Japanese government's repressive and
high-handed methods in silencing those who took an interest in the doctrines of socialism and communism. Takuboku began, just at the end of
his life, to speak out on questions of social injustice. On such subjects,
he used the medium of modern verse rather than the traditional *tanka*, and some of these poems, dealing with oppression and the attempt
of young Japanese to understand it, are highly moving. Takuboku is
sometimes seen as the patron saint of socially committed modern
Japanese literature, and this addition of outward concern to his inner,
more personal despair became another of the forces that were to help
pull apart his health and spirit.

Takuboku, as his *Rōmaji Diary* reveals so clearly, was by no means an
altogether selfless and altruistic person. Rather, he might best be seen
as an intense being, whose thwarted young life turns Pascal's famous
dictum inside out: Takuboku seems to have been both an angel *and* a

beast. Only necessity—the need to sleep, eat, take care of others and himself—seems to have held him back from total incandescence. In the end, I think, it is just this interplay between potential and the needs of a somber reality that give his poetry its energy and, at the same time, its very special kind of restraint.

TRANSLATIONS

Takuboku's *tanka* have attracted translators for many years, and there exist prewar collections in English as well as scattered translations in virtually every anthology of modern Japanese poetry. At present there are two particularly fine book-length collections that complement each other nicely. The first of them, *Takuboku: Poems to Eat*, translated by Carl Sesar, was published by Kodansha International in 1966. These English versions are handsome and sparse, more than living up to the translator's statement that "my one aim in these translations has been to make poems in English." The book includes a cross-section of Takuboku's work from various sources. *Rōmaji Diary and Sad Toys*, translated by Sanford Goldstein and Seishi Shinoda (Charles E. Tuttle, 1985), contains complete English versions of both the diary and Takuboku's last collection, as well as excellent annotations and introductions, from which the prose citations by Takuboku quoted above were taken. Incidentally, those who read excerpts from Takuboku's *Rōmaji Diary* when they first became available in Donald Keene's anthology *Modern Japanese Literature: From 1868 to Present Day* (Grove Press, 1956) will be startled on reading the new and complete translation to find passages of utter frankness in financial and sexual matters that could hardly have been anticipated from the earlier translation.

Howling at the Moon
Hagiwara Sakutarō
Tsuki ni hoeru

Poetry. 1917

As with so many artistic forms in modern Japanese culture, the excitement of contact with the West brought new possibilities of expression to the realm of poetry, and with them fresh opportunities for the extension of the poet's sensibility beyond the limits of the traditional decorums. After a millennium of *waka* and centuries of *haiku*, Japanese translations of romantic German poets by **Mori Ōgai**, and of French symbolist poets by **Nagai Kafū**, among others, served as inspirations for a whole new movement toward the creation of longer, freer poetic forms. **Shimazaki Tōson** was one of the earliest to compose real poems in the new style, but he soon turned to fiction, leaving it to other talents to combine their sensibilities—honed on the great traditions of Japanese poetry—with a fresh desire for new and liberating forms. To such poets working at the turn of the century, *waka* and *haiku*, in their suggestive compactness, provided what they felt was a special congruence with the ideals and practices of French symbolist poetry, particularly with the work of such nineteenth-century poets as Baudelaire, Mallarmé, and Verlaine. In retrospect, therefore, it does not seem surprising that young Japanese poets found themselves able to work in what, although obviously a new medium, was a style with which they could immediately feel comfortable.

Among the younger generation in Japan who began to experiment with these new possibilities, it was Hagiwara Sakutarō (1886–1942) who brought Japanese vernacular and modern-style poetry to a first brilliant flowering with his initial collection, *Howling at the Moon (Tsuki ni hoeru)*, published in 1917. Sakutarō, often ill in his youth, began his career composing *waka*, possibly as a kind of therapy. Later, moving to Tokyo as a young man, he became friends with a number of poets writing in the modern, colloquial style. Fascinated by the potential of the new form, he began to contribute his own experimental work to a number of small journals and magazines. Then, evidently after having gone through a serious mental depression, he suddenly emerged in 1915 to begin composing the morbid, suggestive poetry that makes up the bulk of the verses in *Howling at the Moon*.

The book was a resounding success. Critics and the reading public alike were excited and moved, both by the authenticity of the sentiments revealed in these often autobiographical poems and by the brilliant use of modern colloquial Japanese. For many, it seemed as though Sakutarō had single-handedly made the modern spoken language into a vessel capable of holding a contemporary sensibility.

Sakutarō's images in the collection are at once direct and suggestive. Here, for example, is a short poem from the opening sequence on bamboo, translated, as are all the other quotations, by Hiroaki Sato.

> Something straight growing on the ground,
> something sharp, blue, growing in the ground,
> piercing the frozen winter,
> in morning's empty path where its green leaves glisten,
> shedding tears,
> shedding the tears,
> now repentance over, from above its shoulders,
> blurred bamboo roots spreading,
> sometimes sharp, blue, growing on the ground.

No English translation, however felicitous (as this one is), can convey the precise effect in the original of those repeated images that seem to overlap one on top of the other. Indeed, they spill from one poem into the next, binding each discrete unit together into a larger whole. These images seem at once objective descriptions and psychological projections of the author's shifting, tremulous state of soul.

The poems in *Howling at the Moon* range over a wide variety of subjects, but the poet's ability to combine image and personal projection remains a constant throughout. The famous opening poem begins, "At the bottom of the ground a face emerging. A lonely invalid's face emerging ...," and so appears the poet's persona: awkward, neurotic, the epitome of a man in isolation. It will appear and reappear, in various guises, in a number of poems scattered throughout the collection.

> From the bottom of the earth I stare at,
> a ridiculous hand sticks out,
> a leg sticks out,
> a neck protrudes,
> . . . . . .

Sometimes the figure is in motion.

> Spring has come,
> I've glued *rubber* to the soles of my new shoes,
> so no matter how shoddily made a pavement I walk,
> they won't make that abominable noise,
> besides I'm holding tons of fragile things
> which is what's so risky.
> . . . .

In one poem, "Sad Moonlit Night," from which the title of the collection derives, the image, the projection, and the persona become one.

> A damned thief dog
> is howling at the moon above the rotting wharf.
> A soul listens,
> and in gloomy voices,
> yellow daughters are singing in chorus,
> singing in chorus,
> on the wharf's dark stonework.
>
> Always,
> why am I like this,
> dog,
> pale unhappy dog?

Howling at the Moon

The ordinary world impinges very little upon these poems. Even laborers digging the hard ground in Tokyo seem to exist only to suggest to Sakutarō his state of soul, where "under the sensual twilight shadow, a wholly shriveled heart is plying a shiny *shovel*." Deformations are projected outwards into rotting clams, souring chrysanthemums, and the smell of the decaying soil in the countryside. Yet the "pale fever dream" that these poems represent gives off a splendor of images and a kind of bizarre psychic truth that makes them startlingly effective even now.

After *Howling at the Moon*, Sakutarō published his next collection, *Blue Cat (Aoneko)*, in 1923, in which the individual poems often become musings on the poet's relationships with others, occasionally with strong erotic overtones. It contains as well the sole poem by the poet that might be considered a social commentary of any sort, "The Army." After the publication of this second collection, Sakutarō's interests began to move in the direction of poetic theory, about which he wrote with great eloquence, and to the composition of poetry in more traditional forms. Literary historians of European and American poetry have often noted that lyric poetry appears to be a young man's art: Keats, Shelley, and Rimbaud, among many others, showed a flowering in their early years that, even if they lived long after, was not to be sustained. Sakutarō's career would appear to provide an additional example of this phenomenon. For all his later accomplishments, nothing came close to matching the literary explosion provided by *Howling at the Moon*.

TRANSLATIONS

Hagiwara Sakutarō. *Howling at the Moon*. Trans. Hiroaki Sato. Columbia University Press, 1978. This elegant book, which reproduces the original 1917 illustrations, is a particularly impressive example of modern bookmaking. It includes excellent translations of all poems in both *Howling at the Moon* and *Blue Cat*, as well as a perceptive introduction. A number of translations can also be found in Makoto Ueda's *Modern Japanese Poets and the Nature of Literature* (Stanford University Press, 1983).

Some Prefer Nettles
Tanizaki Jun'ichirō

Tade kuu mushi

Novel. 1928–29

Tanizaki Jun'ichirō (1886–1965) remains for many the most sophisticated and satisfying Japanese novelist of this century. A highly skillful storyteller with an aristocratic irony that brings wit and perspective to every subject he touches, Tanizaki reveals in virtually every work an ability to look into past and present alike and create excitement and, often, erotic suspense. As a novelist his interests ranged widely. He could write a family chronicle such as *The Makioka Sisters* (*Sasameyuki*), or create historical re-interpretations of traditional culture, notably in "A Portrait of Shunkin" (*Shunkin shō*), which deals with a blind woman musician in the Tokugawa period, and "A Bridge of Dreams" (*Yume no ukihashi*), a modern variant on certain themes implicit in Lady Murasaki's *The Tale of Genji*. Tanizaki also wrote satirical accounts on his own contemporary culture, such as *Naomi* (*Chijin no ai*), the mordant and witty story of a man infatuated with a café waitress who "resembles Mary Pickford." Each of these tales has its peculiar delights, but perhaps no single work shows off so many facets of Tanizaki's genius as *Some Prefer Nettles* (*Tade kuu mushi*).

It seems astonishing that the book was completed in 1929. The atmosphere of the novel, and the psychological confusions it wryly chronicles, could apply equally well to the early postwar period. *Some Prefer Nettles* is about many things, but most Western readers are struck by the account it provides of the clash between cultures, a clash that could, and still can, be found between the generations of a rapidly modernizing Japan. Tanizaki chooses for his ironic psychological arena a relationship that is falling apart. Kaname and his wife, Misako, have what they consider a thoroughly modern marriage. Each partner has a full say in how their lives are to be conducted, and each has sufficient room to pursue his or her enthusiasms. At the time the novel opens, Misako has taken to pursuing a lover, and Kaname is considering the possibility of permitting a trial divorce. Their mutual fantasies, however, are complicated by the presence of Misako's father, who, with his mistress O-hisa, represents the values and enthusiasms of a more traditional culture.

Tanizaki uses geography to underscore the differences. Kaname and Misako live in the Westernized city of Kobe, with its European restaurants, film theaters, and ships sailing off to distant ports. Misako's father and O-hisa live in Kyoto, where the old man pursues his interests in traditional culture. To satisfy him, O-hisa must even dress in traditional fashion, like some figure from a woodblock print. Early in the novel, the four meet in Osaka, where the old man takes them to see a famous play by the Tokugawa dramatist **Chikamatsu Monzaemon** as performed by *bunraku* puppets, an art for which the old man feels a particular affinity. Kaname at first rebels at what he sees to be a manifestation of a feudalistic and materialistic culture. Yet as the novel progresses, he becomes more and more caught up in the aesthetic world of the puppet theater and so, by extension, in the older social values that it articulates. The end of *Some Prefer Nettles* will seem unresolved only to readers who regard plot as the purpose of fiction, for in actuality the final atmospheric scene shows Kaname caught in a net, both physically and psychologically, peering through the darkness in search of alternative visions of the world, and of himself. Tanizaki's deepest message, perhaps, is that such visions, once experienced, make mundane decisions difficult.

For all the ironic, often playful tone this very sophisticated narrative provides, *Some Prefer Nettles* has a very special integrity, for it represents in a very real way the author's developing response to his own culture. As a brilliant young writer fascinated by Edgar Allan Poe and Baudelaire, Tanizaki lived in Yokohama and Tokyo, striving to be as up-to-date as possible. He reveled in his modernity, although, curiously enough, he never did manage to go abroad. After the devastating Tokyo earthquake of 1923, however, Tanizaki moved to the Kansai area, near Osaka. His new proximity to Kyoto and the other seats of traditional art and culture began to expand his horizons backward in time, as it were, gaining him an altogether new appreciation for the Japanese past. That sense of discovery brings a special thrust to *Some Prefer Nettles*: Kaname, the protagonist of the novel, discovers the beauties of the Japanese countryside, with its traditional architecture, as well as the art of the *bunraku* puppet theater in almost the same way that a foreign visitor might, and his discoveries mirror Tanizaki's own.

All of Tanizaki's fiction gives great pleasure in the reading, and an increasing amount is now available in English. Along with his tales and novels, Tanizaki's writing for the theater and his essays also strike a provocative note. In particular his long commentary on Japanese aesthetics, *In Praise of Shadows*, claims special pride of place among them, and it, along with the Nobel prize speech of **Kawabata Yasunari**, remains one of the most influential statements on the subject written in this century.

TRANSLATION
Tanizaki Jun'ichirō. *Some Prefer Nettles*. Trans. Edward Seidensticker. 1955. Reprint. Putnam, 1981.

OTHER WORKS BY TANIZAKI JUN'ICHIRŌ
Tanizaki has been widely appreciated, and translated, for several generations. Perhaps the best introduction to the range of his talents is *Seven Japanese Tales* (1963. Reprint. Putnam, 1981), translated by Howard Hibbett, which contains among others the stories "A Portrait of Shunkin" and "A Bridge of Dreams," mentioned above. Edward Seidensticker's masterful translation of *The Makioka Sisters* (1957. Reprint. Putnam, 1981) has long been a classic, and, in more recent years, Anthony Chambers has translated works dealing with modern life, such as the satirical *Naomi* (Knopf, 1985), as well as works set in earlier periods, such as *The Secret History of the Lord of Musashi & Arrowroot* (Knopf, 1982). *In Praise of Shadows*, translated by Thomas J. Harper and Edward Seidensticker, is available in an edition issued by Leete's Island Books in 1977. Readers who enjoy these may next go on to explore the more peculiar pleasures of *The Key* (1961. Reprint. Putnam, 1981), which explores the erotic adventures of a married couple, and the *Diary of a Mad Old Man* (1965. Reprint. Putnam, 1981), Tanizaki's last major work (in which he continues to explore the lures of the flesh), both translated by Howard Hibbett.

Some Prefer Nettles

Rashōmon, Hell Screen, Kappa
Akutagawa Ryūnosuke

Rashōmon, Jigokuhen, Kappa

Stories. 1915, 1918, 1927

Akutagawa Ryūnosuke (1892–1927) was one of the first modern Japanese writers to be discovered in the English-speaking world. Translations of quite a number of his grotesque and fascinating tales became available as early as 1930, and some of these early collections have remained more or less continuously in print. In one sense, this early popularity has done the author a disservice, since these first attempts at rendering his subtle language into English often only approximate the suggestiveness and fluency of the originals.

Early readers of Akutagawa in translation dubbed him a kind of Japanese Edgar Allan Poe, and indeed it is for a certain quality of diablerie that he has maintained his reputation. Akutagawa's own mentors were actually rather different. As a youthful reader, he showed a wide range of literary tastes, ranging from Nietzsche to Tolstoy and Dostoyevsky. Like **Ueda Akinari** many generations before, Akutagawa soon learned to make his art directly from art. Going through old collections of medieval tales, such as *Tales of Times Now Past*, he would select a story or legend, then re-create it in terms of contemporary psychology, employing sophisticated literary devices sometimes gleaned from Western sources. These new stories were by no means mere pastiche. In their transformations the new stories took on a wholly fresh and authentic character.

Despite his enormous fame as an intellectual writer in his day, Akutagawa was forced to work in opposition to certain literary currents. On the one side was the so-called Naturalistic School of writers, who insisted on the primacy of everyday experience, and on the other side the rising school of proletarian writers, who, from their Marxist perspective, found Akutagawa's work effete and self-serving. Akutagawa's celebrated suicide may have been, at least in part, the response of his admittedly somewhat morbid sensibilities to those pressures. Literary history has vindicated him, however, for his work and that of **Tanizaki Jun'ichirō**, his illustrious contemporary who also stood in his own way for art and artifice, have continued to hold their attraction for readers of later generations. The stories and novels of those in the two opposing camps, on the other hand, have been largely forgotten.

Many of Akutagawa's most famous stories deal with the Japanese medieval period. Most well-known, perhaps, is "Rashōmon," or "The Rashō Gate," which, together with "In a Grove" (*Yabu no naka*), formed the basis for the remarkable 1950 Kurosawa film *Rashōmon*. Few who have seen the film can forget that quality of erotic violence that the director brought to the screen; yet, in a reading of the original stories, Akutagawa's expression of his own powerful understanding of the ambiguous nature of truth, as revealed in his elegant and aristocratic language, is equally masterful. The stories, in fact, are even more successful on their own terms than the film, since the reader is left to conjure up the grotesque images himself, rather than be shown them directly, albeit by a master of the art of the film.

Often Akutagawa's stories about medieval Japanese life are slight, just a few pages long. "Rashōmon" itself is a good example of the author's ability to evoke a complex atmosphere with great economy. Another, rather longer piece, "Hell Screen" (*Jigokuhen*), takes up the question of the kinds of sacrifice an artist must make, on every level, in order to create his art. Here, Akutagawa shows with enormous skill how destruction serves to provide the basis for creativity. He was able to sense the brutality and cruelty behind the surface elegance of his original sources, and this tale, with its remarkable twists and turns, mirrors these underlying aspects to perfection.

Much of Akutagawa's reputation in Japan depends on works that directly satirize contemporary society. Several of these have been translated into English. Particularly notable is *Kappa*, a short novel written in 1927, the year that the author died. A Kappa is a mythical water creature, with a slight hollow on the top of his head, familiar to Japanese readers from folklore. In Akutagawa's novel, an inmate in a mental asylum explains how, while hiking in the mountains, he was spirited off to Kappa country, where, rather like Swift's Gulliver, he came to study the peculiar society he found there. On his return, the world in general, of course, regards him as insane, and he is confined. Many of the characters in the Kappa world speak for the author himself, who divides up his dark, cruel views of society among the various persona that appear in the course of the story. The result is a satire that, extending beyond the confines of the 1920s Japan that Akutagawa knew, can stimulate and occasionally shock readers even today.

Other similar works have been translated, including "A Fool's Life" (*Aru ahō no isshō*), but untranslated there remain such well-known and appreciated writings as *Shuju no kotoba* (The Words of a Dwarf). Akutagawa, perhaps more than any major modern Japanese author, needs to be taken up by a new generation of translators. His stories and essays still provide a full measure of satiric bite. To be deprived of modern translations is to be deprived, to some extent, of a full appreciation of one whole aspect of the broad range of modern Japanese literature.

TRANSLATIONS

Kappa: A Satire is available in a translation by Geoffrey Bownas from Charles E. Tuttle (1971). *A Fool's Life*, in a translation by Will Peterson, was published by Grossman in 1970. Both are well worth seeking out. The older anthologies are still in print. A number of individual stories appear in various journals and anthologies. One of them, "An Autumn Mountain," placed in the context of Chinese painting, provides a particularly brilliant conception of the beauty and elusiveness of all great art. It can be found in Ivan Morris, ed., *Modern Japanese Short Stories: An Anthology* (Charles E. Tuttle, 1962).

The Poetry of Miyazawa Kenji
(1896–1933)

Matsuo Bashō made famous the north country of Japan in his *haiku* journal *The Narrow Road to the Deep North*, in which he characterized the particular poetry of that area, still remote and mysterious for so many Japanese. Miyazawa Kenji (1896–1933), one of the greatest of the modern poets, has through his brilliant and idiosyncratic poetry become the modern gatekeeper to the elusive beauty of the north and to the traditions harbored there, which he evoked through the powerful expressiveness of a self-trained and highly original spirit. Like Bashō, Miyazawa seemed throughout his life to be on a quest. A sense of freedom and urgency runs through much of what he wrote. His poetry is at once mystical and earthy.

Miyazawa seemed an unlikely candidate for the literary life. Born in the northern town of Hanamaki in Iwate Prefecture, he studied agriculture with an eye to alleviating the plight of the poor farmers in his area. After a brief stay in Tokyo, where he had gone to further his studies of Nichiren Buddhism, Miyazawa returned to the north country to be present during the final illness of his beloved sister, Toshiko, about whom he wrote some of his most moving poetry. Taking a job at a local agricultural high school, he began to work to improve the lot of the farmers in the region, both in terms of their immediate livelihood and of their broader cultural concerns. Self-denial and overwork, however, led to the poet's early death. Miyazawa was looked on as a kind of saint by the local people, who deeply appreciated what he had done for them during his lifetime. It is doubtful if many would have read or appreciated his poems and touching children's stories, which became widely circulated only after his death.

Spring & Asura (Haru to shura) contains most of Miyazawa's major poems and reveals an astonishing depth of religious conviction, conveyed in an often exhilarating exuberance of language. Miyazawa's commitments to Buddhist belief caused him to place the Lotus Sutra, a central scripture in the Chinese and Japanese tradition, at the center of his meditations. The metaphysical underpinnings provided by this great sacred text run like a thread through his sensibility as expressed in his poetry. Miyazawa's images, however, are altogether his own and lend an invigorating freshness to his verse.

> The hard keyura jewels hang straight down.
> Twirling, shining, the creatures keep falling.
>
> Truly, they are the angels' cries of grief,
> clearer than hydrogen—
> haven't you heard them
> sometime, somewhere?
> You must have heard their cries
> stab heaven like icy spears.
>
> . . . .   (trans. Hiroaki Sato)

Even when his poetry is simple and deeply personal, it resonates with the forces of nature.

> The blizzard drives hard
> and this morning, that catastrophic cave-in
>   . . . Why do they keep blowing
>   the frozen whistle?
> Out of the shadows and the frightening smoke
> a deathly pale man appears, staggering—
> the horrible shadow of myself
> cast from a future of ice.   (trans. Hiroaki Sato)

For Miyazawa, knowing and doing must be one in order for man to find his place in nature.

> The new age points toward a world with a single
>   consciousness, a single living thing.
> To live a righteous and sturdy life we must become

aware of, and respond to, the galaxy within us.
Let us seek happiness for the world. Such seeking is
    itself the way.

(trans. Makoto Ueda)

Even readers who may be resistant to the metaphysics of Miyazawa's personal vision will be moved by the verse he wrote concerning the death of his sister. The poet's fierce affection, his vulnerability to her death, bring him close to the reader, in a kind of awkward embrace.

. . . .

Toshiko,
now so close to death
you asked for a bowl of clean snow
to brighten me for the rest of my life.
Thank you, my brave sister,
I too will go by the straight way
    (Get me some snow, Kenji)
In your delirious fever, panting,
you asked me for the last bowl of snow
that fell from the sky,
the galaxy, the sun, the atmospheric strata
    ... Between two pieces of granite
sleet makes a solifary puddle.
I stand on them, precariously,
keeping the pure, white two-phased balance of snow and water
and get for my gentle sister her last food
from a glowing pine branch
laden with cold transparent drops.

. . . .

(trans. Hiroaki Sato)

Despite the intensity of such moments in his poetry, however, Miyazawa on the whole strikes a powerful note of affirmation, not in terms of his individual ego or his accomplishments as a poet, but rather an affirmation of the healing power of the great forces of Nature to which he found access, and in which, he insisted, we are all, perhaps unwittingly, involved. It may be because the poet's writings can provide the reader with a means of entering Miyazawa's own "deep north" that he has become a sort of cultural hero in Japan. While Miyazawa's poetry is often resistant to quick comprehension, and his juxtapositions of images are often easier to feel than to understand, the totality provides a special species of spiritual clarity, one that is virtually unique.

TRANSLATIONS

Some early, and elegant, adaptations of Miyazawa's poetry can be found in a collection of original work and translations by the American poet Gary Snyder, entitled *The Back Country*, published by New Directions in 1968. These were the first versions to introduce Miyazawa to English-speaking readers. These were followed in 1973 by Hiroaki Sato's splendid collection *Spring & Asura* (Chicago Review Press), still the best selection available. A number of elegant translations, some of poems not included in the Sato volume, can be found in Makoto Ueda's *Modern Japanese Poets and the Nature of Literature* (Stanford University Press, 1983).

Spring Riding in a Carriage, Machine, Time
Yokomitsu Riichi

Haru wa basha ni notte, Kikai, Jikan

Stories. 1926, 1930, 1931

The avant-garde literary movements that began in France after the First World War created new ways to stretch language and to plumb human psychology. Shock effects were felt outside as well as inside Europe, then the center of world culture. America had her Gertrude Stein, and by the mid-1920s it seemed as though Japan would have at least two young novelists of great talent willing and able to break the same kind of fresh ground. One of them, **Kawabata Yasunari**, had only a brief flirtation with international modernism before moving off in very different directions. The other, Yokomitsu Riichi (1898–1947), was also to end his career very differently than he began it, but his modernist phase, which lasted into the 1930s, produced a number of remarkable stories. These works provide, even in translation, a satisfying measure of excellence in a style that represented the high watermark of literary internationalism in Japanese prose before this period of enthusiasms was curtailed by the gloom of Japan's war with China. Perhaps only the great Surrealist poet Nishiwaki Junzaburō (1894–1982) accomplished as much.

Yokomitsu began his career in Japan, not in Europe like Nishiwaki. Ironically, when Yokomitsu did get to Europe, spending some months in Paris in 1936, the realities of the life he experienced there turned him to writing his long, rambling novel *Ryoshū* (The Sadness of Travel; as yet untranslated), in which the protagonist becomes more and more disillusioned with his European experiences. In the 1920s, however, busy discovering Gide, Valéry, and Flaubert, Yokomitsu effected in his earlier experimental writing a powerful opening outward of the possibilities of language, most of them as yet unexplored by his contemporaries.

Scattered throughout Yokomitsu's work of this period are a number of stories that have stood the test of time. Some show his fascination with a style that privileged, as Yokomitsu's gifted translator has put it, the use of "language presenting experience as directly experienced, and not mediated by the mind or the sensibility or the emotions." During another part of his internationalist phase, Yokomitsu went through a Marxist period, much like **Kobayashi Takiji** and others; but unlike them, he attempted to create a literary style quite different from the sort of socialist realism then popular around the world. By the 1930s Yokomitsu's restless explorations led him to attempt the style of the psychological novel.

The stories of Yokomitsu available in translation can be studied as manifestations of these succeeding enthusiasms, but better still, they can be enjoyed for their success in experimenting with new techniques for apprehending and recording reality. As some critics have suggested, Yokomitsu may have failed in his longer novels (all of them untranslated) to spin out his insights on a larger scale, but these briefer visions are often astonishing in their effect.

Perhaps the most universally appreciated story of this kind is "Time," first published in 1931 and long available in an evocative translation by Donald Keene. In it, a troupe of performers (their precise skills are never identified) flee from a rooming house where they cannot afford to pay the bill, dragging themselves over a path that threads a cliff overlooking the sea; they make their escape during a storm that creates a virtual hell, both because of the weather and because of their almost obscene fear and mistrust of each other. The concluding scene in the moonlight, with a hatful of drinking water passed from hand to hand until it reaches the lips of a dying woman from the troupe, has the unsettling force of a hallucination.

Hallucination also plays an important role in a story written the year before—"Machine"—in which the narrator, whose words are nothing if not unreliable, apparently finds himself, and his rivals, pitted against a machine that seems to control their thoughts and responses. Paranoia is mixed with the odors of chromic acid and ferric chloride. An amalgam of crazed psychology and fresh imagery, the story made Yokomitsu famous.

An even wider range of Yokomitsu's abilities can be observed in a collection of early stories translated by the British scholar Dennis Keene, whose close attention to Yokomitsu's linguistic experiments gives his English versions a special relevance. In many of these stories, Yokomitsu has taken events from his own experience and reformed them into the kind of images he sought. His goal is not any smooth narrative line. Rather, he thrusts the reader into the middle of a situation that is unexplained, and for which the reader is unprepared, so that the imagistic moments he creates gain greater force and immediacy.

The milieu of Japanese living in Korea forms the basis for such works as "After Picking up a Blue Stone" and "The Pale Captain." Yokomitsu had lived there as a child, where his father, an engineering contractor, eked out a hand-to-mouth existence. The story "Spring Riding in a Carriage" reflects Yokomitsu's marriage to a young woman he had long admired, which ended with her death from tuberculosis at the age of twenty. Her long and difficult illness drew from him this work, my personal favorite, in which the wife's physical and mental decay intermingle with the twisted and ambiguous emotions of the writer, until their two spiritual trajectories join together to produce the amazing image that concludes and sums up the story. That same theme is explored in still other contexts in "Ideas of a Flower Garden." In Japanese literature written before the war, perhaps only **Masaoka Shiki**, using very different materials, has made the moments preceding death so personal.

TRANSLATIONS

Donald Keene's translation of "Time" can be found in his anthology *Modern Japanese Literature: From 1868 to Present Day* (Grove Press, 1956). "Machine" is available in two translations, one by Edward Seidensticker in the anthology edited by Ivan Morris, *Modern Japanese Stories: An Anthology* (Charles E. Tuttle, 1962), the other in the Dennis Keene volume *Love and Other Stories of Yokomitsu Riichi* (Columbia University Press, 1974). Translations of short works and some theoretical writings by Yokomitsu are contained in Dennis Keene's admirable study of the writer, *Yokomitsu Riichi: Modernist* (Columbia University Press, 1980).

🏵 Black Rain
Ibuse Masuji

Kuroi ame

Novel. 1965–66

Ibuse Masuji, born in 1898, has been a highly respected author in Japan since the 1930s, when his stories and novels first began to garner attention and praise. Always a man of generous spirit, he served as a mentor to a number of young writers, notably **Dazai Osamu**. Ibuse has long been admired for his ability to combine humor and the use of dialect so as to chronicle in a gentle way the passing of older rural styles of life. With the completion in 1966 of *Black Rain* (*Kuroi ame*), however, one of Ibuse's longest and most ambitious narratives, his art reached a special apex.

Written twenty years after the end of the war, *Black Rain* represents Ibuse's attempt to come to terms with Japan's defeat, as symbolized by the bombing and destruction of Hiroshima. This period of two decades was doubtless necessary in order to gain perspective on those cataclysmic events, which for many seemed too large to be encompassed in any artistic form. Just as Tolstoy felt that the real meaning and significance of Napoleon's invasion of Russia could only be comprehended many years after the fact, so Ibuse's special genius required time to grasp and respond to the shattering events of 1945.

Japanese narrative modes, with their stress on the interior flow of human consciousness, would appear inappropriate to render material of this sort. And yet, Ibuse has not transformed his novel into a grand guignol show. Rather, by remaining true to his craft, he has actually made the unthinkable destruction credible and comprehensible in terms of an intimate human response. This credibility, in turn, makes the reader acknowledge the authenticity of the feelings expressed, however painful. Less, in *Black Rain*, is more. On the other hand, some dimensions of the events remain little touched upon. Political and strategic considerations that led to the bombings, for instance, are not referred to in any detail. This is a personal story. True, certain minor characters do remark from time to time on the arrogant stupidity of the Japanese wartime government, mirroring perhaps Ibuse's distaste for the military. The novel, however, is in no way a political tract. It is rather the record of a search for understanding.

Part of that search involves the touching attempt by Shizuma Shigematsu, the protagonist, to prove that his beloved niece Yasuko has not been harmed by her exposure to radiation. Without such assurances, he knows that she will never be able to marry. In this attempt he fails, as she has indeed been tainted. The real movement of the story therefore shows how Shigematsu, suffering through his personal defeat, and the defeat of his country as well, can manage to continue on and seek again the will to live, the ability to leave defeat behind.

Ibuse creates an ingenious narrative structure to show these spiritual transformations. The book moves backward and forward through time, juxtaposing Shigematsu's efforts on behalf of his niece with sections of his wartime diary that describe the bombing. Shigematsu rereads them in the hope of coming to a better understanding of his own responses to his past life. Sections of Yasuko's diaries are also given. Through this device, the reader is provided the opportunity to come to terms with the experiences of both. Mulling over the events, now existing only in his memory, Shigematsu comes to realize that survival and renewal are possible. In a remarkable passage toward the end of the novel, in which Shigematsu hears the emperor's message of surrender on the radio, he watches tiny eels swimming in the water. The represent for him the process of renewal through the simple dignity of nature. With this flash of insight, Shigematsu comes to understand how his own courage must take root and develop. He realizes as well that Yasuko will probably be unable to develop that courage.

In summary, *Black Rain* may appear to be a grim and forbidding book, but Ibuse's enormous skill at characterization and his ever-present sense of humor lighten the narrative considerably. Indeed, the wry and sometimes witty moments that pepper the book are symbols of the kind of response necessary to make survival possible.

Black Rain has received a number of awards in Japan and fully deserves its mighty reputation. Hopefully, potential readers will not be put off by the subject matter. For to read *Black Rain*, like John Hersey's *Hiroshima*, though in a very different way, is to grapple with the terrible problems of this century, which, after all, we have all helped to make. Ibuse's attempt to show that man, if he trusts in the best of nature and the best of nature in himself, cannot be altogether lost reveals to us a message in which he profoundly believes, and his consolations, so beautifully demonstrated in the course of the novel, are necessary for us too.

TRANSLATION
Ibuse Masuji. *Black Rain*. Trans. John Bester. Kodansha International, 1969.

Black Rain is rendered particularly effective in English through the eloquence of John Bester, one of the best translators from the Japanese among those of the postwar period. Mr. Bester has also prepared a collection of shorter pieces by Ibuse, *Lieutenant Lookeast and Other Stories*, published by Kodansha International in 1971. Two new volumes, each containing two short novels, show other aspects of the art of this modern master. *Castaways* (Kodansha International, 1987) has *A Geisha Remembers* and *John Manjirō: A Castaway's Chronicle. Waves* (Kodansha International, 1986) contains *Waves: A War Diary* and *Ise-on-the-Billows.*

Snow Country
Kawabata Yasunari

Yukiguni

Novel. 1935–47

"The train came out of the long tunnel into the snow country." This celebrated sentence, the opening one for the novel *Snow Country* (*Yukiguni*), first published in English in 1956, has by now introduced several generations of readers around the world to the aesthetic world of Kawabata Yasunari (1899–1972). The evocative beauty of this novel helped win Kawabata the Nobel Prize for literature in 1968. An evocation of place outside the confines of ordinary life, this "nihilistic fairy tale," as one critic described it, remains one of the most read and pondered texts in modern Japanese literature. Other novels, *The Sound of the Mountain* in particular, may reach greater depths, but none have ever quite taken over the affection that the public has long felt for *Snow Country*. Its high place among the modern classics is assured, both inside and outside Japan.

Snow Country took a comparatively long time to compose, from 1935 to 1937, with a final installment added ten years later. During those years, Kawabata's interests began to show certain shifts that also appear in the body of the novel. Kawabata began his career in the 1920s as an associate of **Yokomitsu Riichi**, using avant-garde styles he and his colleagues termed "neo-sensualist." Kawabata composed a surrealist filmscript and took a strong interest in the contemporary arts of the West. As time went on, however, he felt himself drawn as a modern man back into the older artistic and aesthetic concerns that helped create the great Japanese tradition. In a sense, *Snow Country* chronicles those changes of attitude in novel form. The author's protagonist, Shimamura, has his own family and life in the city. He has a strong interest in Western ballet, and yet, living in Japan as he does, he can only read about the wonders of this Western art, not see it; indeed, for him that is part of the pleasure. If the excitements of Europe are ultimately inaccessible, however, another remoteness, that of a more traditional Japan, can still be found, and for this reason Shimamura travels from time to time to the remote northern areas of the country, where the weather is rough and old customs and traditions have hung on the longest. Those occasional trips become very important to him. "Shimamura lived a life of idleness, and tended to lose any sense of purpose," Kawabata writes, "and he frequently went out alone into the mountains to recover something of it."

While traveling in these remote spots, Shimamura meets Komako, a young geisha of great beauty, to whom he is inordinately attracted. Shimamura, always the dreamer, forms an aesthetic vision of her, yet Komako's real life is more difficult and complex than he is prepared to believe or understand.

Snow Country shows a certain movement of plot, but the structures of the novel concentrate on showing various aspects of Komako's character. She comes to represent for Shimamura the embodiment of wasted beauty. Through this living metaphor, Kawabata manages to single out a number of deeply felt truths about the human condition that come close to a restatement of the classic concept of *mono no aware*, that self-consciousness of the sad transience of all earthly things. In a sense, Shimamura's function in the narrative is to bring the reader closer and closer to Kawabata's real concern, Komako.

Komako finds many things in her life amount to "wasted effort," from the catalogues she keeps of her reading matter to her doomed affair with the young man Yukio, who is gravely ill. The reader, through Shimamura, comes first to feel a certain sympathy for this wasted effort, then ultimately to realize, through Kawabata's daring insight, that the essence of beauty itself may require the presence of just such a "wasted effort." When Shimamura himself achieves this insight, he knows it is time to leave the snow country, and for good.

Despite suggestions of a complex aesthetic philosophy behind the text, the novel has an immediate appeal, both in the color of its images and in the psychological acumen shown in the various conversations that activate the pace of the story. Kawabata's language, restrained yet highly sensual, has been beautifully rendered in the Seidensticker translation, and the visual and aural images so important to the effectiveness of the text flow with real cumulative power. *Snow Country* has been filmed, but despite the care with which it was made, the suggestive power of Kawabata's words overshadow anything the camera can actually show.

TRANSLATION

Kawabata Yasunari. *Snow Country*. Trans. Edward Seidensticker. 1956. Reprint. Putnam, 1981.

OTHER WORKS BY KAWABATA YASUNARI

A sustained interest abroad in Kawabata's work, beginning in the 1950s, has produced a variety of excellent translations of his representative works. Among them, special attention might be given to *Thousand Cranes* (1958. Reprint. Putnam, 1981), which uses the traditions of the tea ceremony to suggest the nihilism of modern Japan, and *The Sound of the Mountain* (1970. Reprint. Putnam, 1981), a masterful study of old age and death. Others well worth reading include *The Lake* (Kodansha International, 1974), *The House of the Sleeping Beauties and Other Stories* (Kodansha International, 1969), *The Master of Go* (1972. Reprint. Putnam, 1981), and most recently available in English and a longtime favorite in the Kawabata canon, *The Old Capital* (North Point Press, 1987), an evocative tale of two sisters living in Kyoto, whose destiny draws on elements adapted from certain classical themes in Japanese fiction.

Twentieth-Century Theater

The great classic theaters of Japan—*nō*, *bunraku*, and *kabuki*—have long had their Western partisans, but the modern theater has only recently attracted the attention that, from a literary point of view, it certainly deserves. Fortunately a number of translations of the work of a variety of the best dramatists have become available in recent years. Hopefully, the best of the large dramatic literature produced in Japan since the turn of the century can begin to find readers and performances abroad.

Once travel to Europe became possible at the end of the nineteenth century, young Japanese intellectuals began to explore European traditions at firsthand. They found there two elements that were missing, they felt, from their own dramatic traditions. One was identified as the portrayal of inner psychological aspects of the characters on the stage, which they traced back to the influence of Shakespeare. The other involved the fact that the theater in Europe could serve as a vehicle for statements on social and political issues. These qualities they saw exemplified in the work of Ibsen. Slightly later, they were to be captivated by the poetic atmosphere of Chekhov. These three great European figures, then, were to form the models for Japanese playwrights until the postwar years, when other models, notably Bertolt Brecht, were to be introduced in turn.

From its beginning in the early years of this century, the modern theater movement in Japan was considered a serious and a committed endeavor. Although many popular forms of entertainment that owed much to Western theatrical modes sprang up as well, few serious writers ever paid much heed to them. Of all these ventures, probably only the films called on some of the writing talent available at the time. By the 1920s many of the important playwrights saw themselves as socially committed, if not outright Marxists, and the dramas they composed showed these predilections. Much of this prewar work now seems dated, but the best still carries a powerful social message. *Vol-*

canic Ash by Kubo Sakae (1901–58) is perhaps the most outstanding. Complex in design, humanistic in philosophy, much of its power is still unabated. One notable exception to this trend toward leftist social commitment was the work of Kishida Kunio (1890–1954), whose writing was much affected by his experiences in France after World War I, when he worked with the famed French director Jacques Copeau. Kishida's comedies and dramas, sometimes written in a lyrical vein, captured nuances of social behavior in the Japanese middle and upper classes. In this endeavor he succeeded brilliantly, and his best plays, such as *Mr. Sawa's Two Daughters, Paper Balloon*, and *A Diary of Fallen Leaves*, are linguistically elegant and theatrically effective.

World War II brought most theatrical activities to a halt. By the late 1940s, however, younger dramatists were beginning to make their mark. Some novelists also wrote for the stage, notably **Abe Kōbō** and **Mishima Yukio**. Other writers devoted their energies almost exclusively to the stage. Among the senior dramatists of the postwar period, pride of place surely goes to Kinoshita Junji (b. 1914), who combines his interests in traditional Japanese drama and what he terms Shakespearean psychology to create such plays as the beautiful *Twilight Crane*, an evocation in modern terms of a medieval folk tale, which has become perhaps the most beloved of all modern Japanese plays. Kinoshita's strong social commitments can be seen in his 1970 *Between God and Man*, an account of the Tokyo war crimes trials, and in the play that is doubtless his masterpiece, *A Japanese Called Otto*, still untranslated, which gives the author's moving interpretation of the real significance of the Soviet Sorge spy ring active in Tokyo just before World War II.

The other senior writer who combines lyrical gifts with social concerns is Tanaka Chikao (b. 1905), whose 1959 *Head of Mary* is a trenchant poetic fantasy that deals with the spiritual aftermath of the destruction of Nagasaki by the atomic bomb.

A number of younger writers active since the 1960s have written in more or less conventional modern modes, but with skill and eloquence. Yamazaki Masakazu (b. 1934) has taken up both historical and contemporary subjects, and his drama based on the life of Zeami, the great poet of the medieval nō theater, is a modern classic. Yashiro Seiichi (b. 1927) often writes colorful dramas exploring from a modern psychological perspective the lives and personalities of historical figures. His 1973 drama *The Hokusai Sketchbooks* is particularly successful in this regard, at once amusing, thoughtful, and informing.

The development of a powerful avant-garde theater movement in Europe with the coming to prominence of such writers as Samuel Beckett, Eugène Ionesco, and Fernando Arrabal helped stimulate a still younger generation of Japanese playwrights, several of whom have developed into major figures in the theatrical world. The novelist Abe Kōbō, mentioned above, began to compose a series of plays that owe much to the "theater of the absurd." His works, notably *Friends*, first presented in 1967, have been translated and staged abroad. Betsuyaku Minoru (b. 1937) inhabits something of the same artistic territory, but his plays are more uncompromising, more daring, and in my view even more successful. His first important play, *The Elephant*, written in 1962, takes as its theme the victims of the atomic bomb, but nevertheless contains remarkable scenes of wry humor. Of his later plays available in translation, perhaps *The Move*, first staged in 1971, is most representative. The wandering family he shows there knows neither destination nor purpose, but their activities on the stage are never less than absorbing. The interactions of the characters in the plays of Satoh Makoto (b. 1943) are even more absurd, and show a powerful political and even metaphysical thrust.

A number of the finest contemporary playwrights in Japan have yet to achieve translations. At this writing, there are no English versions available of Shimizu Kunio, whose poetic and theatrical skills reveal a remarkable personal vision. Kara Jūrō, the brilliant and iconoclastic dramatist who often staged his frenetic plays in a tent, is likewise unrepresented. Inoue Hisashi, whose rich and humorous work has received both high critical and popular esteem for the past decade, is unavailable as well. Hopefully, translated versions of the best work of these and other striking writers will appear before too long. Plays of this quality can provide particularly effective access into the concerns, fears, and solaces of contemporary Japanese life.

TRANSLATIONS
Kubo Sakae's *Volcanic Ash*, translated by David Goodman, is available in the Cornell University East Asia Papers, no. 40. A volume of Kishida's plays will also be available from the same source (forthcoming). A. C. Scott's translation of Kinoshita Junji's *Twilight Crane* is available in *Playbook* (New Directions, 1956). Eric Gangloff's translation of Kinoshita's *Between God and Man: A Judgment on War Crimes, a Play in Two Parts* was published by Tokyo University Press and the University of Washington Press in 1979. Two anthologies, Ted Takaya's *Modern Japanese Drama: An Anthology* (Columbia University Press, 1979) and David Goodman's *After Apocalypse* (Columbia University Press, 1986), contain many of the other dramas mentioned above. *Zeami* and another play by Yamazaki Masakazu are available in J. Thomas Rimer's *Mask and Sword: Two Plays for the Contemporary Japanese Theater* (Columbia University Press, 1980).

The Factory Ship
Kobayashi Takiji

Kani kōsen

Novella. 1929

The works of modern Japanese literature most familiar to Western readers are often romantic and elegiac, and in them the pull of traditional aristocratic attitudes helps to color perceptions of the present. In this regard, the works of a **Kawabata** or a **Tanizaki** reign supreme, as indeed, in light of Japanese literary tradition, it is perhaps inevitable that they should. Yet, read with an eye for any contemporary social content, these elegant, introspective novels give little heed to, and therefore in some senses present a false image of, life as it was actually lived by ordinary Japanese during the period between the two world wars. Japan had by this time established her own colonial empire and was straining to maintain her economic hegemony. In time, however, there was a response by writers to the dark side of Japanese culture during this period, a response which provided the basis for a grim and realistic modern literature as important in its way to an understanding of twentieth-century Japan as the work of **Akutagawa** or **Shiga Naoya**. Yet, on the whole, the ensuing literary outpouring of socially committed poetry, drama, and fiction, despite some works of excellent accomplishment, has attracted relatively little attention among translators until fairly recently. As a result, many works regarded in Japan as central to the modern tradition—one thinks immediately, for example, of celebrated novels touching on social themes by two distinguished women writers, Hayashi Fumiko and Miyamoto Yuriko—have remained hidden to readers unable to manage the lengthy Japanese originals.

Literature of social commentary during the interwar period might be roughly divided up into two kinds, the first showing a humanitarian sense of malaise, or occasionally outrage, at the pitiful conditions of the lower classes, and the second, an overtly Marxist literature that analyzes social difficulties in those terms. We are fortunate indeed to have a specimen in translation of a short novel that combines elements from both these categories, the celebrated 1929 *Factory Ship* (*Kani kōsen*) by Kobayashi Takiji (1903–33). Presenting as grim and uncompromising a tale as one might imagine of the economic degradation of modern man, this book chronicles a Japan virtually unrepresented in classical or high modern literature, where such subjects lay outside the bounds of literary decorum. Indeed, most writers had no access in their personal experience to the kinds of lives portrayed therein. In the useful introduction to his translation of *The Factory Ship*, Frank Motofuji quotes from **Natsume Sōseki**'s preface to the first of those accounts that might be termed a "proletarian novel," Nagatsuka Takashi's *Earth* (*Tsuchi*) of 1910. "The work describes," Sōseki wrote, "the life of wretched farmers without education or refinement who, like maggots, are merely born and are attached to the soil and mature on it.... *Earth* portrays vividly for us the vulgarity and shallowness, the deep superstitiousness, innocence, cunning, unselfishness, and avarice —qualities that are unimaginable to me and to every writer in the literary world." Sōseki championed Nagatsuka and acknowledged that, indeed, Japanese writers and intellectuals seemed unable to move with assurance in a society so deeply stratified, so profoundly divided.

One reason for the success of Kobayashi's book is that he, to a greater extent than any of his like-minded predecessors, could bridge that gap through his own experience. Born into a destitute farming family living in a poor area of northern Japan, later to be made familiar through the poetry of **Miyazawa Kenji**, Kobayashi moved as a child to the seaport town of Otaru in Hokkaido, a hour's train ride from Sapporo, the largest city on the island. Hokkaido had been opened to settlement since the latter half of the nineteenth century, but the cold and unfamiliar climate made life there difficult, and economic success, at least for ordinary farmers and laborers, was virtually impossible. Kobayashi finished his schooling in Otaru at a time of great social strife; in 1918 alone there were four major strikes in Hokkaido's developing industries. Attempts by workers to unionize were met with stiff resistance from the government.

Kobayashi showed artistic interests as a child, but rebuffed by his father, he eventually took a job as a bank clerk, only then finding the time to write. Living in the midst of social unrest and human squalor, Kobayashi sought to understand the personal dimensions of the struggle he was forced to witness. Talking with newspaper writers, reading accounts of the victims of violence, and joining with protest groups, he found himself increasingly well-informed as well as occasionally under surveillance by the police, who rightly suspected him of being sympathetic toward the Communist party.

Kobayashi wrote a number of interesting stories and novels during his brief life, all of them showing compassion for the common laborer. By the time he came to compose his masterpiece, *The Factory Ship*, his commitment to the techniques of "proletarian writing" gave him the idea of making the workers themselves a kind of collective hero, since the momentum of the story would involve the coming together of a number of desperate men seeking to right intolerable conditions.

The Factory Ship deals with the crew of a crab-canning boat, one of many that worked the cold, inhospitable seas between northern Japan and the Kamchatka peninsula in Siberia, a part of the Soviet Union. The idea for the story had come to Kobayashi after reading a newspaper account of the horrors perpetrated on the crew of one of these vessels, and the novel was completed on the basis of subsequent research. Vivid and authentic in every detail, its message is powerful. Kobayashi sketches a number of striking characters, portrayed in all their gruffness, with an eye that is both sharp and sympathetic; he then follows them through their travails until they are able to learn, slowly and painfully, to unite in a common effort to improve their working conditions. The supervisors may seem to be cast altogether in the role of villains, yet the author has created no cartoon of his own imagining. The novel is a piece of inspired reportage.

The Factory Ship makes painful reading, as one shockingly brutal act follows another. But in the dynamics of the book, a powerful note of affirmation is struck in the portrayal of the men's will to survive and to work together. The cast of characters is sufficiently diverse—students tricked into signing on the trip, day laborers out of work and trying to earn enough money to keep themselves alive, farmers dispossessed of their land—so that the human interactions are continuously varied and revealing.

For Kobayashi, with his humanistic and socialistic sympathies, the real villain of the piece is not Asakawa, the cruel supervisor, who flogs his men and steals the crabs from other boats in order to turn a higher profit. Indeed, the company dismisses him out of hand for allowing a strike to occur. Rather, in Kobayashi's view, it is the vast, unseen capitalist machine itself, allied to the militaristic government, which must take the ultimate blame. "This story is a page from the history of infiltration of capitalism into new territories," writes Kobayashi at the end of his account.

The publication of *The Factory Ship* turned Kobayashi, already regarded as a powerful writer, into a celebrity, and that notoriety in turn forced him underground, helped by the Communist party. He continued in concealment to write powerfully of the lot of the lower classes until, arrested by the police on February 20, 1933, he was evidently beaten to death the same day. Even those who admired his work at the time never knew it well, for *The Factory Ship* and other of his published pieces were heavily censored by the government before going into print. The full text of *The Factory Ship* was not available until 1948.

Much has happened to change altogether the functioning of the world economy since the dark days of 1929. Many readers may be tempted to see no more in *The Factory Ship* than the fading virtues of a period piece. The author's narrative skills are such, however, that he makes those dreadful moments come vividly alive. Read as an account of the way in which one group of men can tyrannize another, the novel will always tell an accurate, if frightening, human truth.

TRANSLATION

Kobayashi Takiji. *The Factory Ship*. Trans. Frank Motofuji. University of Tokyo Press, 1973.

An earlier translation of *The Factory Ship*, included in a volume entitled *The Cannery Boat and Other Japanese Short Stories*, was published in 1933 by International Publishers of New York. The unnamed translator used the bowdlerized, censored version of the original Japanese text. This earlier version thus remains a historical curiosity, but it is not a reliable version of the novel. The Motofuji translation also contains another moving short novel, *The Absentee Landlord*. Incidentally, the novel *Earth* by Nagatsuka Takashi, mentioned above, was published in translation by Kawamura Yasuhiro in 1986 by Liber Press in Tokyo.

🍄 The Counterfeiter
Inoue Yasushi

Aru gisakka no shōgai

Novella. 1951

Inoue Yasushi (b. 1907) is widely regarded in Japan as perhaps the most distinguished author of his generation. Like his older compatriot **Ibuse Masuji**, Inoue continues to compose stories and novels of the highest quality. Fortunately, Inoue has attracted the enthusiasm and talent of a number of excellent translators, so that some indication of the range and, more importantly, the depth of his work can be observed through French, German, and English renderings of his novels and stories.

At first encounter, the potential appeal to Western readers of Inoue's writings may seem somewhat limited. While his work is not difficult in terms of style, a certain amount of close attention is needed from readers learning to respond to his celebrated re-creations of life in classical China and early Japan. All of Inoue's work will amply repay in fascination and pleasure any efforts expended on the reader's part, but his remarkable historical works are composed in a grave kind of poetic mode which does require some adjustment. In this regard, Inoue carries on the intellectual traditions of older Japanese literature, exemplified in the modern period by writers and thinkers such as **Mori Ōgai**. Inoue tends to adopt the same attitudes toward his historical material, and to apply the same literary techniques. In his choice of subject matter, Inoue is highly adventuresome, and his empathy with other periods and mentalities seems nothing short of astonishing. He is perhaps the last of the masters whose work connects to the great traditions of Chinese and Japanese classical literature.

Inoue is generally regarded as a postwar writer, unlike **Kawabata** or **Tanizaki**, much of whose important work was published before the war. His more contemporary reputation springs, no doubt, from the fact that he began to write relatively late in life. After his university training, Inoue became a journalist, working with the *Mainichi Newspapers*. During the war, he served for a time as a foot soldier in China, a fact that may well have strengthened his interests in the civilization he would later write about with such skill and insight. Inoue did not begin to publish any of his fiction until 1948. One of his first works, *The Hunting Gun*, made an enormous splash and put him, in his early forties, in the forefront of the "new" or "younger" writers. By that time his contemporary **Dazai Osamu** was already dead. From then until now, Inoue has written copiously, sometimes on historical themes, sometimes on contemporary life, but always masterfully.

As a means of entering into Inoue's special world, I can think of no doorway more beguiling or enticing than his short novel *The Counterfeiter* (*Aru gisakka no shōgai*), written in 1951. The story is narrated in the first person by a writer who has been asked to compose the official biography of a well-known modern Japanese painter famous for his work in the more traditional styles of *Nihonga*. As the narrator undertakes his investigation, he finds, as did Mori Ōgai in his own research on the life of the doctor and scholar Shibue Chūsai, that unexpected characters and relationships begin to manifest themselves. He learns that the artist, proud and aloof, evidently had few friends and managed to have only one confidant, a certain Shinozaki. Who was this Shinozaki? The narrator is determined to find out, and the focus of the story shifts to this shadowy and increasingly fascinating figure.

The narrator's inquiries soon lead him to the realization that Shinozaki had been, at least for a time, creating forgeries in the style of his mentor. But as Shinozaki himself is also dead, details are hard to come by. The investigations, which continue off and on for many years, take the narrator to various out-of-the-way spots in Japan, some described with a remarkable sense of the poetry of landscape. As the shadowy figure of the forger draws closer, his life takes on other hues and colors. By the time the narrator, and so the reader, has learned of Shinozaki's interest in fireworks, the author has reached a point where he is able to raise, in the most natural and inevitable way, questions concerning the purposes of art and the larger commitments that anyone can make in the course of their lives. The story stretches in a remarkable curve from prose to poetry, from common sense to inspired intuition. In one sense, *The Counterfeiter* may be counted a highly skillful literary performance: the seams of its construction, by which the reader is moved from one plane of consciousness to the next, are virtually invisible. Here, art has concealed art; mere skill is transcended. This short novel is a masterpiece of modern fiction, Japanese in some of its techniques and cultural grounding, universal in the questions it poses.

TRANSLATION
Inoue Yasushi. *The Counterfeiter and Other Stories.* Trans. Leon Picon. Charles E. Tuttle, 1965.

OTHER WORKS BY INOUE YASUSHI
I mentioned above that *The Counterfeiter* might best be regarded as an effec-

tive introduction to Inoue's work. Since the story is set in modern times, relatively little cultural background is needed for an appreciation of the author's conception. The same is true of the two shorter pieces in the same volume, "Obasute" and "The Full Moon," although both draw for their evocative power on certain strains in classical Japanese literature. Another useful bridge to Inoue's work is his novel based on contemporary life, *The Hunting Gun*, available in a translation by Sadamichi Yokoo and Sanford Goldstein, first published by Charles E. Tuttle in 1961. Inoue's long and celebrated 1956 novel that concerns the postwar period, *Hyōheki* (Wall of Ice), is now available in French and German translations but not, as of this writing, in English.

A good introduction to the kinds of historical understanding shown by Inoue is provided by a collection of his short pieces entitled *Lou-lan and Other Stories*, translated by James T. Araki and Edward Seidensticker and published by Kodansha International in 1979. In this volume, which contains six stories ranging in subject matter from modern Japan to ancient China, Inoue mixes older and newer modes of consciousness. *Tun-huang* (Kodansha International, 1978), translated by Jean Oda Moy, on the other hand, is a more extended work that reveals Inoue's superb historical imagination as he re-creates the period when a great horde of Buddhist treasures was hidden in the Tun-huang caves in China, probably in the eleventh century.

My personal favorite among Inoue's historical works with which I am acquainted is *The Roof Tile of Tempyō*, translated by James T. Araki and published by University of Tokyo Press in 1975 (available in the United States from Columbia University Press). Here, Inoue draws on his profound empathy for both ancient Chinese and Japanese culture by recounting the lives of the Japanese Buddhist monks who made the perilous voyage over rough seas to T'ang-dynasty China in order to bring back Buddhist texts and teachings as well as other elements of high Chinese culture. The period of the narrative is very generally contemporary with the compilation of the *The Anthology of Ten Thousand Leaves*.

The Setting Sun
Dazai Osamu

Shayō

Novel. 1947

From the perspective of Western readers, the thrust of much modern Japanese fiction would seem to move unerringly toward the psychic interior, rather than spiraling outward to record a variety of human responses to the events of the day. Dazai Osamu (1909–48) generally follows the same pattern, yet he is so much a product of his era, and in particular of the wartime period through which he lived, that the best of his work fuses individual and context irrevocably together. Dazai has thus become, in the minds of his Japanese readers, a chronicler of the nihilistic aftermath of that terrible time, and he has achieved the status of literary hero. Indeed, the very word *shayō* (setting sun), drawn from the title of his 1947 novel, has given rise to the word *shayōzoku*, the "impoverished aristocracy," as a standard Japanese-English dictionary has it. Dazai has thus entered the fabric of his language.

In some ways, it is true, Dazai Osamu was typical of the intelligentsia of his time. Born in 1909 into a good family who owned considerable property in the north of Japan, he followed the route laid down by custom for a young person destined and eager to join the ranks of the intelligentsia. He was enrolled as a student at Tokyo University by 1930, where he came into contact with European-derived modes of Marxist thought, flirted with social action, attempted studies in French literature, dropped in and out of school, and slowly began to write. Unstable emotionally, he was helped by others to restrain his suicidal tendencies, and found support for his writing from such respected older figures in the literary world as **Ibuse Masuji**. Dazai's talent was great, and much of his earlier work shows a mastery of style and substance; yet his real reputation was made, and has been sustained, by his last two longer novels, *No Longer Human* (*Ningen shikkaku*) and *The Setting Sun* (*Shayō*), both written after the war, shortly before his successful suicide in 1948.

Dazai's life and work, many Japanese critics have pointed out, are closely intertwined. The more a reader knows of Dazai's life, so the argument goes, the more Dazai can and should be admired for finding a literary means to bare his soul. Perhaps; yet a reader of *The Setting Sun* needs no such background to be drawn into the world of a decaying family as represented by its three survivors—the mother, last in the line of an aristocratic gentility, a class that the end of the war will extinguish altogether; Naoji, her son, leftist intellectual manqué and drug addict; and Kazuko, his sister: gauche, lovable, and, in her strange way, a brave herald of the new times that inevitably must follow. There are other peripheral characters of occasional importance to the story, but they live only insofar as they impinge on the psychic lives of those three. The trio may well represent three aspects of the author's own being; on the page, however, thanks to Donald Keene's evocative translation, they each possess a life of their own.

Much of the story of the destruction of the family is lived through and narrated by Kazuko. Through her, the reader learns of her mother, "the last aristocrat," who dies as the war draws to its dreadful close. The older woman is described, not in the abstract, but in specific and often touching terms, as in the opening pages where she "flutters the soup spoon to her mouth." Kazuko describes her mother on her deathbed as a "Pietá," one of the numerous references to Western art, literature, and thought that dot the text and reveal (no doubt unwittingly on the author's part) how much the Japanese intelligentsia of that time had come to know and share in the body of Western cultural traditions.

With her mother's death at the end of the war, Kazuko forces herself to shake off her innocence and her lethargy, to learn how to take hold of her life. "Victims," she proclaims toward the end of the novel, "we are victims of a changing morality." To escape the passive role of victim, she decides to have a child, and chooses for its father a former drinking companion of her brother. Although Uehara, another disillusioned intellectual, is not attractively sketched, the brief glimpses of him that the author provides indicate something of the nihilism and despair that characterized Tokyo in its hours of ruin and defeat. Kazuko, however, feels that she has triumphed over them all. "My child," she says, "is my revolution."

Naoji, whose intense love and admiration for his sister runs through the novel like a steady musical rhythm, possesses as clear a vision as his sister, both of the past and of the present, but the sharpness of that understanding is what eventually drives him to suicide. His long last letter to his sister is one of the most moving passages in Dazai's corpus of writings. Naoji turns a spiritual searchlight onto every aspect of his life and finds all he sees as wanting. While Kazuko's naiveté may shield her from such a pitiless vision, Naoji, who cannot bear hypocrisy, sees only the failure within himself. And that failure is not only his own, but a failure of his generation and his society as well; thus his account of his own decline and fall seems less a case study than a literary document that reveals a powerful resonance with his time. Naoji feels, as did many a member of the socially committed intelligentsia, that some kind of revolution, some sort of movement from the bottom, must surge up and displace the rotting superstructures that had carried the country into war. With his background, however, Naoji realizes that in such a movement he could take no honest part.

Dazai's novel contains no plan of action and no objective overview of the political and moral situation in which the characters find themselves. Kazuko and Naoji are hopelessly caught in the complexities, social and personal, of their situation. Dazai's ability to create pathos derives from his remarkable ability to sketch their portraits without simplification or sentimentality. Passionately written and beautifully crafted, *The Setting Sun* stands as a witness to the moment when, in defeat, Japan was poised at the crossroads. Japan's situation today represents a further point along the road taken since 1945, and readers who wish to retrace that road will find Dazai a powerful guide. It is no wonder that *The Setting Sun* has never gone out of print, either in Japanese or in English.

TRANSLATION
Dazai Osamu. *The Setting Sun.* Trans. Donald Keene. New Directions, 1956.

Donald Keene's translation of *No Longer Human*, published by New Directions in 1958, comes even closer than *The Setting Sun* to providing a chronicle of Dazai's personal decline. Phyllis Lyons provides translations of five short stories and *Return to Tsugaru*, an unconventional travel journey undertaken by the novelist in 1944, in her *Saga of Dazai Osamu* (Stanford University Press, 1985). Another translation of *Return to Tsugaru*, with copious photographs and notes, was prepared by James Westerhoven and published by Kodansha International in the same year. A selection of stories including several not otherwise available was translated by James O'Brien and published under the title *Dazai Osamu: Selected Stories and Sketches* in the Cornell East Asia Paper series, no. 33 (undated).

Fires on the Plain
Ōoka Shōhei

Nobi

Novel. 1951

Novels truly capable of describing the trials of soldiers in wartime are apparently difficult to write; too often rage or ideology seems to cut into the clarity of the author's intentions. Perhaps both of these, rage and ideology, serve a purpose of sorts, that of providing a screen between the author and the full impact of the horror he has experienced, creating a merciful degree of aesthetic distance. One novel that conveys a full measure of chilling horror is Ōoka Shōhei's *Fires on the Plain* (*Nobi*), first published in Japanese in 1951. Ōoka's account, which served as the basis for the macabre 1952 film by Ichikawa Kon, is without question the most remarkable novel to come out of the Pacific War.

Some Western writers and critics have speculated as to how an otherwise obscure writer could have produced a work of this power and economy of language. Ōoka is not known as a one-novel writer in Japan, however, having composed a number of highly regarded works on a variety of themes. *Fires on the Plain* was not his first novel, and by no means his last. Born in 1909 and still active today, Ōoka underwent an encounter with Christianity during his teenage years, a fact readily apparent from certain of the scenes and themes in *Fires on the Plain*. He then turned to develop an intense attachment to French literature, partly through the influence of his mentor, the renowned critic Kobayashi Hideo. Acquiring a special fascination for the novels of Stendhal, he admired in particular the sort of detached clarity with which the French nineteenth-century master described powerful political and social events in such works as *The Charterhouse of Parma* and *The Red and the Black*. Ōoka was himself to be confronted by a series of cataclysmic events when drafted in 1944 and sent as an ordinary soldier to fight in the Philippines. *Fires on the Plain* is only one of the novels Ōoka wrote concerning his encounters with war and death on those islands, and indeed many Japanese readers prefer *Prisoner of War (Furyoki)*, a more closely autobiographical account.

Fires on the Plain, eloquently translated by Ivan Morris, chronicles two levels of destruction, that of the Japanese war effort on Leyte and that of the physical and spiritual well-being of the protagonist, Tamura, whose hallucinatory first-person narrative constitutes the text. Everything the reader comes to learn and understand is conveyed through Tamura's words, and as the soldier sinks to new levels of degradation, the more his account becomes unpinned from ordinary logic. Here, the shift of language from laconic prose into a kind of terrible poetry is perhaps a simple device, even classical in nature, but the effect of the visions that make up the final third of the book are uniquely effective, and impossible to describe or paraphrase. They must be read whole to be understood.

In the beginning, the reader observes, as it were, Tamura watching himself. By the climax of *Fires on the Plain*, however, Tamura and the reader alike are caught up in a series of terrifying hallucinations, culminating in a cannibalistic adventure entitled by the author, with irony and deep understanding, "In Praise of Transfiguration." What leads Tamura to these depths of horror are a series of grotesque events, narrated with what indeed might be described as a kind of Stendhalian clarity. The soldier, who has been on leave from his unit because of illness, cannot, like many others he meets, gain admittance to the only field hospital available. He wanders away and eventually finds himself in an abandoned Filipino plantation. Spotting a cross on a building in the valley below, he goes down a hillside and stumbles into a deserted town, there to both create death and suffer as a witness of its ghastly results. From this point onward begins Tamura's descent into madness.

However powerful the incidents portrayed in the course of the novel, it is Ōoka's ability to create a character capable of reflecting on himself, his actions, and his motives that propels the narrative to its climax. Early in the book, Tamura ponders, in the abstract, over the meaning of life as opposed to death. Here, Ōoka shows his cultivated Japanese literary sensibilities. The possibility of repetition, Tamura decides, gives human beings the sense that they are alive.

Again, was it not this same presentiment of death that made it seem so strange to me now that I should never again walk along this path in the Philippine forest? In our own country, even in the most distant or inaccessible part, this feeling of strangeness never comes to us, because subconsciously we know that there is always a possibility of our returning there in the future. Does not our entire life-feeling depend on this inherent assumption that we can *repeat indefinitely* what we are doing at the moment?

Here is revealed an underlying paradigm that can be traced back, in literary terms at least, to the work of the great poet **Saigyō** (1118–90), who felt death in much the same terms.

Did I ever think
In old age
I would cross it again?
So long I've lived,
Saya-between-the-Hills

(trans. Burton Watson)

In the same manner, Tamura's intuitive sense of the beauty and evanescence of flowing water serves as a cruel new version of the opening of *An Account of My Hut* by Kamo no Chōmei (1153–1216).

> Death was no longer an abstract notion, but a physical image. Already I could see my dead body lying here on the riverbank, with the stomach blown out by my hand grenade. Soon it would decay and be resolved into its various elements. I knew that my flesh was composed two thirds of water: before long that water would begin to flow—yes, it would merge with this very river and flow downstream.

Even the visions of hands and of flowers that dominate the final hallucinations possess a kind of poetic decorum and lyric power that make them bearable to the reader. In the end, perhaps, it is the literary tradition itself that serves as Ōoka's personal screen, protecting him from the horrors he observed. His literary perceptions organize and give shape to these terrifying visions; and in doing so, he may slightly adjust and intensify their focus, so that the reader can neither reject or avoid them.

Fires on the Plain, for all its power, is not perhaps a perfect novel. I myself find the epilogue, subtitled "A Madman's Diary," a superfluous appendage. It seems unnecessary to explain again in modest prose what has already been conveyed in fearful poetry. Nevertheless, this is a great work of imaginative literature, one that lingers long in the mind.

TRANSLATION
Ōoka Shōhei. *Fires on the Plain*. Trans. Ivan Morris. Charles E. Tuttle, 1957.
The Saigyō translation in the text is from *From the Country of Eight Islands: An Anthology of Japanese Poetry* (Doubleday, 1981).

Silence
Endō Shūsaku

Chinmoku

Novel. 1966

The complexities of modern Japanese culture are nowhere more clearly or more artfully visible than in the writings of Endō Shūsaku (b. 1923), whose works, ranging in subject matter from the political to the spiritual, from light entertainment to narratives on grand themes of universal concern, have given him a wide and appreciative readership in Japan and, thanks to a number of excellent translations, an enthusiastic following abroad. Selecting a representative work from those available in English is not easy, but most readers would in the end agree that *Silence* (*Chinmoku*) is the inevitable choice, both because of its high novelistic skills and because the book captures a major strain in Endō's thought.

Endō is Catholic and thus a member of a small but highly educated minority in Japan. Early in his career, a period of study in Europe forced him to realize the tensions within himself. On one side, he acknowledged the pull toward a universal set of beliefs, through his allegiance to the Church; on the other, he reaffirmed his membership in a culture so different from that of Europe that compromise seemed necessary and inevitable. It is the nature of such compromise that *Silence* explores, often to harrowing effect.

Endō has written that because he received baptism as a child, his Catholicism served as a kind of ready-made suit, one which, although he sometimes wanted to discard it, he could never completely remove. In seeking out his real self, Endō encountered what he termed "the 'mudswamp Japan' in me," that swamp which represents (in the words of William Johnston, the translator of *Silence*) a culture that can "suck up all sorts of ideologies, transforming them into itself and distorting them in the process." In *Silence*, the reader can watch the process lived out in the psychology and actions of Endō's characters, who are doomed from the beginning to spiritual disgrace.

When Christianity was brought to Japan in the middle of the six-teenth century, the first Catholic missionaries found apt and sophis-ticated pupils. High-ranking officials began to adopt the faith, and seminaries were built for the training of Japanese clergy. So success-ful were these efforts that the noted British historian C. R. Boxer could speak of Japan's "Christian century." Japan was then in a period of protracted civil wars, and when the nation was eventually unified in 1600, Tokugawa Ieyasu promulgated an edict of expulsion, fearful as he was, and perhaps rightfully, of the politically dangerous potential of the foreign missionaries. Despite the huge numbers of Japanese now converted to Christianity, some of them holding high rank, a sys-tematic and cruel attempt was made by Ieyasu's successors to hunt out and destroy priests and laity alike. There were only two options open to Christian believers: martyrdom or apostasy. Endō, having studied the records and documents of the period with care, used both historical sources and his own powerful imagination to re-create this fearful time in Japanese history.

Such considerations may seem rather abstract, but the novel itself is precise and gripping. The protagonist of *Silence*, Sebastian Rodrigues, sets out with some companions in an attempt to locate his former men-tor, the much admired priest Christovao Ferreira. On the ship that is taking them to Japan, where priests have already been forbidden en-trance, they first come in contact with Kichijirō, a venal, fawning, preposterous creature who will later assume a Judas-like role. Rodrigues goes into hiding immediately upon landing but is soon apprehended by the authorities. Their attempts to force the priest to apostatize are por-trayed with sympathy and powerful dramatic flair. In his despair, Rodrigues ponders on what he calls the silence of God, a silence with respect to all those things that the deity had seemingly allowed to come to pass. Endō's imaginative skill extends as well to the peasants who are made to suffer for their faith. At one point, an interpreter blames their plight on men like Rodrigues: "Because of your dream," he screams at the priest, "just because you want to impose your selfish dream upon Japan." When Rodrigues finally meets his old teacher Ferreira, now in disgrace, the novel reaches both its dramatic and its spiritual climax. In combining both together so skillfully, Endō expounds with powerful resonance the real implications of the plight of these men. There are many Western characters scattered through modern Japanese fiction, but none delineated with such naturalness and sympathy.

As many critics and commentators have pointed out, Endō's concerns are by no means limited to the historical period he has sketched here with such skill. Rather, he uses such incidents to show how the deepest, and often unarticulated, assumptions of Japanese culture move in different directions from those of the West. That fact, Endō seems to suggest, needs to be discovered and rediscovered as the modern world pushes Japanese and Western culture in ever closer, and sometimes arbitrary, proximity. In *Silence*, the message is delivered with depth, precision, and an inexorable cumulative force.

TRANSLATION

Endō Shūsaku. *Silence*. Trans. William Johnston. Originally published by Sophia University, Tokyo, in 1969 and now available from various publishers.

OTHER WORKS BY ENDŌ SHŪAKU

Endō has attracted gifted translators and enjoys as wide a readership in the West as any major postwar Japanese novelist. As a companion piece to *Silence*, readers may wish to explore his play *The Golden Country* (Charles E. Tuttle, 1970), which covers some of the same ground in a suitably theatrical fashion. *The Sea and Poison: A Novel* (1973. Reprint. Taplinger, 1980) confronts the problems of individual responsibility in wartime. *Volcano* (1978. Reprint. Taplinger, 1980) is a remarkable parable of two men who study a dormant volcano in an implicit quest to grasp the meaning of nature and of their own lives. *Wonderful Fool* (1974. Reprint. Harper & Row, 1983) is full of humor in its account of a clumsy but likable young Frenchman living in Japan, who represents for Endō a living embodiment of giving love. Endō's 1980 novel *The Samurai* (Harper and Row, 1982), which deals with the visits by Japanese Catholics to Rome in 1613, has enjoyed a particularly wide success among readers in English. Endō has also written a highly respected life of Jesus, recently made available in English translation (*A Life of Jesus*; Paulist Press, 1979).

The Woman in the Dunes
Abe Kōbō

Suna no onna

Novel. 1962

Many readers with a taste for European avant-garde writing find Abe Kōbō (b. 1924) both attractive and approachable, for he appears to examine some of the territory first explored by such writers as Samuel Beckett and Eugène Ionesco. His vision of present-day Japan finds similar pockets of absurdity and humorous nonsense, which are, after all, highly viable ways of ordering or understanding the peculiarities of our contemporary reality. By the same token, Abe is occasionally dismissed as a kind of mutant of that same European avant-garde, a writer who merely models his work on the creations of his slightly older Western contemporaries. Such a judgement, I feel, misses the mark: the atmosphere Abe creates, and the uses to which he puts his vision, have something authentically his own.

Abe's background certainly made him unusual from the start. Brought up outside Japan, in Manchuria, he led an existence cut off from any real Japanese roots, rendering him, as he once wrote, a kind of displaced person and thus, in his view, a genuinely contemporary man. Perhaps this lack of involvement with the values prevalent in the home islands during his childhood helped underscore in his mind the follies of the war period. Abe began his career as Marxist playwright, and his reputation as a leader in the field of modern Japanese theater remains high.

The versions of Abe's novels available in English date from after this brief Marxist period and belong to a later, somewhat absurdist phase of his work. The subject matter ranges widely, and Abe often employs elements from popular forms such as science fiction or the detective story, into which he infuses his ironic and skillful view of man's own unique irrationalities. Whatever the "meaning" that a reader may attach to Abe's bizarre narratives, most will agree that he is always a superb storyteller, never failing to hack an intriguing trail through strange terrains. Nowhere is this more evident than in his most popular success, *The Woman in the Dunes* (*Suna no onna*), written in 1962. It is no wonder that the novel attracted the ingenious director Teshigahara Hiroshi, whose 1963 film of the novel was a worldwide success. Yet, however brilliant the images Teshigahara concocted for the screen, Abe's original story remains more striking still. In the film, the very fact of the physical space between the screen and the audience creates a certain distance between the viewer and Abe's protagonist Niki Jumpei, caught up in the mysterious village in the sand. In reading the novel, however, the reader comes as close to suffocation as does Jumpei himself.

The concept of the book is certainly clever. Jumpei, a teacher, collects insects as a hobby and decides to go to the sand dunes in some remote spot of the countryside to gather some unusual specimens. He becomes entrapped in a house at the bottom of a sandpit and finds that he has apparently been "chosen" to take the place of the dead husband of the woman who lives there. It is his daily task to shovel away the encroaching sand so that the apparently meaningless life of the little community can continue. The novel traces the evolving emotional responses of this rueful Robinson Crusoe as he adapts, rejects, then ultimately comes to terms with this most peculiar world. Abe uses every emotion, from pride and fear to sexual desire and despair, to force his protagonist, and so his reader, into an acute self-awareness of the absurdity of the human condition.

Faced with the ever-changing forms of the sand, Jumpei is forced to recall the shifting realities of his former life. His adventures in the village, Abe seems to suggest in one particular scene, may have been inevitable. Indeed, the book could possibly be read as a projection of Jumpei's inner thoughts and fantasies, re-created on some highly refracted plane. Thus, the absurdity of the village may be a perfect match for Jumpei's own personal world. The story is so compelling, however, that it is perhaps only after several readings that Abe's enormous skills of construction become apparent.

As ingenious as such concepts may be, however, without extremely skillful writing they would probably seem merely jejune. Indeed, in *The*

Woman in the Dunes, there is scarcely a sentence that does not contribute to the whole. But that is not all. Much has been made in recent years of the sort of writing perfected by novelists such as Gabriel García Márquez in his *One Hundred Years of Solitude*, a manner that some have termed "magic realism." Márquez can take totally fantastic and improbable events and, by describing them in accurate and homely detail, make them believable, just as a "superrealistic" street scene by a contemporary painter like Richard Estes takes on archetypical properties. Abe employs some of these same techniques. Each gesture, each thought, each description follows naturally, inevitably. The tactile sense of place that Abe creates is surely among the most skillful achieved by any modern novelist. Yet this peculiar verisimilitude makes the bizarre world of the dunes all the more unreal. The reader, like poor Jumpei himself, can grasp naturally and in sequence each feeling, each event, but the larger meanings remain stubbornly inexplicable. In one sense, of course, this is the message of the novel.

The Woman in the Dunes is by no means altogether grim and frightening, however. There is a good deal of wry humor and some well-wrought observations on the vagaries of ordinary human nature. Even a decrepit dog gets a striking description. Nevertheless, the shadow of a sense of wonder always hovers behind. The novel is a remarkable performance by a master showman.

TRANSLATION
Abe Kōbō. *The Woman in the Dunes*. Trans. E. Dale Saunders. 1964. Reprint. Random House, 1972.

OTHER WORKS BY ABE KŌBŌ
In addition to Abe's plays, listed elsewhere, quite a number of his successful novels are now available in English. Notable among them are *The Face of Another* (Knopf, 1966), in which the protagonist enters his former surroundings with a new identity, *The Ruined Map* (1969. Reprint. Putnam, 1981), a science-fiction–like metaphysical adventure, and *The Box Man* (1974. Reprint. Putnam, 1981), an amusing and grotesque satire on contemporary society, in which a man abandons his ordinary life to live in a portable house like some medieval Buddhist hermit, all the better to observe what he takes to be an increasingly mad world.

The Temple of the Golden Pavilion
Mishima Yukio
Kinkakuji

Novel. 1956

No other twentieth-century Japanese writer has attracted so much sustained attention in the West as Mishima Yukio (1925–70), and few Japanese writers, with the possible exception of **Natsume Sōseki**, have had such a large and representative proportion of their works rendered into English. In addition, books and essays on Mishima's writing, complex life, and flamboyant death by ritual suicide have been written by such diverse and prominent figures in the West as Henry Miller and Marguerite Yourcenar. A number of Mishima's novels, including *The Temple of the Golden Pavilion* (*Kinkakuji*), have been filmed in and out of Japan, and his own life has been the subject of a widely circulated 1985 commercial film by Paul Schrader simply entitled *Mishima*. There is no other Japanese writer whose name could assure that kind of recognition.

Although Mishima composed in virtually every literary form, and maintained in particular a high reputation in Japan as a dramatist, it is as a novelist that he is most appreciated in the West. To choose from his many novels in translation a single representative work is not an easy task. Of the various possibilities, which range from the intensely personal, such as the semi-autobiographical *Confessions of a Mask* (*Kamen no kokuhaku*), to a book like *Runaway Horses* (*Honba*), which makes skilled and imaginative use of Japanese historical material, perhaps his 1956 *Temple of the Golden Pavilion* can be said to strike a reasonably happy balance between the personal and the objective. For many critics in Japan, this relatively early novel remains the author's representative masterpiece.

The Golden Pavilion, like Mishima's later *After the Banquet* (*Utage no ato*), written in 1960, belongs to that class of work in which a set of objective facts serves as the basis for an imaginative story. *After the Banquet* deals with the financial power that lurks behind conservative politics in postwar Japan. *The Golden Pavilion* represents a fictionalized account of the infamous destruction of the famous Kyoto landmark, the Kinkakuji, set to the torch by a disturbed young man, a Buddhist acolyte, in 1950. The three-storied pavilion, situated on a pond in the midst of the grounds of a Buddhist temple, was originally built for Ashikaga Yoshimitsu (1358–1408), the great medieval shogun and patron of the arts whose love of the theater gave great impetus to the development of the nō drama. Following that disastrous fire in 1950, incidentally, the building was completely reconstructed along the lines suggested in the original designs.

Mishima, much intrigued by the incident, carried out a certain amount of research on the acolyte's life and the circumstances of the fire, then set out to construct his novel, presumably in an attempt to explore the motivations that eventually pushed the young man to carry out such a nihilistic act. In writing his story, Mishima was to make use of narrative methods well known to him from classical Japanese literature, when historical fact often served to justify fictional imagination. Japanese readers of *The Golden Pavilion* knew the outcome of the story before they began, just as those who saw the domestic dramas of **Chikamatsu** in the Tokugawa period knew the ultimate outcome of a lover's suicide before they entered the theater. The emphasis in both cases focuses on how the final incident came to pass; suspense of plot is replaced by an analysis of character and circumstance.

In re-creating his historical figure, however, Mishima read a great deal of himself into the stuttering Mizoguchi, so that the novel becomes a highly personal vision as well as a historical account. Early in the novel, Mizoguchi, who serves as narrator, states that "my first problem was that of beauty," and Mishima sets up a strong set of tensions between the mentality of the central character and his peculiar opponent, a shifting image of the Golden Pavilion itself, which in his mind assumes various guises, some friendly, some antagonistic. In many ways, the young narrator might be said to possess an erotic fixation on the building. Like Salome in Oscar Wilde's famous play, who has John the Baptist beheaded, Mizoguchi also destroys what he loves most—not flesh, in his case, but wood and paper.

From the beginning, Mizoguchi's stutter has kept him from a normal life. "It is the first sound," he remarks, "that I have trouble in uttering."

> The first sound is like a key to the door that separates my inner world from the world outside, and I have never known that key to turn smoothly in its lock. Most people, thanks to their easy command of words, can keep this door between the inner world and the outer world wide open, so that the air passes freely between the two; but for me this has been quite impossible. Thick rust has gathered on the key.

Incident after incident in the novel reveals Mizoguchi attempting to keep that door open, only to find it relentlessly shutting against him. A series of women he encounters may have the potential to lead him into the ordinary, exterior world, but none of the relationships evolve in a satisfactory way. As a boy, Mizoguchi is drawn to a lovely girl who lives in his village, but she only laughs at him. Degraded, he comes to feel her equal only after she herself becomes an outcast because of her relationship with a runaway soldier. Mizoguchi detests his mother, who can only scheme and urge him to hope that he will one day become the head of the temple. Other women are only visible to him in the sort of erotic vignettes of which Mishima was an experienced and masterful creator. Mizoguchi's sole successful physical encounter is with a prostitute. Even in the realm of friendship, his good and pure friend Tsurukawa appears in the end to have drawn away from him and closer to the clubfooted Kashiwagi, a sardonic, ironic young man who seems a black-comic objective correlative of Mizoguchi's own twisted thoughts.

The novel moves in classical rhythms, beginning slowly and moving inexorably to its devastating climax, when the building goes up in flames. Afterward, perhaps *only* afterward, a measure of common sense becomes possible for Mizoguchi. "I noticed the pack of cigarettes in my other pocket. I took one out and started smoking. I felt like a man who settles down after finishing a job of work. I wanted to live." So Mishima ends the book.

At once subjective and objective, highly personal yet cunningly shaped and crafted, *The Temple of the Golden Pavilion* shows perfectly those qualities of narrative skill, erotic fixation, and linguistic brilliance that have made Mishima such a popular novelist in the West, more so perhaps than in Japan. In some of his works, the facade separating the subject matter from Mishima's private obsessions may appear too arbitrary. Here, however, the narrative events and the author's concerns combine with resonant skill. If the novel does not reach the level of high art, its superb construction and moments of human insight make it prodigious, troubling entertainment.

TRANSLATION
Mishima Yukio. *The Temple of the Golden Pavilion.* Trans. Ivan Morris. 1959. Reprint. Putnam, 1985.

OTHER WORKS BY MISHIMA YUKIO
Much of the author's work is already translated, and more continues to appear. Among the most widely read are his 1949 *Confessions of a Mask* (New Directions), an account of a young man's developing homoerotic impulses as he grows to maturity, followed by the 1950 *Thirst for Love* (Putnam), which chronicles the love of a city woman for a handsome peasant. *Forbidden Colors* (Knopf), written in 1951, deals with the homosexual subculture of postwar Tokyo. Mishima's trip to Greece produced the 1954 *Sound of Waves* (Knopf), an elegant reworking of the ancient Greek legend of Daphnis and Cloe in Japanese pastoral terms. Translations of two later novels, *After the Banquet* (Putnam), mentioned above, and the author's 1963 *Sailor Who Fell from Grace with the Sea* (Putnam), were followed by an English version of his 1967 *Spring Snow* (Knopf), the first in a series of four novels entitled collectively *The Sea of Fertility*, which Mishima finished the day he committed suicide. The other three novels in the quartet are entitled *Runaway Horses* (1968), *The Temple of Dawn* (1970), and *The Decay of the Angel* (1971), all three now available from Washington Square Press. Mishima's autobiographical essay *Sun and Steel* (1968), published in English by Kodansha International, provides considerable insight into the personality of a man who would put himself to death in a manner he felt befitting a samurai.

The Doctor's Wife
Ariyoshi Sawako

Hanaoka Seishū no tsuma

Novel. 1966

Ariyoshi Sawako (1931–84) is often identified as one of the finest of postwar Japanese women writers, but to categorize her in that fashion seems to do little to define or suggest the range of her prodigious talents. Better surely to say that she is one of Japan's most evocative and elegant modern novelists and that she is also a woman.

Ariyoshi was brought up in the Wakayama area of the Kii Peninsula south of Osaka, an area with old and venerable traditions, and her interests in the traditional arts and theater provide a focus for many of her earlier stories and novelettes, some of them, like the 1958 "Village of Eguchi" (*Eguchi no sato*), of great and evocative sophistication. Another of these early works, "Jiuta," written in 1956, evokes the world of traditional musicians, while the 1961 "Ink Stick" (*Sumi*) concerns the power of ancient culture over the modern artist. Ariyoshi visited the United States and Europe in 1959–60, and perhaps because of this experience, and for other, related reasons, some of her most representative later works deal with social concerns: the complex role of women in Japanese society, environmental pollution, domestic politics, and the problems of aging. To read such works as these gives an extraordinary glimpse into the real issues that beset modern and contemporary Japan. More importantly, they show her consummate narrative skill in demonstrating how her characters face the challenges of their natural and psychological environments. In almost every case, their abilities to fight in some fashion these situations give them a quiet, tenacious humanity.

Perhaps no novel in translation shows off Ariyoshi's skills as quickly or as well as *The Doctor's Wife* (*Hanaoka Seishū no tsuma*), written in 1966. In one sense, the book is a historical novel, making use of documents of the period to re-create certain aspects of the life and career of a noted physician from her native Wakayama Prefecture,

Hanaoka Seishū (1760–1835), the inventor of an anesthetic permitting successful surgical operations even before such feats were practiced in the West. Like **Mori Ōgai** writing about the physician Shibue Chūsai, Ariyoshi makes use of a variety of materials to reconstruct her story. While Ōgai remains visible throughout his account, however, Ariyoshi conceals her presence, and then through a prodigious feat of artistic empathy, wills herself into the lives of the two women of the story, Seishū's mother, Otsugi, and his wife, Kae. Ariyoshi brings to her narrative a strong sense of the involved relationships in a traditional Japanese family between mother-in-law and young wife newly brought into the household. Ariyoshi being a modern novelist, the almost relentless self-consciousness of her characters perhaps renders them articulate in a fashion unusual for their time. They seem, in many ways, very contemporary people. Nevertheless, their emotions are altogether genuine. Ariyoshi advances her arguments in the byplay between what is felt and what is said among the various women who inhabit the inner universe of the story.

As with any good novel, a summary of the plot alone is a betrayal of larger considerations. In one sense, *The Doctor's Wife* concerns the heroism and self-sacrifice of a wife anxious for her brilliant husband to succeed. On another level, it concerns the rivalries that beset any group of women in a society that places them in subordinate social roles. Kae, the central figure, is the daughter of the head of a prominent family. As a girl, she has always admired Otsugi, the daughter of a wealthy landowner from a neighboring area. Otsugi, ill as a child, had been given as a bride to a poor country doctor, Hanaoka Naomichi, since he was able to cure her unsightly affliction. Kae's fascination with the elegant and glamorous Otsugi culminates when Kae herself is chosen to become the bride of Otsugi's son Seishū, who, like his father Naomichi, has taken up the study of medicine. Kae marries him in absentia and works happily for long hours in the Hanaoka household. Once her young husband returns from his period of study in Kyoto, however, Kae is reduced to a long and painful struggle with her mother-in-law, Otsugi, for the primacy of affection of this young man, whose allegiances are almost by definition divided between his wife and mother. The relationship between the two women takes many harrowing turns, none more gripping than their rivalry over who can best aid Seishū in his experiments with his anesthetic potions. Otsugi and Kae both love and hate each other, and in a remarkable moment toward the end of the book, Ariyoshi makes it clear that Kae has, even unwittingly, absorbed much of the older woman's aristocratic demeanor, even something of her physical grace.

However intense the involvement of the two women in the doctor's medical affairs, their role, as Ariyoshi is quick to point out, is almost negligible as far as the outside world is concerned (as the title of the novel suggests). After all, in the eyes of a larger society, they are mere women. "If you stand directly in front of Seishū's tomb," the concluding lines of the novel read, "the two behind him, those of Kae and Otsugi, are completely obscured." It is only through an imaginative penetration into the heart of the doctor's family that Ariyoshi could divine the truth.

The beauty of this novel, however, does not merely lie in the author's ability to set the record straight or to resuscitate a sense of Tokugawa social relationships. Ultimately, its attraction comes as a natural and inevitable result of Ariyoshi's patient and painstaking re-creation of vivid moments in the lives of her characters, moments that allow them to see, even if briefly and imperfectly, both into and beyond the limits of their own personal destinies.

TRANSLATION
Ariyoshi Sawako. *The Doctor's Wife*. Trans. Wakako Hironaka and Ann Siller Kostant. Kodansha International, 1978.

OTHER WORKS BY ARIYOSHI SAWAKO
The early short stories mentioned above are available in various issues of the *Japan Quarterly*, a well-known journal covering various aspects of Japanese contemporary affairs, life, and culture available in most larger libraries. "The Village of Eguchi" is in the October-December 1974 issue, "Jiuta" in the January–March 1975 issue, and "The Ink Stick" in the October-December 1975 issue. All three are well worth seeking out. Among the full-length works presently available in translation is the 1959 *River Ki* (Kodansha International),

which, like *The Doctor's Wife*, examines with compassion the tensions and satisfactions of women in traditional Japan. Her 1972 *Twilight Years* is, along with **Inoue Yasushi**'s *Chronicle of My Mother*, among the most moving accounts in postwar Japanese literature of the problems of old age (both books available from Kodansha International). Several of Ariyoshi's novels and stories have been filmed or adapted for the stage.

The Silent Cry
Ōe Kenzaburō

Man'en gannen no futtobōru

Novel. 1967

Of all the postwar Japanese writers presently available in English translation who embrace the challenges of the international modern literary tradition, Ōe Kenzaburō (b. 1935) is surely the most accomplished, if not the most immediately accessible. His consciousness is securely placed during and after the Occupation period, and he captures a political dimension of Japan's unique and problematic status in the world. Ōe writes on a variety of topics, ranging from problems of the atomic bomb and the Korean minorities to the kind of contemporary malaise that arises from living in an ever more wealthy consumer society. By comparison, even such writers as **Ibuse Masuji** and **Abe Kōbō**, who also take up such themes on occasion, appear merely to hint at such problems obliquely. What is more, Ōe weds this contemporary sense of social concern to a prose style that, in the words of his gifted translator, John Bester, has the power to prod his reader, "forcing him to make unexpected associations, or emphasizing the author's analytical self-awareness." Dense, allusive, "difficult," Ōe has chosen the mode of fiction to push his language to the frontiers of expression and thought alike. He succeeds brilliantly. A reviewer once described one of his novels as a toothache, but one that went right to the roots so that one was forced to take cognizance of the reality of the pain.

Ōe continues to write, and no overview of his career at this point in time is possible. As a milestone along the way, however, his 1967 novel *Man'en gannen no futtobōru* (translated as *The Silent Cry* in 1974) stands as a conspicuous marker. No other work in English reveals so much of the range of Ōe's ambitions or the variety of strategies by which he hopes to attain them.

The Silent Cry is assuredly not easy to digest. Quickly the reader is drawn into a juxtaposition of dream, reverie, and action that seems at first altogether bewildering. And the characters that Ōe has created are as uncomfortable with themselves as they are with each other. However, while the reader may enter their world kicking and screaming that he doesn't want to know about them, he or she will emerge at the end with a sense of Ōe's remarkable vision of what travails, and what heroism, are needed when an individual decides to come to terms with himself, with his own history, and with the society by which he is surrounded.

I say "he" because the novel represents a kind of chronicle of the relations between two brothers. The older, Mitsusaburō, is a scholar and a writer; his younger brother, Takashi, like one of his illustrious ancestors, feels a strong pull toward political action. The women provide powerful vignettes, particularly in the case of Natsumi, Mitsusaburo's alcoholic wife; Jin, "the fattest woman in Japan"; and Momoko, a follower of Takashi in the "uprising" he leads in the mountain village where once his ancestors ruled as local officials. Most powerful of all is a woman who never actually appears in the novel, the demented sister of the two brothers, whose life can only be guessed at until Takashi gives his own shocking account of her existence in a final confession just before his death. All these women must fend for themselves, caught as all of them are in the taut net of relationships cast by the two brothers. Some lose, and some win. Natsumi's victory seems particularly striking, as she is able to tell her husband, Mitsusaburō, at the end of the novel that "I'm going to start thinking again ... thinking for myself, independently of you." Within the orbit of the personalities of these two men, however—so different on the surface yet so joined at the root—the others can achieve little autonomy.

To describe the subject matter of the book is in a sense to betray it, as the events portrayed are interlaced with memories, dreams, nightmares, and desires—none of which can be simply reduced to any linear plot line. Certain of the themes in the novel, the birth of a deformed child, for example, appear in other of Ōe's works and come close to revealing the depths of his own personal experience. In a very general sense, it can be said that *The Silent Cry* describes an attempt by Takashi to stage a kind of political uprising in the village, a duty he assigns himself as the final descendant of a long and illustrious line. Takashi is to some extent attempting to reenact in contemporary terms an event that took place a hundred years before, now a part of the valley's history. The uprising fails. Takashi makes his confession to his brother, then kills himself, leaving all those around him, as one character puts it, to carry on as best they can.

The real subject matter of Ōe's novel, however, bears only a tangential relationship to these surface events, extraordinary as they may be in and of themselves. Questions of self-identity and self-knowledge are paramount, and Takashi's powerful drive to tell the truth in his final confession—the absolute truth—mirrors a concern for sincerity that had surfaced in Japanese plays and novels as early as the Tokugawa period. Many a **Chikamatsu** hero has gone to his death in order to pay homage to the same ideal. Ōe's extraordinary understanding of the difficulties, spiritual and social, of carrying out such a charge reveal all the more his own contemporary convictions about the difficulties of living in modern society, where all are apparently caught in a mental world in which insight clashes with reverie and desire.

Yet to describe *The Silent Cry* in such general terms is to miss its most salient quality, that of a palpable specificity of image, place, even language, a specificity that allows the narrative, often dense and self-reflective, to reverberate with meaning. There is a tactile quality about every scene; the places and characters have their grotesque elements, but they are altogether real nonetheless. Within the environment that Ōe creates, every word, every gesture, every event, however outrageous, will seem by the end of the novel to have assumed its inevitable place in the scheme of the narrative. From the stench of dead chickens to a naked body in the snow, every aspect of foreground and background alike imposes itself on the reader. Ōe's dark poetry cannot be pushed aside. Through the lens of his hyperrealistic yet meta-physical language, the landscape of Japan, and of Japanese litera-ture, looks entirely different. Indeed, it may never look quite the same again.

TRANSLATION
Ōe Kenzaburō. *The Silent Cry*. Trans. John Bester. Kodansha International, 1974.

OTHER WORKS BY ŌE KENZABURŌ
John Nathan, another fine translator of postwar Japanese fiction, has rendered into English both an important novel of Ōe, *A Personal Matter* (Grove Press, 1968), and a collection of four of his longer stories entitled *Teach Us to Outgrow Our Madness* (Grove Press, 1977), which includes the famous story "Prize Stock," in which a black American flyer is captured in a remote Japanese village during World War II.

After Ōe

Ōe Kenzaburō, born in 1935, is the youngest of the authors contained in the original body of this book. When this guide was first compiled, a decade ago, Ōe was still considered an avant-garde writer, and while he remains indisputably one of the finest in his generation, there have been a series of developments in Japanese literature, particularly in fiction, which indicate a change in the direction taken by so many of the younger writers. As a result, the concerns of Ōe's generation seem, if by no means superceded, certainly sidetracked. What follows is a brief sketch-map of some of the newer developments in Japanese fiction. Thanks to the efforts of many translators and publishers, there are far more authors and works available than I can mention here. Similar changes have occurred in Japanese drama and, to some extent, in Japanese poetry as well, but translations of these works are fewer and more sporadic in their appearance and so are regretfully not included.

Literature is inevitably created in a context, and two central changes in the nature of postwar Japanese society doubtless helped bring about these divergences in the developing literary profile.

First, for many writers, notably such modern masters as **Dazai Osamu**, the end of the Pacific War in 1945 marked a kind of ground zero, in which older cultural values now seemed soiled, bankrupt. By the middle of the 1960s, an improving economic climate and a growing psychic distance from the war period created a younger generation of readers more willing to look on the past, and certainly the present, with a certain ironic humor, a quality missing for so many years in Japanese writing. The audiences for fiction grew larger during this time, and the distinctions between serious and popular literature began to blur. Two superb novels serve to document this change.

The first of them, *The House of Nire* (*Nireke no hitobito*) by **Kita Morio** (b. 1927), was published between 1962 and 1964 and is available in a fine two-volume translation by Dennis Keene (Kodansha International, 1984–85). Kita's father, Saitō Mokichi, was a famous poet of the prewar period and one of the first Japanese to study psychiatry in Europe. Kita's re-creation of the life of his family during several generations, while certainly not without shadows, is filled as well with humor and insight into the vagaries of life and the complications of prewar Japan. Kita treats everything from the woman suffrage movement to the Tokyo earthquake of 1923 with brilliance, wit, and, when necessary, considerable compassion. His characterizations are vivid and invariably compelling. The novel developed an enthusiastic following in Japan and helped launch the author's subsequent career as a humorist. No better, or more surprising, means for contemporary English-language readers to glimpse the flow of the earlier part of the century in Japan has ever been written. The tonality of the book remains fresh, its appeal authentic.

The second of these two highly popular and influential books that appears to mark such a striking change in the Japanese literary temperament was written in 1972 by another highly regarded modern master, **Maruya Saiichi** (b. 1925), and is entitled *Singular Rebellion* (*Tatta hitori no hanran*, also translated by Dennis Keene and published by Kodansha International in 1986). This is a book that deals with the present, not the past, and, while probing in its portrayal of the mores of contemporary Japan, provides a fresh, wry, and sometimes rather relaxed view of contemporary society. The male narrator of the novel, who tells the story of his charming and very modern wife and her amazing mother, a brilliantly conceived comic character who, remarkably enough, is just to be released from prison as the book begins. A delightfully nihilistic old lady, she even joins the students in throwing rocks in the antiwar demonstrations of the late 1960s.

For writers of a serious bent, such as Ōe and many others of his generation, the efforts of students and others to protest against the Vietnam war (and in particular the fact that the United States was using bases available to them in Japan) represented a movement of the utmost seriousness. Maruya does not make fun of such views directly, and indeed may agree with them, but the fact that he is able to find some humor in the conduct of those who lived through these complex years marks a new departure. It is one that would be taken up by a younger generation of writers who, perhaps disillusioned by the failure of politics to change the structures and policies of the nation, were to turn away altogether from such overt efforts. Politics and high cultural debate, at least as revealed in Japanese fiction, was in the 1970s and after to be increasingly replaced by humor, satire, and an increased interest in, indeed commitment to, the power of international popular culture, which with Japan's increasingly affluent society seemed to grow ever more seductive. In that regard, it might be said that Ōe, with his earnest concerns, may represent the last of the great modern writers in Japan; the younger writers, on the whole happy to define themselves as postmodern, developed their interests and skills in a very different way. They were, for better or for worse, enjoying themselves.

Translations require time and so invariably follow behind any new shift in literary trends, and it was therefore not until the beginning of the 1990s that the general English-language reading public could gain a full sense of the shifting ground of contemporary fiction in Japan. This was possible through the publication of two entertaining, if occasionally unsettling, anthologies of stories by younger Japanese writers. They are both still well worth reading, both for enjoyment and for the light they shed on these newer concerns. The first of them, edited by Helen Mitsios (Atlantic Monthly Press, 1991) was entitled *New Japanese Voices: The Best Contemporary Fiction from Japan* and included short stories by a number of writers mentioned below. The second, edited by Alfred Birnbaum, was entitled *Monkey Brain Sushi* (Kodansha International, 1991) and was even brasher, containing a story written in *manga* (comic book) form as well as a number of stories which included, at least in terms of prior Japanese fiction, some rather scatological elements. As with *New Japanese Voices*, this collection served to introduce writers who have since become widely available in English translation and some of whom have developed substantial international reputations. A number of these writers are mentioned below.

Looking over the range of contemporary writing available in translation, there appears to me to be a continuum, moving from what some critics have termed the "cool" writings of the younger generation, through a middle ground where this "coolness" is filtered through a more rigorous attention to more traditional elements of literary craft. At the other end of the spectrum can be found the work of writers who continue, in their own ways, to aim for the highest reaches of literary ambition. Space does not permit any attempt at a full documentation of all the contemporary Japanese writers now available in translation, but the works described below continue to interest a wide variety of readers, including, of course, myself and may hopefully provide suitable points of departure.

The so-called "cool" range of writers shows a number of common characteristics. They take an active interest in international popular culture. Their characters sometimes live abroad or at the least have foreign friends. The characters they create appear to have little if anything to do with current intellectual or political concerns and seemingly live in a kind of fantasy world, often of their own making. Incidents in these works are often sexually explicit in a fashion difficult to imagine within the framework of earlier modern Japanese fiction. These writers are also interested in video, film, and other means of expression, and, in fact, some have worked in these media themselves.

Among the authors most representative of this genre of contemporary writing, there is no one who better personifies these trends than **Murakami Ryū** (b. 1952), whose books spin along at a startling, sometimes beguiling narrative pace, and his flavorful accounts continue to attract considerable attention. Of these "cool" writers, he has written most explicitly about his lack of interest and concern in politics. In his 1987 novel *69* (translated by Ralph F. McCarthy, Kodansha International, 1993), his attitudes towards the antiwar demonstrations of the late 1960s have moved from Muraya's mildly satiric views to ones of cheerful indifference. The book is certainly a chronicle of the period, but the views of his student narrator are, however amusing, quite startling for readers who took or continue to take that grim period seriously. Perhaps his most successful novel so far available in translation is his 1980 *Coin Locker Babies* (*Koin rokka beibizu*) (translated by Stephen Snyder, Kodansha International, 1995). In this long and somewhat delirious account, two baby boys are variously abandoned and brought up together in an orphanage. One grows up to be an athlete, the other a transsexual entertainer. They manage to keep their friendship, then attempt to seek out their destinies in the labyrinths of a grotesque and satirical vision of a contemporary Tokyo underworld. Despite the overt sexuality stirred in with the curiously mixed flavors of a frenetic cornucopia of contemporary culture, *Coin Locker Babies* remains funny, and curiously charming, a kind of teddy-bear Rabelais that delights far more than it shocks.

Another writer who inhabits something of the same world is **Shimada Masahiko** (b. 1961), whose 1989 novel *Dream Messenger* (*Yumetsukai*, translated by Philip Gabriel and published by Kodansha International in 1992) remains at present the most substantial of his works available in English. Like Murakami, Shimada retains his popularity in Japan but is as yet relatively less well known abroad. This translation may change things. In the kaleidoscope of the author's imagination, characters from various cultures interact in a "manhunt" that takes them from Tokyo to New York. The author's wit, urbanity, and playful sexuality mark his work as uniquely his own, although the plot of the novel, with its concept of "rent children" and dream doubles, is quite impossible to summarize. Hopefully more of his work will be made available in English.

Yamada Eimi (or as she is sometimes called, **Amy Yamada**) is another writer with an interest in international settings and characters. A number of her works are now available in English. Her 1991 novel *Trash* (*Torasshu*, translated by Sonya L. Johnson, Kodansha

International, 1994) is perhaps the best place to start, as the concerns so well expressed here can be found in many of her other short stories and longer narratives. Yamada, who presently lives in the United States, sets her story in New York, where her heroine is in love with Rick, an African-American, who loves her but mistreats her during his drunken rages. Fascinating as the duel between them remains, many of the most touching episodes deal with her relations with Jesse, Rick's son, whom she befriends and, by the end of the novel, has been able to draw close to. The style is stripped down, and the novel is peopled with "New York" characters that even Woody Allen might have had some trouble conjuring up, but the heroine's growth from dependence to independence presents the reader with a striking vision of a growing wholeness, and her own shifts in sensibility are beautifully and delicately recorded.

Another writer who might be said to fit into this category goes by the beguiling name of **Yoshimoto Banana** (b. 1964). Long a best-selling author in Japan, she first became widely known abroad with the publication of her 1988 book *Kitchen* (*Kitchin*, translated by Megan Backus, Grove Press, 1993), and there are now several more of her works available in English. My own personal favorite remains her 1991 *N.P.* (*NP*, translated by Ann Sherif, Grove Press 1994), in which the heroine becomes involved with the family of a writer who has committed suicide after the composition of the final story in a series he produced. Despite the dark-sounding subject matter, the tonality is light, even quixotic, and the heroine's shifting visions of reality altogether her own. Nobody's fool, she is still open to wonders of the world and to the pull of a nostalgia which is strong yet never sentimental. Despite the special brand of naivete the heroine exhibits in the course of the novel, Yoshimoto, herself the daughter of one of the great left-leaning intellectuals of the previous generation, Yoshimoto Takaaki (b. 1924), displays an ability of observation and a craft of expression that are abundantly clear and satisfying, even in translation.

All of these writers show skill, even cunning, in their strategies of writing and conceptualization, but those I would place in a middle group seem, at least on the appearance of their work available in English, to connect themselves somewhat more closely to the relatively fastidious traditions of the older generation of writers. Here I will mention two such novelists who certainly deserve their wide readership in English.

Tsushima Yūko (b. 1947) has been taken up by feminist critics, who find her concerns of particular interest and relevance. As the daughter of the revered novelist **Dazai Osamu**, Tsushima's credentials are powerful and her writings of the highest interest to all readers of any gender or generation. Several of her novels and stories are now available in English translation, but I would myself suggest beginning with her 1980 *Woman Running in the Mountains* (*Yama o hashiru onna*, translated by Geraldine Harcourt, Pantheon Books, 1991). This account of the travails of an unwed mother, who must suffer the travails of a drunken father and an increasingly sick mother as she tries to bring up her baby alone, is told with an insight and a lack of sentimentality that for me make Okada-san, with her unthinking responses to life and her occasional flashes of compassion and emotional insight, one of the most authentic and fully contemporary heroines I have encountered in the fiction of any country.

By far the most popular and widely translated of all contemporary Japanese authors is **Murakami Haruki** (b. 1949). His numerous novels often possess protagonists of the laid-back, apolitical sort that seem to have developed from the example of the protagonist of Maruya Saiichi's *Singular Rebellion* some twenty years or more before, or perhaps from Murakami's appreciation for such authors as Raymond Carver, whose work he has translated into Japanese. Murakami makes use as well of elements usually found in science fiction as well as in detective stories, a trait which has earned him a wide circle of readers both in Japan and abroad, but has not endeared him to the more austere of the Japanese literary critics. On the surface, his novels and stories seem almost resolutely apolitical, and only in his newest novel to be translated into English, the 1994–95 *Wind-up Bird Chronicle* (*Nejimaki-dori kuronikuru*, translated by Jay Rubin, Alfred A. Knopf, 1997) does he dwell at all on such still difficult subjects as the role of the Japanese in Asia during the Pacific War. And it must be admitted that for some critics, both in Japan and abroad, Murakami's foray into history and politics was not considered altogether a success.

To show the range of Murakami's enthusiasms and interests, I myself would be apt to recommend his 1985 *Hard-boiled Wonderland and the End of the World* (*Sekai no owari to hādo-boirudo wandārando*, translated by Alfred Birnbaum, Kodansha International, 1991). Here Murakami runs two stories in close parallel. One relates the highly fanciful adventures of a computer data processor, living in some Tokyo set in the near future, who gets mixed up in a complex and highly fanciful scheme with his newfound friend the Old Man and his daughter, and one so bizarre that it makes the most complicated of **Abe Kōbō**'s bizarre urban visions seem mere child's play. The other involves a protagonist who has somehow come to a strange, medieval town from which he cannot easily escape; he is asked to read the skulls of unicorns in order to locate ancient dreams in a mysterious library tended by a woman who is apparently there for him alone. These sections are highly poetic and their eerie effectiveness difficult to sum up in any objective fashion. Over both these stories there hovers a kind of foreboding intensity, and Murakami's strategy, of course, is to reveal the implicit connections between the two, which emerge as the novel progresses. The texture of the narrative is hard to describe, but in this excellent translation, the sense of playfulness and foreboding combine in ways that mark this novel as an architectural achievement of the first rank.

Finally, there remain a group of writers whose work seems, on the whole, quite unconcerned with contemporary fashions, pop culture, and adventures in a fanciful urban underworld. Two of the very best are at last represented by recent translations in English of some of their more important works.

Furui Yoshikichi (b. 1937) developed a powerful reputation in Japan beginning in the early 1970s, but significant samples of his work have only become available in English in the last year or two. Furui was a student of German literature, and has translated significant works by such modern giants as Hermann Broch and Robert Musil into Japanese. Some have classified him as belonging to an "introverted generation," but there remains an implicit political edge, perhaps of disgust or despair, in some of his work.

Both of the two collections recently made available reveal the depths of Furui's art in elegant and nuanced English. The first of them, *Child of Darkness*, translated by Donna George Storey, was published by the Center for Japanese Studies at the University of Michigan in 1997. The title of the translation refers to the heroine of the major novella in the collection, the 1970 *Yōko*, named for the heroine, a mysterious woman found sitting in a ravine by the male narrator. Her mental illness serves as a means for the author to explore the construction of human identity, and the fluid nature of human consciousness makes itself felt in the other shorter narratives in this collection as well.

Ravine and Other Stories is an equally fluent and satisfying translation by Meredith McKinney (published in 1997 by Stone Bridge Press) of the title story ("*Tani*," 1980) and three others. "Ravine," like *Yōko*, begins in the mountains and fits itself, among other places, into the long history of narrative that deals with the power of nature over men of the sort that **Kawabata Yasunari** described with such eloquence in novels such as *The Sound of the Mountain* and *Snow Country*. As in the other stories, dream, fantasy, and spiritual indwelling also function to move these strange, mesmerizing stories from fact into myth. Furui is a master of his chosen fictional world, and his work, at least in terms of these translations, ranks him among the finest writers of the postwar period.

Myth also plays a part in the powerful writings of another acknowledged master of postwar prose, **Nakagami Kenji** (1946–92), whose relatively early death cut short the life of one of the most powerful and disturbing writers of twentieth-century Japan. Despite his high reputation, Nakagami's work was only known in the West through a handful of translations of his short stories until the publication in 1998 of a collection entitled *Snakelust* (*Jain*, translated by Andrew Rankin, Kodansha International, 1998). "Snakelust" is one of seven stories and tales included in the volume, and this collection goes a long way in both indicating the range of Nakagami's concerns (some might say "obsessions") and revealing his powerful literary strategies in coming to terms with them.

Nakagami was born in Shingū, a small port town on the large peninsula to the south of the mountain ranges south of Kyoto, not too far from the Ise Shrine. The area is poor, wild, and removed from the amenities of contemporary urban life. There have been other fine writers from this general area, notably **Satō Haruo**, but none to my knowledge who have made this territory, and the myths that inhabit it, the focus of such sustained and successful literary creation. In contemporary terms, this area may be of little national significance, but the mountains of Kumano, which tower behind Shingū, have long harbored the sites of famous Shintō shrines and the trails once used for Buddhist pilgrimages in the medieval period that give the area even today a haunted and archaic atmosphere. It is qualities just such as these which haunt the stories.

Nakagami began as a laborer, and his painful early years, which included his brother's suicide, helped form, or deform, his convictions about the basic instability of human nature. His stories, whether set in the past or the present, move from the contemporary world, often gross, crude, and frustrating, into a mythical realm where sexuality and purity fuse, then break apart. The events portrayed seem on the surface to be the subjects for melodrama, but they are redolent instead of the shifting, unarticulated relationships between man and nature. In this regard, if in no other, his work bears some comparison with that of Furui, yet Furui's fastidious understatement is altogether at variance with the driving force of Nakagami's narratives.

The title story "Snakelust" deals with a young man and his common-law wife who murder his parents, and is representative of the contemporary stories in the collection. "Tale of a Demon," on the other hand, reads like a medieval Japanese tale (with a few touches worthy of **Ueda Akinari**), yet with the hidden and suggestive sexual elements in his classic tales now made explicit. In all seven of them, Nakagami reveals himself a master storyteller; once read, his powerful narratives are impossible to forget.

It will by now be clear to any reader who has read the body of the guide that the trajectories of contemporary Japanese literature have spun off in any number of new directions, ones that could scarcely have been imagined two decades or more ago. Yet, whether cool or classic, the best of these newer works are successful in their own terms and are certainly worthy of enthusiastic exploration by readers of every generation.

Some New Translations

Among a variety of translations which have appeared since 1988, when the first edition of this book appeared, I have found the following particularly worth noting.

CLASSICAL WORKS

Collection of Old and New Japanese Poetry

Although no new translations of the *Kokinshū* have appeared, readers with an interest in early classical poetry may enjoy looking at *Poems to Sing: The Wakan Rōeishū*, translated and edited by Joanthan Chaves and J. Thomas Rimer, published by Columbia University Press in1997. Compiled in the early eleventh century by a leading poet of his time, Fujiwara no Kintō (966–1041), this collection contains, arranged by themes, a selection of highly appreciated Chinese poetry by both Chinese and Japanese poets, along with 31-syllable *waka* on similar themes by Japanese poets. The collection served as a central source book for the composition and appreciation of poetry in both languages until the end of the nineteenth century.

The Poetry of Saigyō

Thanks to the efforts of Burton Watson, a sampling of the full range of poetry by this master of the entire *waka* tradition is now available in *Saigyō: Poems of a Mountain Home,* published by Columbia University Press in 1991. The volume contains perhaps one-tenth of Saigyō's total work, but the poems have been beautifully selected, both for their intrinsic beauty and significance and for their potential to reveal their beauty in translation. This is a major and highly satisfying contribution to our understanding of the power of Japan's classical literary heritage.

The Tale of the Heike

Shortly after the appearance of the original edition of this guide, a new translation by Helen McCullough of *The Tale of the Heike* was published by Stanford University Press in 1988. The translation, without the copious notes provided in the Tsuchida/Kitagawa version, described in the body of the guide, reads a bit more quickly, possibly due to its somewhat more laconic style, but for a careful reader some important and often intriguing textual details may seem slighted. The best solution is doubtless to read both translations in tandem.

Nō Theater

Continued interest both by scholars and readers has made possible an ever greater number of new translations of these lyrical dramas. For the general reader, perhaps the most important publication in recent years is *Japanese Nō Dramas,* with beautiful translations by Royall Tyler and published by Penguin Classics in 1992. Translations of twenty-five plays are included, ranging from such classics as *Matsukaze* and *Atsumori* to a number of unusual but compelling texts. Those seeking more scholarly annotated editions can turn to *Twelve Plays of the Noh and Kyōgen Theaters,* edited by Karen Brazell and published in 1988 by Cornell University's excellent East Asia Series. The Series is also in the process of publishing a multivolume series of meticulous translations by Shimazaki Chifumi, which include extensive notes and background material, with the texts both in English and romanized Japanese. Finally, in the same series, Mae Smethurst has translated five unusual plays, in versions as close to the original as possible, in her 1998 *Dramatic Representations of Filial Piety*.

Ihara Saikaku

Saikaku's writings in translation continue to attract readers, and the newest contribution to the growing list of his major works available in English is Paul Schalow's highly effective translation of the 1687 *The Great Mirror of Male Love* (*Nanshoku ōkagami*), published by Stanford University Press in 1990. This collection of stories, which deals with homosexual love affairs arising in various situations and social classes, has, despite its original popularity in the Tokugawa period, never been fully translated into English until now. The stories, touching and amusing by turns, are not only highly readable in and of themselves but help lead to a greater understanding of the society of the time.

The Narrow Road to the Deep North

Those who have long admired Donald Keene's translation of several sections from Matsuo **Bashō**'s greatest travel diary, as contained in his 1955 *Anthology of Japanese Literature*, will be delighted to have available his elegant rendering of the entire text, so beautifully attuned to the elusive original, in *The Narrow Road to Oku*, published in an illustrated, bilingual edition by Kodansha International in 1996.

The Poetry of Ryōkan

Along with the excellent translations of Ryōkan's poetry, in both Chinese and Japanese, by Burton Watson and John Stevens, a new collection by Abe Ryūichi and Peter Haskel, entitled *Great Fool: Zen Master Ryōkan*, published by the University of Hawaii Press in 1996, contains both essays by the compilers and a number of effective alternate translations of some of the work found in the earlier compilations, as well as additional poems, letters, and other writings new to English. Those who already enjoy the work of this great Buddhist recluse of the Tokugawa period will find this new collection of special interest.

MODERN WORKS

Mori Ōgai

While the 1972 Kingo Ochiai and Sanford Goldstein translation of Ōgai's novel *Wild Geese* is quite satisfactory, readers may wish to read as well the translation by Burton Watson published in 1995 in the series published by the Center for Japanese Studies of the University of Michigan. Watson's work as a translator of both Chinese and Japanese texts has long been held in high regard, and his version of the novel has its own particular and effective poetry. Those wishing to read other novels from this period in Ōgai's career may enjoy *Youth and Other Stories*, edited by J. Thomas Rimer and published by the University of Hawaii Press in 1994. The volume contains translations by a number of fine scholars and includes both Ōgai's early romantic tales set in Europe, as well as novellas such as the title work, his engrossing 1910 account of student life in Tokyo at the beginning of the century (*Seinen* in the original Japanese).

Masaoka Shiki

In the past two years, two collections of the work of this most beloved of modern poets have been made available in English. The first, entitled simply *Masaoka Shiki: Selected Poems*, is a selection by Burton Watson published by Columbia University Press in 1997, which includes moving samples of his 17-syllable *haiku*, 31-syllable *tanka*, and poems in classical Chinese. The second, a translation by Sanford Goldstein and Seishi Shinoda entitled *Songs from a Bamboo Village*, concentrates on English versions of Shiki's *tanka* and provides as well a lengthy biography and notes on each poem. Both provide romanized versions of the original texts.

Tanizaki Jun'ichirō

Tanizaki's sophisticated and ironic works continue to attract readers and translators alike. Several of his most admired works have been made available for the first time in recent years and have proven themselves attractive to a wide public. Among the best of these new translations are an evocative and highly personal memoir of the author's own early life, first published serially in 1955 and 1956, entitled *Childhood Years* (*Yōshō jidai*), translated by Paul McCarthy and published by Kodansha International in 1988. The same translator and publisher also produced a very well-received English-language version of the 1937 *A Cat, a Man, and Two Women* (*Neko to Shōzō to futari no onna*) in 1990. Alfred A. Knopf published two additional volumes in 1994, a translation by Howard Hibbett of the once notorious 1930 *Manji*, here rendered as *Quicksand*, which deals with sexual partnerings considered bizarre in its day, as well as a translation by Anthony Chambers of two of the master's most striking and unsettling historical novellas, his 1932 *The Reed Cutter* (*Ashikari*) and the 1950 *Captain Shigemoto's Mother* (*Shōshō Shigemoto no haha*).

Kawabata Yasunari

Although a good deal of Kawabata's representative work has been rendered into English, more collections continue to appear. The most recent of these, entitled *The Dancing Girl of Izu & Other Stories*, was translated by Martin J. Holman and published by Counterpoint in 1998. The 1926 title story ("*Izu no odoriko*" in the original) has long been known and admired through an abbreviated translation by Edward Seidensticker. Here the story is presented complete, along with a number of stories from the prewar period that in the more personal accounts reveal new facets of Kawabata's own experience and character.

Twentieth-Century Theater

Those interested in more recent developments in the modern and contemporary theater in Japan will find excellent translations of some of the most admired plays by such top dramatists as **Shimizu Kunio**, **Betsuyaku Minoru**, **Kara Jūrō**, and others in the collection *Alternative Japanese Drama*, translated and edited by Robert Rolf and John Gillespie and published by the University of Hawaii Press in 1992.

The book includes a generous number of photographs from the Japanese original productions.

Dazai Osamu

Dazai's reputation continues to stimulate the production of new translations of his always intense tales, stories, and novellas. Among the best collections to appear during the past decade is *Blue Bamboo: Tales of Fantasy and Romance*, seven stories translated by Ralph F. McCarthy and published by Kodansha International in 1993. Evocative renderings of another half-dozen stories can be found in *Crackling Mountain and Other Stories*, translated by James O'Brien and published by Tuttle in 1989. Ralph F. McCarthy's English renderings of some of the author's autobiographical writings in *Self-Portraits* were published by Kodansha International in 1991. The photographs contained in this volume are of particular interest to those curious about Dazai, his family, and the period in which he lived.

Ōoka Shōhei

Readers drawn to Ōoka's harrowing and poetic *Fires on the Plain* will find his 1952 *Taken Captive* (*Furyoki*) of particular interest. The translation, by Wayne Lammers, was published by John Wiley & Sons in 1996. The account, a literary reorganization of the author's own experience as a prisoner of war captured by the American army, here becomes not only a vivid rendering of the encounter between two nations at war but a fascinating mirror in which the complications of modern Japanese culture are strikingly captured.

Endō Shūsaku

In the past decade a number of translations of Endō's work have appeared. As a result, something of the full range of the work of this popular and often profound novelist, who died in 1996, is now available in English. Three very important contributions to this legacy should be mentioned here. The earliest is his 1965 novel *Foreign Studies* (*Ryūgaku*), translated by Mark Williams and published by

Simon and Schuster in 1990, which includes three separate yet subtly related stories about the Japanese encounter with European culture, two of them concerning Japanese living in France (as did Endō) in the early postwar years. It remains to my mind the most compelling account of the confusions and cross-cultural adventures met by the Japanese in the West as any yet available in English.

The second, his 1986 novel *Scandal* (*Sukyandaru*), translated by Van Gessel and first published in the United States by Dodd, Mead & Company in 1988, is for me his most stylistically adventuresome book, which deals with the confession of a novelist, much like Endō himself, who faces the nature of evil in the most personal way, yet one he cannot grasp or come to terms with himself. Endō's last work, his moving 1993 *Deep River* (*Fukai kawa*), translated by Van Gessel and first published in the United States by New Directions in 1994, takes his Japanese protagonist to India where he encounters both a version of Hindu spirituality quite distant from his own faith, as well as an opportunity to face the significance of his own past. Some reviewers of this translation have made the case that *Deep River* may be Endō's greatest achievement, a final elegy to the themes of religious sensibility that have occupied him throughout his career.

Abe Kōbō

Abe, who died in 1993, had a long and vigorous career as a novelist and playwright. Although certain individual plays of Abe have been heretofore available, Donald Keene's collection *Three Plays by Kōbō Abe*, published by Columbia University Press in 1997, best captures the author's droll, absurdist vision of the contemporary universe. The photographs of Japanese productions provided are striking.

Among Abe's works of fiction made available in English in recent years, readers will find of particular interest a collection of his stories entitled *Beyond the Curve*, translated by Juliet Winters Carpenter and published by Kodansha International in 1991, as well as two novels, his 1984 *The Ark Sakura* (*Hakobune Sakuramaru*), translated by Carpenter and published by Alfred A. Knopf in 1988, and his final laconic 1991 vision of an urban hell, *Kangaroo Notebooks* (*Kangarū nōto*), translated by Maryellen Toman Mori and published by Knopf in 1996. *The Ark Sakura*, which deals with the adventures involved in setting up a nuclear fallout shelter deep in an abandoned stone mine, has been singled out by some reviewers for its moments of brilliant satire and sardonic humor, but the thrust of Abe's ironic vision of society may seem to run out for some readers before the end of this lengthy novel.

Mishima Yukio

Of the works of Mishima translated in recent years, the most striking is his 1964 novel *Silk and Insight* (*Kinu to meisatsu*), translated by Hiroaki Sato and published by M.E. Sharpe in 1998. The novel, long regarded in Japan as one of Mishima's masterpieces, is, like his *Before the Banquet* and *The Temple of the Golden Pavilion*, an account based on actual historical events, in this case a famous labor dispute. Mishima's concerns are less openly aesthetic than in many of his other works, and the various characters he has created seem vivid, the tensions between them authentic.

Those who enjoy Mishima's shorter works should seek out *Acts of Worship: Seven Stories*, translated by John Bester and published by Kodansha International in 1989. The title story, *"Mikumano mōde"* in the original, is particularly effective and takes the reader to the relatively remote area in Japan that forms the subject of many stories by **Nakagami Kenji.**

Ōe Kenzaburō

Since receiving the Nobel Prize for literature in 1994, international interest in Ōe has resulted in the publication of a number of new translations of his work, from all periods of his career. Before this date, the author's long-term concerns with international politics, particularly those surrounding the bombing of Hiroshima and its effect on the postwar ideologies of Japan and the world, were reflected in his collection of essays entitled *Hiroshima Notes* (*Hiroshima nōto*), translated by Toshi Yonezawa and first published by YMCA Press in 1981.

Among the various works of Ōe recently made available in English are his compelling novella about the psychological and sexual state of a young right-wing terrorist, written in 1961 and entitled *Seventeen* (*Sebuntin*), here coupled with a translation of *J* (*Seiteki ningen*, literally "Sexual Humans"), written in 1963, which chronicles the politics of sexual assault. Both are available in a collection entitled simply *Two Novels: Seventeen, J*, translated by Luk Van Haute and published by Blue Moon Books in 1996.

Other recently translated novels include *A Quiet Life* (*Shizuka na seikatsu*), written in 1990, translated by Kunioki Yanagishita and William Wetherall and published by Grove Press in 1996. His 1976 *An Echo of Heaven* (*Jinsei no shinseki*) is a wrenching tale partially set in Mexico concerning the suicide of two handicapped children, which was translated by Margaret Mitsutani and published by Kodansha International in 1996. Ōe's particularly complex and demanding *The Pinchrunner Memorandum* (*Pinchi rannā chōsho*) was translated by Michiko Wilson and Michael Wilson and published by M.E. Sharpe in 1994. His early 1948 novel about juvenile delinquents during the Pacific War, *Nip the Buds, Kill the Kids* (*Memushiri kouchi*), translated by Paul St. John Mackintosh and Maki Sugiyama and published by Marion Boyars in 1995, has also been widely reviewed.

Of particular relevance is Ōe's collection of essays, *Japan, the Ambiguous, and Myself*, which contains his Nobel Prize acceptance speech and three other lectures in English versions by various translators. The collection, published by Kodansha International in 1995, provides a strong statement on Ōe's part about those ambiguities, political and psychological, he locates in contemporary Japanese culture. The Nobel Prize speech in particular is a useful source to gain the measure of Ōe's concerns and thus a key to reading some of his more demanding stories and novels.

Another Classical Master: Buson

Yosa Buson (1716–83)

As I mentioned in the original edition of this guide, I very much regretted the fact that at that time there was no entire volume devoted to translations of the great Tokugawa poet Yosa Buson. Now Makoto Ueda, long acknowledged as a distinguished translator and commentator on Japanese poetry, has produced just such a volume, entitled *The Path of Flowering Thorn*, published by Stanford University Press in 1998. This study, which combines biography with copious translations, as well as reproductions of drawings and paintings by Buson who was also revered as a superior painter, goes a long way towards filling the gap. Like **Bashō**, for whom Buson had the greatest respect, Buson was also a traveler. Yet, however far-flung his adventures continued to be, he was always drawn back to Kyoto and the beauties of its classical culture. Ueda discusses the various other types of prose and poetry written by Buson in addition to his *haiku* and provides sufficient commentary on his translations when the sometimes elusive verses do not convey their diverse meanings and tonalities in English.

Perhaps the most significant aspect of this new study is the introduction it provides to the world of the Tokugawa literati, the *bunjin*, with their strong interest in the literature and art of classical China and Japan. As in the stories of **Ueda Akinari**, Buson's poetry gives a glimpse of the best of this "classical" art, which can combine fresh and personal inspiration with a reverence, solemn or sometimes playful, to the beauties of the past.

More Modern Masters

The ever-increasing number of effective translations of twentieth-century Japanese literature has made available the work of a much larger group of authors than was the case a decade or so ago. In addition to the thirty authors represented in the section of the original edition of this book entitled "Thirty Modern Works," the following additional selection of writers from that same period will hopefully be of interest to a wide variety of readers. For ease in locating or selecting an old, or new, favorite from among them, I have simply listed these writers alphabetically. There are, of course, many more candidates than can be included here, but these writers, when added to those described in the original edition, can help reveal something of the remarkable range of accomplishments in the Japanese literature of this century.

Enchi Fumiko (1905–86)

Enchi is a writer of formidable insights into the pains engendered by the restricted role, some might say plight, of educated women in twentieth-century Japan who, despite their education, intuition, and often intellectual brilliance, are forced by society to take a secondary place to men in social, marital, sexual, and psychic spheres. These painful tensions are nowhere more visible than in her 1957 *The Waiting Years* (*Onnazaka*), translated by John Bester and published by Kodansha International in 1971. Here the heroine must suffer through both her husband's infidelities and her son's stupidities until the narrative reaches a violent climax, both shocking and seemingly inevitable.

A considerable scholar of classical Japanese literature, Enchi's translation into modern Japanese of **Murasaki Shikibu**'s *The Tale of Genji* has received high praise and helps indicate the considerable knowledge and insight into the Japanese classical literary traditions that inform her powerful 1958 novel *Masks* (*Onnamen*), translated by Juliet Winters Carpenter and published by Alfred A. Knopf in 1983. In this novel, the author has borrowed with enormous skill devices from both the classical *nō theater* and *Genji* in order to introduce such elements as a "secret" sister who remains hidden away, as well as a character who owes much to the imperious and jealous character of Lady Rokujō, first described by Murasaki Shikibu more than a millennium ago. *Masks* is a brilliant and disturbing recasting of classical themes and motifs, as effective in its way as similar experiments by **Tanizaki Jun'ichirō**.

Hayashi Fumiko (1903–51)

Enchi seems an aristocrat in her demeanor; Hayashi began her career as a day laborer and reveals in her various writings a side of modern Japanese life, particularly as pertains to working women, that remains as touching, penetrating, and sobering as when she first wrote them. For many years there were only scattered stories by this famous writer available in English, but two recent volumes, both published in 1997, have finally made significant portions of her work available to a wider readership.

Joan E. Ericson's *Be a Woman: Hayashi Fumiko and Modern Japanese Women's Literature*, published by the University of Hawaii Press, contains extensive excerpts from her brilliant early work *The Diary of a Vagabond* (*Hōrōki*, 1928–30), which she compiled and adapted from her journals. The book may be said to represent a kind of fictionalized autobiography, mixing prose with poetry, as the author describes the poverty of her existence and the men in her life, all rendered with an enormous gusto and frankness which startled her first readers and even now puts her very much at odds with those writers who concentrated on describing characters drawn from the upper classes, with their surface gentilities. The book also contains a 1949 story entitled "Narcissus" ("*Suisen*"), which chronicles the tensions between a mother and her son in a fashion that only a mature writer could have imagined.

The second volume, translated by Janice Brown and published by the Cornell East Asia Series, is entitled *I Saw A Pale Horse* (*Aouma o mitari*) and contains Hayashi's 1929 collection of poems, many adapted from those contained in *The Diary of a Vagabond*, as well as a group taken directly from the *Diary*. Although Hayashi was a fine poet early in her career, this aspect of her work, as Janice Brown points out, has not been given its due until recently. Read together, these two books do much to bring into focus the trenchant talents of this remarkable woman, long a popular favorite in Japan but still too little known in the West.

My own favorite work of Hayashi Fumiko is her novel *The Floating Cloud* (*Ukigumo*), written between 1949 and 1951, which charts the trajectory of the heroine Yukiko from a wartime job in Indochina through the decadence of the early postwar period in Tokyo and her liaison with an American soldier, to her final illness and death on a small island near Kagoshima, off the coast of Kyushu. A brilliant and penetrating portrait of a group of characters who embody the sadness of those years, it is no wonder that the famous film director Naruse Mikio chose the novel as the basis for his film by the same name, his celebrated masterpiece of 1955.

There is an elusive and somewhat awkward translation by a Y. Koitabashi published by Information Publishing Ltd. of Tokyo in 1957, but it is well worth seeking out for the poignant glimpse it provides of the difficulties of early postwar Japan and of the psychic wounds of those who had to live through that period as best they could.

Ishikawa Jun (1899–1987)

One of the superior novelists of Japan in this century, Ishikawa holds pride of place for many Japanese readers because of his intellectual acumen, sophisticated and urbane artistic interests, and his ironic view of Japan before, during, and after the Pacific War. Some have likened him to France's André Gide. It is thanks to the sustained efforts of the scholar and translator William J. Tyler that Ishikawa's work can now be known and appreciated abroad.

Tyler's translation of Ishikawa's 1936 *The Bodhisattva, or Samantabhadra* (*Fugen*), published by Columbia University Press in 1990, seems to me a total success in rendering Ishikawa's complex, sometimes playful cultural layerings, in which the appeal of Marxism for the protagonist (hardly unusual for that period) is blended with his equal fascination for the work of an obscure medieval French poet, Christine de Pizan (who wrote of Joan of Arc), juxtaposed in turn with references to those two mystic Chinese Buddhist figures Han Shan and Shi Te. However unlikely such combinations may appear on the surface, Ishikawa's use of each to show contrasting facets of his protagonist's personality is compelling and persuasive, an accomplishment certainly aided by the elegance of the translation.

Tyler's new collection of translations is entitled *The Legend of Gold and Other Stories* and was published by the University of Hawaii Press in 1998. Of the six selections, I am most taken with "Mars' Song" ("*Marusu no uta*"), an ingenious piece of antiwar writing from 1938, and "The Jesus of the Ruins" ("*Yakeato no Iesu*") of 1946, which presents an unusual vision of a ruined Tokyo at the end of the war period.

Izumi Kyōka (1873–1939)

Kyōka, with his mysterious and fanciful tales, has long been considered one of Japan's great modern romantic writers, but it has only been with the relatively recent appearance of a collection of four stories chosen and translated by Charles S. Inouye and entitled *Japanese Gothic Tales*, published by the University of Hawaii Press in 1996, that Kyōka's peculiar and compelling genius can be widely appreciated outside of Japan.

The collection contains what is perhaps Kyōka's masterpiece, "The

Holy Man of Mount Kōya" ("*Kōya hijiri*"), written in 1900, the strange tale of a man lost in the wilds of this holy mountain and his encounters with a strange woman who seems to represent both the religious and the erotic impulses inherent in humankind. It is a tale worthy of the classic stories of **Ueda Akinari**, yet filled with the kind of unsettling insights that seem possible for writers only in our century. This is a story, and a collection, not to be missed.

Stephen W. Kohl has produced another translation of the story, the title of which he has rendered as "The Saint of Mt. Koya." Published in 1990 by "The Committee of the Translation of the Works of Izumi Kyoka" in Kanazawa, Japan (the author's birthplace), the book is not easy to find except in libraries, but for those who enjoy Kyōka's evocative work, it is well worth seeking out for Kohl's translation of another famous novella entitled "The Song of the Troubadour" ("*Uta andon*," composed in 1910), a haunting tale concerning what the reader comes to understand are the supernatural relationships between a musician and a geisha, and a story that shows Kyōka's deep appreciation of the classical **nō theater** as well.

Kōno Taeko (b. 1926)

Made famous by her story "Crabs" ("*Kani*"), published in 1963, Kōno has gone on to earn the plaudits of many, including **Ōe Kenzaburō** and **Endō Shūsaku**, who have praised her "unsparing gaze" as well as her "carnal understanding." Kōno's attitude towards her protagonists, mostly women of her generation in Japan, are as unsettling as they are revelatory.

Translations of individual stories by Kōno have appeared from time to time in journals and anthologies, but with the publication in 1996 by New Directions of a translation of nine stories by Lucy North, with an additional contribution by Lucy Lower, entitled *Toddler-Hunting & Other Stories*, the range of her skill and insights have become clear.

Kōno certainly rejects the received idea of the "good wife" in Japanese society. Her protagonists show an aversion to normal marriage, and certainly to girl children, notably in the title story "Toddler-Hunting" (*"Yoji-gari,"* written in 1961), which, with its erotic overtones, may prove more than a bit strong for some tastes. My particular favorite in the collection is a chilly but more understated story, "Night Journey" (*"Yoru o yuku,"* 1963), which sketches the ambiguous relationships between two couples and concludes with an unsettling scene in a Buddhist graveyard. In this case, less is more.

Nishiwaki Junzaburō (1894–1982)

Nishiwaki, translator of T. S. Eliot into Japanese, scholar of Anglo-Saxon, and sometime colleague of Ezra Pound, was a brilliant poet in his own right and stands at the apex of Japan's modernist movement. His poems, filled with complex allusions, both to Japanese and Western works of art and literature, are extremely difficult to translate, and it is thanks to the extensive sympathies and knowledge of the scholar and translator Hosea Hirata that we have an entire volume of his poetry, plus a lengthy commentary, *The Poetry and Poetics of Nishiwaki Junzaburō: Modernism in Translation* (Princeton University Press, 1993). Hirata places the poet in his national and international context, provides translations from eight of his collections, and gives as well a not surprisingly difficult but frequently absorbing commentary on the poems themselves. With or without the commentary, the beauty of these translations is compelling, and the necessary notes are provided with taste and discretion. An exemplary presentation of the work of one of Japan's greatest poets of this century.

Satō Haruo (1892–1964)

Satō's high place in the literature of interwar Japan is altogether secure. His enormous talent was sufficiently clear early in his career that he was helped along by his more famous contemporary **Tanizaki Jun'ichirō**, only to have their relationship rapidly dwindle after Satō married Tanizaki's former wife shortly after her divorce. In some ways, from our contemporary vantage point, both writers have something in common in their choice of sophisticated subject matter, but the tonality is different: Satō's bent is lyrical, while Tanizaki is ironic and sometimes playful.

Thanks to the recent appearance of two volumes of work by Satō, a variety of his most appealing work is now available for the first time in English. The first volume, *The Sick Rose*, published by the University of Hawaii Press in 1993, contains what is perhaps Satō's most consistently admired work, his early novella *Gloom in the Country* (*Den'en no yūutsu*, 1918), as well as a kind of sequel, *Gloom in the City* (*Tokai no yūutsu*, 1922). Both of these are lyrical and introspective. The third story included in the volume, "Okinu and her Brother" ("*Okinu to sono kyōdai*") of 1918, is a far more objective rendering of certain events and characters appearing in the two novellas. "The Sick Rose" ("*Yameru bara*"), with its references to Goethe and Edgar Allan Poe, helps establish a prevailing mood of a very modern melancholy, which grows from rootlessness but stops short this side of nihilism. It is no wonder that this inward-looking account seemed so contemporary to its first readers, and its rueful charm still remains persuasive.

The second volume, entitled *Beautiful Town*, contains the title story ("*Utsukushii machi*," 1919) and five other beguiling stories which capture the essentials of a wide range of emotional attitudes and physical locales, including Paris. More importantly still, it contains a full translation of Satō's celebrated essay "A Discourse on 'Elegance'" ("*Fūryū-ron*") of 1924, a masterful statement on traditional aesthetics worthy of comparison, in its way, to Tanizaki's "In Praise of Shadows."

Shiba Ryōtarō (1923–96)

For much of his long career, Shiba has remained one of the most popular and respected authors of his generation, but unaccountably virtually none of his work has appeared in translation. One of the reasons for this neglect may well be that some of the works the author prized most highly are those based on Japanese history, and translations of such accounts are both difficult to manage and slow to interest non-Japanese readers, who more often than not understandably lack the background to grasp the niceties of the author's accomplishments.

Hopefully that situation may change, thanks to the recent appearance of a translation of Shiba's 1967 novel *The Last Shogun* (*Saigo no shōgun*), translated and adapted by Juliet Winters Carpenter and published by Kodansha International in 1998.

The shōgun in question is Tokugawa Yoshinobu (1837–1913), who witnessed the downfall of the feudal Japanese system and the rise of a modern, Westernized Japan during the reign of the Emperor Meiji, who died a year before Yoshinobu, in 1912. Garnering details from what must have been a remarkable variety of public and private sources, Shiba chronicles Yoshinobu's stern upbringing, then goes on to sketch his complex emotional life, and evokes as well the complex intrigues that eventually caused his retirement with the coming of the new government. The account is never less than compelling, and thanks to the notes and other useful background information provided, the reader, after a little initial effort, will be altogether fascinated. One hopes that this translation will be successful in finding an appreciative audience, and that other works by this master of historical re-creation can be made available in translation as well.

Uno Chiyo (1897–1996)

Uno Chiyo has long been appreciated as an example of a flamboyant Japanese "modern" woman; indeed, the complexities of her emotional life are such that they may have tended to overshadow her considerable accomplishments as a writer. She is perhaps most celebrated for her liaison, remarkable both for its suddenness and its intensity, with a leading Japanese painter in the Western style, Tōgō Seiji (1897–1978), whom she interviewed and fell in love with in the same day, abandoning her husband and any hope of marital respectability. Her version of this episode is brilliantly and provocatively captured in her 1935 masterpiece *Confessions of Love* (*Iro zange*), translated by Phyllis Birnbaum and published by the University of Hawaii Press in 1989. No more informed evocation of the artistic life of Tokyo in the 1920s exists.

In her biography of Uno, entitled *The Sound of the Wind: The Life and Works of Uno Chiyo*, published by the University of Hawaii Press in 1992, Rebecca Copeland has also included three of her stories, which touch on such varied subjects as puppets and the traditional bunraku theater (an art which seized Uno by happy surprise), the life of a neglected wife, and the narrator's memories of a love affair that long seemed over. These beautiful stories more than confirm Uno's reputation as a writer capable of rendering her sense of self, and of her femininity, for her generation.

The Art of the Essay

As in modern European literature, the art of the literary essay has long served as an important means of expression in the history of Japanese letters during the last hundred and forty years, particularly in the realm of aesthetics. Regrettably, relatively few examples of this trenchant and informative genre have yet appeared in English translation.

One of the most important of all such twentieth-century works is *The Structure of Iki* (*Iki no kōzō*), first published as a small book in 1930. This study on late Tokugawa aesthetics remains the most widely appreciated work of its author, the philosopher **Kuki Shūzō** (1888–1941), who, after studying philosophy in Europe with Heidegger and others, lived for a time in Paris, where he became friends with the young Jean-Paul Sartre. He wrote this study shortly after returning to Japan. While there is an entire book devoted to this text and its significance in modern Japanese culture (Leslie Pincus, *Authenticating Culture in Imperial Japan: Kuki Shūzō and the Rise of National Aesthetics*, University of California Press, 1996), an English translation of the text itself has only recently been made available, in a version by a noted scholar of modern Japanese art, John Clark. The translation was published in 1997 by Power Publications in Sydney, Australia.

Two other writers, translations of whose work are perhaps more easily obtainable, can also make important contributions to our greater understanding concerning the powerful trajectories of intellectual life in twentieth-century Japan.

The first of these is a collection of literary and cultural criticism by the writer **Kobayashi Hideo** (1902–83), most often regarded as the single most important Japanese critic of the century, and so, like an Edmund Wilson or a Michel Foucault, one impossible to avoid or to escape. A man of high enthusiasm and prodigious learning, Kobayashi was as apt to write on Rimbaud as on **Akutagawa** or **Tanizaki** as on Marx. Paul Anderer has made a useful selection of essays and excerpts from a number of Kobayashi's writings in his anthology *Literature of the Lost Home: Kobayashi Hideo—Literary Criticism 1924–39*, published by Stanford University Press in 1995. Reading through these well-chosen selections provides a map of the enthusiasms and confusions of Japanese intellectual and artistic life during the entire span of Kobayashi's long life, revealing his resolute commitment to a cosmopolitan view of the artistic world in which he found himself. Reading them can be a bracing experience.

Kobayashi's visions, so powerful in their pronouncements and convictions, must now, in the eyes of many younger writers, be transcended or at the least put aside. One of the most gifted critics of our own period who seems convinced of this fact is **Karatani Kōjin** (b. 1941), whose prodigious reputation in Japan can now be better understood by the readers of his *Origins of Modern Japanese Literature* (*Nihon kindai bungaku no kigen*), a collection of essays originally collected and published in Japanese in 1980, then made available in English in a translation edited by Brett DeBary in 1993, published by Duke University Press. Karatani's fresh and often iconoclastic views of the nature and paradoxes he finds inherent in modern Japanese literature (and the visual arts) are of the greatest interest, particularly since, while using on occasion the insights of such European writers as Nietzsche, Heidegger, and Foucault, Karatani can often invert them so as to re-examine or question certain Western assumptions as well. Among the seven essays included, I was particularly struck with "The Discovery of Landscape," which deals, among other things, with the work and ideas of **Natsume Sōseki**, and "Sickness as Meaning," in which Karatani makes some striking observations on **Masaoka Shiki**'s mental situation during his painful illness. As these essays were originally written for Japanese readers, a number of untranslated writers and works are mentioned as well, some of which, on the basis of Karatani's observations, surely deserve English-language versions.

There is another book of Karatani's available in English, entitled *Architecture as Metaphor: Language, Number, Money*, published by MIT Press in 1995. The general subject matter of that work, however, lies outside the scope of this guide.

Further Readings

For those who would enjoy deepening their knowledge and appreciation of Japanese literature, the following books may prove useful. There are many other works of great value in addition to those listed here, including articles in scholarly journals. I have chosen these in particular since they supplement directly the purposes of the present book.

GENERAL WORKS

Shūichi Katō. *A History of Japanese Literature*, 3 vols. Vol. 1, *The First Thousand Years*; vol. 2, *The Years of Isolation*; vol. 3, *The Modern Years*. Kodansha International, 1979–83. An excellent and thought-provoking treatment of the subject, which includes a good deal of material in the area of intellectual history as well.

Donald Keene. All three volumes of Donald Keene's evocative and thorough history of Japanese literature have now appeared. The first in the series is entitled *Seeds in the Heart* and describes the history of Japanese literature from its beginnings to the late sixteenth century. Henry Holt and Company, 1993. The second is entitled *World Within Walls: Japanese Literature of the Pre-Modern Era, 1600–1867* and was published by Holt, Rinehart & Winston in 1976. Two volumes make up *Dawn to the West*, which deals with literature since 1868. Vol. 1 covers fiction, Vol. 2 poetry, drama, and literary criticism. Holt, Rinehart & Winston, 1984.

Jun'ichi Konishi. Three in a projected series of five volumes on the history of Japanese literature have now appeared. Konishi is one of the finest scholars at work in contemporary Japan, and his analysis, while detailed and rigorous, is always fascinating to read and is grounded in a sensitive understanding of Western literature as well. Vol. 1, *The Archaic and Ancient Ages*; vol. 2, *The Early Middle Ages*; vol. 3, *The High Middle Ages*. Princeton University Press, 1984, 1986, 1991.

Masao Miyoshi. *Accomplices of Silence: The Modern Japanese Novel*, University of California Press, 1974. A striking and still controversial treatment of certain structural elements in modern Japanese fiction that differentiate modern Japanese narrative from its Western counterparts. A crucial and revealing study. Admirers of Miyoshi's general approach to literature may also profit from reading sections in his newer book, *Off Center: Power and*

Culture Relations between Japan and the United States, published by Harvard University Press in 1991, in which he discusses such writers as Ōe Kenzaburō, Mishima Yukio, and Tanizaki Jun'ichirō, all described in the body of this guide.

Benito Ortolani. *The Japanese Theatre: From Shamanistic Ritual to Contemporary Pluralism,* revised edition, Princeton University Press, 1995. A highly valuable synthesis of the newest scholarship on every aspect of the long history of the Japanese drama and theater. The bibliography, which includes citations of material available in all major Western languages, is extremely useful.

Makoto Ueda. *Modern Japanese Poets and the Nature of Literature,* Stanford University Press, 1983. A sensitive and synthetic treatment of eight modern poets central to the traditions of Japanese poetry in this century. The translations running through the book are particularly attractive.

_____. *Modern Japanese Writers and the Nature of Literature,* Stanford University Press, 1976. Six great modern novelists are given a thorough analysis, and the quotations from their fictional writings and essays make this study an invaluable resource.

USEFUL ANTHOLOGIES

A number of individual works of Japanese literature, some of them of the highest quality, are contained in anthologies or collections. I mention here only those most important for the purposes of the present volume.

Karen Brazell, ed.. *Traditional Japanese Theater: An Anthology of Plays,* Columbia University Press, 1998. An exciting anthology of representative plays from the long tradition of classical Japanese theater, ranging from *nō* **theater** and *kyōgen* to puppet plays and *kabuki* dramas. Along with familiar material, there are some unusual contributions of the highest interest. Excellent glossaries of theatrical terminology and fine photographs.

Lane Dunlop, ed. *Autumn Wind and Other Stories,* Charles E. Tuttle, 1994. A first-rate collection of unusual stories and tales of the greatest interest from all periods of twentieth-century literature. Those who enjoy Dunlop's elegant translations will enjoy as well his earlier collections, in particular *A Late Chrysanthemum: Twenty-One Stories from the Japanese,* first published by North Point Press in 1986.

Theodore Goosen, ed. *The Oxford Book of Japanese Short Stories,* Oxford University Press, 1997. Another fine anthology of modern stories in English by diverse translators, traversing the entire range of modern writers from Mori Ōgai to Ōe Kenzaburō.

Donald Keene, ed. *Anthology of Japanese Literature: From the Earliest Era to the Mid-Nineteenth Century,* Grove Press, 1955. An indispensable collection of classic texts in translation and a sensitive sampler of the best in classical Japanese literature, in a variety of genres.

Ivan Morris, ed. *Modern Japanese Stories,* Charles E. Tuttle, 1962. An excellent group of shorter works by modern masters, many of whom are discussed in this volume.

Hiroaki Sato and Burton Watson, eds. *From the Country of Eight Islands: An Anthology of Japanese Poetry,* Doubleday, 1981. A veritable cornucopia of Japanese poetry, from the earliest sources to the present-day avant-garde. A surprising amount of this work is not otherwise available in translation, and the variety is prodigious. An exciting and satisfying collection.

For those particularly interested in postwar and contemporary Japanese literature, there are, in addition to those collections mentioned in the section "After Ōe," two additional anthologies that can be particularly recommended. Howard Hibbett's *Contemporary Japanese Literature,* published by Knopf in 1977, and the two-volume *Showa Anthology,* edited by Van C. Gessel and Tomone Matsumoto, published by Kodansha International in 1985. Both of these collections contain important and representative shorter works by a variety of writers, a number of whom are mentioned in this guide.

STUDIES OF INDIVIDUAL WORKS AND AUTHORS

A number of valuable works deal more specifically with individual works or writers. Some of those have been mentioned in the essays contained in the guide, and those citations, for reasons of space, are not repeated here. Again, for reasons of space, I have not annotated each individual entry except where necessary.

■ CLASSICAL JAPANESE LITERATURE

An Anthology of Ten Thousand Leaves (Man'yōshū)
   Ian Hideo Levy. *Hitomaro and the Birth of Japanese Lyricism,* Princeton University Press, 1984.
Chikamatsu Monzaemon
   C. Andrew Gerstle. *Circles of Fantasy: Convention in the Plays of Chikamatsu,* Harvard University Press, 1984.
Collection of Old and New Japanese Poetry (Kokinshū)
   Helen Craig McCullough. *Brocade by Night: "Kokin Wakashū" and the Court Style in Japanese Classical Poetry,* Stanford University Press, 1985.

Robert Brower and Earl Miner. *Japanese Court Poetry*, Stanford University Press, 1961. The study also deals with other works in the canon of court poetry.

Earl Miner. *An Introduction to Japanese Court Poetry*, Stanford University Press 1968. A clear and attractive introduction to the entire tradition.

Ihara Saikaku

Howard Hibbett. *The Floating World in Japanese Fiction*, Oxford University Press, 1959; available in the United States through Charles E. Tuttle.

Matsuo Bashō

Earl Miner and Hiroko Odagiri. *The Monkey's Straw Rain-Coat and Other Poetry of the Bashō School*, Princeton University Press, 1981.

Haruo Shirane. *Traces of Dreams: Landscape, Cultural Memory, and the Poetry of Bashō*, Stanford University Press, 1998.

Makoto Ueda. *Bashō and His Interpreters: Selected Hokku with Commentaries*, Stanford University Press, 1992.

Nō Drama

James Brandon, ed. *Nō and Kyōgen in the Contemporary World*, University of Hawaii Press, 1997.

Thomas B. Hare. *Zeami's Style: the Noh Plays of Zeami Motokiyo*, Stanford University Press, 1986.

Donald Keene. *Nō: The Classical Theatre of Japan*, Kodansha International, 1966.

Kunio Komparu. *On the Art of the Nō Drama: Principles and Perspectives*, Weatherhill/Tankosha, 1983.

J. Thomas Rimer and Masakazu Yamazaki. *On the Art of the Nō Drama: The Major Treatises of Zeami*, Princeton University Press, 1984.

The Tale of Genji

Richard Bowring. *The Tale of Genji*, Landmarks of Literature Series, Cambridge University Press, 1988.

Norma Field. *The Splendor of Longing in the Tale of Genji*, Princeton University Press, 1987.

Ivan Morris. *The World of the Shining Prince*, Penguin Books, 1969.

Andrew Pekarik, ed. *Ukifune: Love in "The Tale of Genji,"* Columbia University Press, 1982.

William J. Puette. *Guide to "The Tale of Genji,"* Charles E. Tuttle, 1983.

Haruo Shirane. *The Bridge of Dreams: A Poetics of "The Tale of Genji,"* Stanford University Press, 1988.

The Treasury of Loyal Retainers (Chūshingura)

James R. Brandon, ed. *Chūshingura: Studies in Kabuki and the Puppet Theatre*, University of Hawaii Press, 1982.

Ueda Akinari

Blake Morgan Young. *Ueda Akinari*, University of British Columbia Press, 1982.

Studies on these writers are often mentioned in the category of "General Works." A few additional suggestions follow.

Akutagawa Ryūnosuke

Beongcheon Yu. *Akutagawa: An Introduction*, Wayne State University Press, 1972.

Arishima Takeo

Paul Anderer. *Other Worlds: Arishima Takeo and the Bounds of Modern Japanese Fiction*, Columbia University Press, 1984.

Ishikawa Takuboku

Yukihito Hijiya. *Ishikawa Takuboku*, Twayne, 1979.

Izumi Kyōka

Charles Shirō Inouye. *The Similitude of Blossoms: A Critical Biography of Izumi Kyōka (1873–1939): Japanese Novelist and Playwright*, Harvard University Press, 1999.

Kawabata Yasunari

Van C. Gessel. *Three Modern Novelists: Sōseki, Tanizaki, Kawabata*, Kodansha International, 1993.

Kōda Rohan

Chieko Mulhern. *Kōda Rohan*, Twayne, 1977.

Kōda Aya (1904–90), the daughter of Kōda Rohan and a novelist in her own right, is the subject of a searching biography by Alan M. Tansman (Yale University Press, 1993), which includes considerable information on Rohan himself as well as translations of several of her own striking stories.

Mishima Yukio

Napier, Susan J. *Escape from the Wasteland: Romanticism and Realism in the Fiction of Mishima Yukio and Ōe Kenzaburō*, Harvard University Press, 1991.

John Nathan. *Mishima: A Biography*, Little, Brown, 1974.

Henry Scott-Stokes. *The Life and Death of Yukio Mishima*, Farrar, Straus & Giroux, 1986.

Roy Starrs. *Deadly Dialectics: Sex, Violence, and Nihilism in the World of Mishima Yukio*, University of Hawaii Press, 1994.

Marguerite Yourcenar. *Mishima: A Vision of the Void*, Farrar, Straus & Giroux, 1986.

Mori Ōgai

Richard Bowring. *Ōgai and the Modernization of Japanese Culture*, Cambridge University Press, 1979.

Marvin Marcus. *Paragons of the Ordinary: The Biographical Literature of Mori Ōgai*, University of Hawaii Press, 1993.

J. Thomas Rimer. *Mori Ōgai*, Twayne, 1975.

Natsume Sōseki

Doi Takeo. *The Psychological World of Natsume Sōseki*, Harvard University Press, 1976.

Van G. Gessel. *Three Modern Novelists: Sōseki, Tanizaki*, Kawabata, Kodansha International, 1993.

Edwin McClellan. *Two Japanese Novelists: Sōseki and Tōson*, University of Chicago Press, 1969.

Beongcheon Yu. *Natsume Sōseki*, Twayne, 1969.

Angela Yiu. *Chaos and Order in the Works of Natsume Sōseki*, University of Hawaii Press, 1998.

Ōe Kenzaburō

Napier, Susan J. *Escape from the Wasteland: Romanticism and Realism in the Fiction of Mishima Yukio and Ōe Kenzaburō*, Harvard University Press, 1991.

Michiko Wilson. *The Marginal World of Ōe Kenzaburō: A Study in Themes and Techniques*, M.E. Sharpe, 1986.

Shiga Naoya

William F. Sibley. *The Shiga Hero*, University of Chicago Press, 1979.

Shimazaki Tōson

Edwin McClellan. *Two Japanese Novelists: Sōseki and Tōson*, University of Chicago Press, 1969.

Tanizaki Jun'ichirō

Anthony H. Chambers. *The Secret Window: Ideal Worlds in Tanizaki's Fiction*, Harvard University Press, 1994.

Van C. Gessel. *Three Modern Novelists: Sōseki, Tanizaki, Kawabata*, Kodansha International, 1993.

Ken Ito. *Visions of Desire: Tanizaki's Fictional Worlds*, Stanford University Press, 1991.

Yokomitsu Riichi

Dennis Keene. *Yokomitsu Riichi: Modernist*, Columbia University Press, 1980.

USEFUL REFERENCE BOOKS

As more and more Japanese literature in translation becomes available, the following publications will be of particular use in seeking out translations, biographical material, and other matters of possible interest to the general reader.

Van C. Gessel, ed. *Japanese Fiction Writers, 1868–1945*, Dictionary of Literary Biography, Vol. 180, Gale Research, 1997.

_____, ed. *Japanese Fiction Writers Since World War II*, Dictionary of Literary Biography, Vol. 182, Gale Research, 1997.

The Japan P.E.N. Club, ed. *Japanese Literature in Foreign Languages 1945-1995*, Japan P.E.N. Club, 1997.

John Lewell. *Modern Japanese Novelists: A Biographical Dictionary*, Kodansha International, 1993.

INDEX
(Numbers in bold type indicate extended discussions)

Abe, Kobo	**THE FACE OF ANOTHER** **THE RUINED MAP** **SECRET RENDEZVOUS**
Agawa, Hiroyuki	**CITADEL IN SPRING** **THE RELUCTANT ADMIRAL**
Ariyoshi, Sawako	**THE DOCTOR'S WIFE** **KABUKI DANCER** **THE RIVER KI**
Boehm, Deborah	**A ZEN ROMANCE**
Booth, Alan	**LOOKING FOR THE LOST** **THE ROADS TO SATA**
Dazai, Osamu	**BLUE BAMBOO** **SELF PORTRAITS**
Enchi, Fumiko	**THE WAITING YEARS**
Endo, Shusaku	**THE SAMURAI** **SILENCE**
Hamill, Pete	**TOKYO SKETCHES**
Ibuse, Masuji	**BLACK RAIN** **CASTAWAYS** **SALAMANDER** **WAVES**
Ikenami, Shotaro	**THE MASTER ASSASSIN** **BRIDGE OF DARKNESS**
Ikezawa, Natsuki	**STILL LIVES**
Inoue, Yasushi	**LOU-LAN** **TUN-HUANG**
Ishikawa, Yoshimi	**STRAWBERRY ROAD**
Kaiko, Takeshi	**INTO A BLACK SUN**
Kawabata, Yasunari	**HOUSE OF THE SLEEPING BEAUTIES** **THE LAKE** **THE TALE OF THE BAMBOO CUTTER**
Kita, Morio	**GHOSTS**
Kizaki, Satoko	**THE PHOENIX TREE** **THE SUNKEN TEMPLE**
Komatsu, Sakyo	**JAPAN SINKS**
Kuroyanagi, Tetsuko	**TOTTO-CHAN**
Maruya, Saiichi	**A MATURE WOMAN** **RAIN IN THE WIND** **SINGULAR REBELLION**
Matsumoto, Seicho	**POINTS AND LINES** **THE VOICE**

MONKEY BRAIN SUSHI New Tastes in Japanese Fiction
Edited by Alfred Birnbaum

Fresh and irreverent, 11 remarkable stories introduce the brightest and boldest voices in Japanese fiction.
"A lively, electric picture of contemporary Japanese society."—*Booklist*

Hardcover: 312 pages, 140 x 210 mm, ISBN 4-7700-1543-7
Paperback: 312 pages, 113 x 182 mm, ISBN 4-7700-1688-3

THE SHOWA ANTHOLOGY
Modern Japanese Short Stories
Edited by Van C. Gessel & Tomone Matsumoto

Covering 60 years of literature, this anthology presents both established authors as well as numerous skillful writers almost unknown in English.
"...lyric, comic, tragic, satiric, fantastic and experimental—all the stories shine."—*Publishers Weekly*

Paperback: 464 pages, 113 x 182 mm, ISBN 4-7700-1708-1

THE MOTHER OF DREAMS AND OTHER STORIES
Portrayals of Women in Modern Japanese Fiction
Edited by Makoto Ueda

An anthology of stories about women in Japanese society. Includes works by Dazai, Oe, Abe, and other celebrated Japanese writers.
"This appealing anthology reflect[s] traditional women's roles while showing what radical changes have taken place...especially since World War II."—*Publishers Weekly*

Hardcover: 280 pages, 148 x 210 mm, ISBN 0-87011-775-0
Paperback: 280 pages, 110 x 182 mm, ISBN 0-87011-926-5

THREE MODERN NOVELISTS
Soseki, Tanizaki, Kawabata

Van C. Gessel

This concise volume traces the lives and careers of three literary giants and their varying responses to Japan's increasing internationalization.
"Deftly outlined and memorably presented." —Donald Richie, The *Japan Times*

Paperback: 208 pages, 113 x 188 mm, ISBN 4-7700-1652-2

A READER'S GUIDE TO JAPANESE LITERATURE
New Edition

J. Thomas Rimer

A stimulating guide to 20 classic and 30 modern works, with plot summaries, characterizations, background, and other helpful insights to help the reader enjoy the special flavors of these masterpieces.
Paperback: 216 pages, 113 x 182 mm, ISBN 4-7700-2359-6

A WILD SHEEP CHASE

Haruki Murakami   Translated by Alfred Birnbaum

Unusual characters, a mysterious sheep, and a race across Japan reveal a wild, contemporary imagination that is witty, irreverent and delightful.

Paperback: 312 pages, 113 x 182 mm, ISBN 4-7700-1706-5, Territories: Japan only

HARD-BOILED WONDERLAND AND THE END OF THE WORLD

Haruki Murakami   Translated by Alfred Birnbaum

Set in the near future, this unnerving tale of technological espionage is a fable for the modern age.

Hardcover: 416 pages, 156 x 235 mm; ISBN 4-7700-1544-5
Paperback: 416 pages, 113 x 182 mm, ISBN 4-7700-1893-2, Territories: PB Japan only

DANCE DANCE DANCE

Haruki Murakami   Translated by Alfred Birnbaum

An ordinary man on an extraordinary journey through a high-tech, high-rise world with a host of bizarre companions, a mysterious woman who invades his dreams, and the search for. . .?

Hardcover: 352 pages, 152 x 226 mm, ISBN 4-7700-1683-2

ALMOST TRANSPARENT BLUE

Ryu Murakami   Translated by Nancy Andrew

A youth in college, his older mistress, and a melange of odd friends— a novel full of rapidly sketched scenes that glide from everyday reality to the hallucinatory.

"A Japanese mix of *A Clockwork Orange* and *L'Etranger*."—*Newsweek*

Paperback: 128 pages, 110 x 182 mm, ISBN 0-87011-469-7

COIN LOCKER BABIES

Ryu Murakami   Translated by Stephen Snyder

This startlingly imaginative work follows the histories of two boys who, as infants, were left to die in adjacent coin lockers, and set off on parallel quests of vengeance.

"A frontal assault on all five senses...a great big pulsating parable."— *Washington Post*

Paperback: 400 pages, 113 x 182 mm, ISBN 4-7700-2308-1

JAPAN, THE AMBIGUOUS, AND MYSELF
The Nobel Prize Speech and Other Lectures

Kenzaburo Oe
Translated by Kunioki Yanagishita & Hisaki Yamanouchi

Oe's message for mankind—his faith in human decency, in the renunciation of war, and in the healing power of art.
"[A] brave, reasoned and passionately honest book."—Donald Richie
Hardcover: 128 pages, 120x 188 mm, ISBN 4-7700-1980-7

AN ECHO OF HEAVEN

Kenzaburo Oe   Translated by Margaret Mitsutani

A penetrating portrait of a woman driven by a series of personal tragedies to search for a way to understand the mystery of her life.
Hardcover: 240 pages, 152 x 228 mm, ISBN 4-7700-1986-6

THE SILENT CRY

Kenzaburo Oe   Translated by John Bester

A man in search of his identity becomes caught in a vortex of sexuality and violence.
"Oe's major mature work...an imaginary world where life and myth condense to powerfully portray the human predicament."—The Nobel Committee
Hardcover: 288 pages, 143 x 215 mm, ISBN 4-7700-0450-8
Paperback: 288 pages, 113 x 182 mm, ISBN 0-87011-466-2

THE CATCH and Other War Stories

Kenzaburo Oe, Haruo Umezaki, Tamiki Hara, Fumiko Hayashi

A superb collection of war stories condemning war, made unforgettable by Oe's most powerful piece of shorter fiction.
"Some of the finest stories ever translated."—*The Guardian*
Paperback: 162 pages, 113 x 182 mm, ISBN 0-87011-457-3

A HEALING FAMILY

Kenzaburo Oe
Translated by Stephen Snyder   Illustrated by Yukari Oe

An intimate portrait of the Nobel Prize-winning author's handicapped son, the unexpected courage we can all find in ourselves, and the meaning of family.
Hardcover: 160 pages, 140 x 210 mm, color illustrations, ISBN 4-7700-2048-1

A DARK NIGHT'S PASSING

Naoya Shiga   Translated by Edwin McClellan

A young man's passage through a sequence of disturbing experiences to a hard-won truce with the destructive forces in himself. "...One of the outstanding monuments of Japanese literature... a superb translation."—*Choice*

Paperback: 408 pages, 110 x 182 mm, ISBN 0-87011-362-3

CITADEL IN SPRING

Hiroyuki Agawa   Translated by Lawrence Rogers

An autobiographical account of fighting on the losing side in the Pacific War. The story of a young man who has lost everything yet manages to come to terms with loss and despair.

Hardcover: 256 pages, 148 x 210 mm, ISBN 0-87011-960-5

THE RELUCTANT ADMIRAL
Yamamoto and the Imperial Navy

Hiroyuki Agawa   Translated by John Bester

The definitive account of the man who planned Pearl Harbor and died a dramatic death in the South Pacific.
"One of the most comprehensive and enlightening biographies available of a wartime leader"—*New York Times*

Paperback: 408 pages, 110 x 182 mm, chronology, index, ISBN 0-87011-512-X

THE SAMURAI

Shusaku Endo   Translated by Van C. Gessel

An exciting historical novel that retraces the steps of four samurai sent as envoys in 1613 to Mexico and Europe and the trials of faith, ambition, and loyalty they faced.

Paperback: 272 pages, 113 x 182 mm, ISBN 4-7700-1996-3, Territories: Japan only

SILENCE

Shusaku Endo   Translated by William Johnston

"Silence is a remarkable work, a somber, delicate, and startlingly empathetic study of a young Portuguese missionary during the relentless persecution of the Japanese Christians in the early seventeenth century."—*John Updike*

Paperback: 312 pages, 110 x 182 mm, ISBN 0-87011-536-7
Territories: Japan & EU. (not available UK.)

A MATURE WOMAN

Saiichi Maruya   Translated by Dennis Keene

A witty and entertaining look at the role of women in Japan in the 90s, bribery, and coercion at the highest levels of society.
"As gripping as a thriller."—*The Times*

Hardcover: 328 pages, 152 x 228 mm, ISBN 4-7700-1864-9
Paperback: 328 pages, 113 x 182 mm, ISBN 4-7700-2183-6

RAIN IN THE WIND   Four Stories

Saiichi Maruya   Translated by Dennis Keene

A subtly comic and satirical world of half-solved puzzles, sudden depths, and the mind at last confronting truths it prefers not to acknowledge.

Hardcover: 240 pages, 148 x 210 mm, ISBN 0-87011-940-0
Paperback: 240 pages, 113 x 182 mm, ISBN 4-7700-1558-5

SINGULAR REBELLION

Saiichi Maruya   Translated by Dennis Keene

A quiet middle-aged businessman marries a beautiful young model. Her granny, fresh out of jail for murder, moves in with them... A comic story of singular choices made in a conformist society.
"A circus...of the picaresque"—*Kobo Abe*

Paperback: 420 pages, 110 x 182 mm, ISBN 0-87011-989-3

GHOSTS   A Tale of Childhood and Youth

Morio Kita   Translated by Dennis Keene

A man obsessed with memories of the past struggles to interpret dream images of his mother and sister, lost during the war.

Hardcover: 200 pages, 148 x 210 mm, ISBN 4-7700-1559-3
Paperback: 200 pages, 113 x 182 mm, ISBN 4-7700-1743-X

THE SIGNORE   Shogun of the Warring States

Kunio Tsuji   Translation and Introduction by Stephen Snyder

Narrated by an Italian companion of the Signore, the dramatic story of the charismatic and tragic warlord of Napoleonic ambition and complexity whose brilliant but short life changes Japanese history.

Paperback: 210 pages, 110 x 182 mm, ISBN 4-7700-2066-X

THE DOCTOR'S WIFE

Sawako Ariyoshi
Translated by Wakako Hironaka & Ann Siller Kostant

A novel based on the life of the first doctor in the world to perform surgery for breast cancer under a general anesthetic.
"An excellent story."—*Choice*

Paperback: 192 pages, 113 x 182 mm, ISBN 0-87011-465-4

KABUKI DANCER A Novel of the Beginnings of Kabuki

Sawako Ariyoshi   Translated by James R. Brandon

Based on fact, this fictional story of the dancer who created kabuki captures the miraculous moment in which an art form appears.
"A valuable addition to the works of Ariyoshi in English."—*Asian Theatre Journal*

Hardcover: 288 pages, 152 x 226 mm, ISBN 4-7700-1783-9

THE RIVER KI

Sawako Ariyoshi   Translated by Mildred Tahara

A river's current links the moods and fortunes of three women over three generations.
"A vivid portrait of a family in a changing society."—*Observer*

Paperback: 248 pages, 110 x 182 mm, ISBN 0-87011-514-6

THE WAITING YEARS

Fumiko Enchi   Translated by John Bester

A brilliant but unnerving portrait of women caught in a web of shifting relationships within an upper-class family in the years following the Meiji Restoration.
"A subtle dissection of the attitudes of Japanese women."—*Pacific Citizen*

Paperback: 208 pages, 110 x 182 mm, ISBN 0-87011-424-7

THE END OF SUMMER

Harumi Setouchi   Translated by Janine Beichman

This award-winning autobiographical novel tells of a woman in her late thirties, who for eight years has been the mistress of a married man, but is forced to reexamine her whole emotional life when an old lover reappears.

Paperback: 152 pages, 110 x 182 mm, ISBN 4-7700-1746-4

BLACK RAIN

Masuji Ibuse   Translated by John Bester

Based on actual diaries and interviews with the survivors of Hiroshima, *Black Rain* is a literary masterpiece about friends, neighbors, and a city that suddenly ceased to be.

Paperback: 304 pages, 110 x 182 mm, ISBN 0-87011-364-X

CASTAWAYS Two Short Novels

Masuji Ibuse   Translated by David Aylward & Anthony Liman

Castaway John Manjiro travels the world and returns to a secluded island nation on the brink of westernization. Plus the story of a woman's exile after the political downfall of her lover.

Hardcover: 160 pages, 148 x 210 mm, 5 maps, ISBN 0-87011-808-0
Paperback: 160 pages, 110 x 182 mm, 5 maps, ISBN 4-7700-1744-8

SALAMANDER and Other Stories

Masuji Ibuse   Translated by John Bester

This collection of short stories displays Ibuse's engaging style to full advantage, from biting satire to wry lyricism.
"A brilliance and humour which is frequently memorable."—*Times Literary Supplement*

Paperback: 136 pages, 110 x 182 mm, ISBN 0-87011-458-1

WAVES Two Short Novels

Masuji Ibuse   Translated by David Aylward & Anthony Liman

During the twelfth-century war between the Heike and Genji clans, a young warrior is forced to abandon the comforts of court life.
"His subtle ironies and unsentimental sympathy are a reminder of the strengths of Japanese fiction."—*New Statesman*

Paperback: 176 pages, 110 x 182 mm, ISBN 4-7700-1745-6

INTO A BLACK SUN

Takeshi Kaiko   Translated by Cecilia Segawa Seigle

"At last the sights, sounds and smells of wartime Vietnam have been rendered by a master... No other account of Vietnam has been so vivid, so intimate or so moral."—Edmund White, *New York Times*

Paperback: 224 pages, 113 x 182 mm, ISBN 0-87011-609-6

SNAKELUST

Kenji Nakagami   Translated by Andrew Rankin

Seven stories from one of Japan's most exciting and original postwar
writers that depict the brutalized lives of people from the ghetto and
the dark side of human nature—cruelty, prejudice, deformity, lust.
"A dark, mysterious lyricism in a world entangled with love and hate."
—Jun Eto

Hardcover: 144 pages, 140 x 210 mm, ISBN 4-7700-2354-5

STILL LIVES

Natsuki Ikezawa

A premier collection by Japan's "current master of short fiction,"
these captivating stories attain the highest level of imagination, yet
remain always anchored in a reassuring normality.

Hardcover: 232 pages, 152 x 226 mm, ISBN 4-7700-2185-2

MY BOY   A Father's Memories

Makoto Shiina   Translated by Frederik Schodt

One of Japan's most popular adventurers and writers recounts
delightful tales of freedom and love shared with his free-spirited,
escapade-prone son.

Hardcover: 168 pages, 140 x 210 mm, ISBN 4-7700-1693-X

DREAM MESSENGER

Masahiko Shimada   Translated by Philip Gabriel

A wealthy woman hires a beauty-queen-turned-securities-analyst to
find her lost son—now a "professional friend" who visits people's
dreams.

Hardcover: 304 pages, 152 x 226 mm, ISBN 4-7700-1535-6

A SPRING LIKE ANY OTHER

Takashi Tsujii   Translated by Beth Cary

Takashi Tsuji is the pseudonym for Seiji Tsutsumi, poet, novelist and
former head of one of Japan's largest retail empires. His beguiling
novel offers "a searing self-portrait and an intimate look at an affluent
Japanese family in disarray."—*Translation Review*

Hardcover: 272 pages, 140 x 210 mm, ISBN 4-7700-1550-X

A CAT, A MAN, AND TWO WOMEN

Jun'ichiro Tanizaki   Translated by Paul McCarthy

This wonderful collection is distinguished by its lightheartedness, and comic realism.
"A masterpiece... Don't miss this piece of brilliant drollery."—
Washington Post Book World

Paperback: 180 pages, 110 x 182 mm, ISBN 4-7700-1605-0

CHILDHOOD YEARS A Memoir

Jun'ichiro Tanizaki   Translated by Paul McCarthy

Set against the modernization of Japan and World War II, the personal diary of Tanizaki's early years offers a moving and intense look at one of Japan's foremost modern novelists.

Hardcover: 196 pages, 148 x 210 mm, ISBN 0-87011-863-3
Paperback: 196 pages, 110 x 182 mm, ISBN 4-7700-2322-7

BLUE BAMBOO Tales of Fantasy and Romance

Osamu Dazai   Translated by Ralph F. McCarthy

Stories that combine fantasy and romance with Dazai's own psychological concerns reveal the optimistic, humorous, and idealistic side of a writer too often been typecast as dark, pessimistic, and self-absorbed.

Hardcover: 184 pages, 140 x 210 mm, ISBN 4-7700-1738-3

SELF PORTRAITS

Osamu Dazai   Translated by Ralph McCarthy

20 autobiographical stories describe with uncommon honesty and self-deprecating humor the women, the suicide attempts, the drinking, and the struggle against a staid literary establishment of Japan's most engaging *enfant terrible*.

Hardcover: 232 pages, 148 x 210 mm, b/w photos, ISBN 0-87011-779-3,

---

THE DARK ROOM

Junnosuke Yoshiyuki   Translated by John Bester

A middle-aged man revels in a free and easy life of casual sex, until he finds himself hovering on the edge of commitment and love which loom like a dark room.
"The translation is superb."—*Oriental Economist*

Paperback: 172 pages, 110 x 182 mm, ISBN 0-87011-361-5